QUEEN MARY

QUEEN MARY

David Duff

COLLINS
8 Grafton Street, London W1
1985

William Collins Sons & Co. Ltd
London · Glasgow · Sydney · Auckland
Toronto · Johannesburg

BRITISH LIBRARY CATALOGUING IN PUBLICATION DATA

Duff, David
Queen Mary.
1. Mary, *Queen, consort of George V, King
of Great Britain*   2. Great Britain – Queens
Biography
I. Title
941.083'092'4   DA574.A2

ISBN 0-00-217240-2

Photoset in Linotron Sabon by
Rowland Phototypesetting Ltd
Bury St Edmunds, Suffolk
Made and printed in Great Britain by
William Collins Sons & Co. Ltd, Glasgow

CONTENTS

LIST OF ILLUSTRATIONS

[7]

PREFACE

The idea of writing this life story of Queen Mary resulted from a long conversation which I enjoyed with Lady Cynthia Colville, for thirty years lady-of-the-bedchamber to Her Majesty. Always eloquent, Lady Cynthia sketched out for me the portrait of a woman of extraordinary strength, courage and loyalty, amply illustrated by the number of problems which had faced her during her life and explaining how she overcame them. Lady Cynthia raised in my mind many thoughts as to the character of the Queen and the workings of her mind behind the façade which she presented to the public, and to a lesser extent her family.

Queen Mary was the image of a princess and a queen, her upright, unchanging figure a national emblem from 1893 to 1953. When she died it was said of her that the last of the great Victorians had passed away. She endured three major wars and saw the ages of progress pass from the origins of the safety bicycle to those of the jet aircraft. Having lost her fiancé, Prince Albert Victor, Duke of Clarence and Avondale, who was in direct line to the throne, her marriage to his younger brother, the Duke of York, who became King George V, was one of convenience, but she developed the union into a great love story, so much so that her husband openly admitted that he feared he would become seriously ill if he was separated from her for any length of time. On every occasion that he returned to the palace after an engagement, his first action was to call her name and hurry to her room.

The romantic side of Queen Mary's life centred on the person of her eldest son, David. In him, as a youth and young man, she envisaged the ideal sovereign for Britain and the Empire. His popularity as a world figure has probably never been rivalled, and it was with great pride that she received the glowing reports of him which came first from the trenches of the First World War and then from the tours which he undertook to every corner of the British Isles and across the world. That he failed her during the 1930s caused her deep humiliation, happily to be offset by the sterling performance of her second son, King George VI, aided by his wife Elizabeth.

I have dealt in considerable detail with Queen Mary's background and childhood, for both had a deep effect upon the forming of her character. She was the great-granddaughter of King George III, and her mother, the Duchess of Teck, before her marriage Princess Mary of Cambridge, never allowed her to forget it. In her struggle to keep up her royal position, and handicapped by a penurious husband, the Duchess was permanently short of money: this shortage led to the enforced exile of the Teck family to Florence. Humiliating as this was to the seventeen-year-old Princess May of Teck, she learned much from her stay in Italy, and there was born her love and penchant for the arts and history.

Owing to her parents' close relationship to many of the small courts of Europe, Queen Mary obtained a unique knowledge of European royalty. Many of the palaces and castles in which she stayed had changed little from the eighteenth century, and her knowledge of the Continental background stood her in good stead when she married the Duke of York, who had made his career in the British Navy and was woefully ignorant of the way of life of the reigning Continental families. Throughout his reign, King George V relied absolutely on his wife for details of the royal family's Continental connections.

For Queen Mary's interests in charity and her work during the First World War, I have relied on Kathleen Woodward's *Queen Mary*, a now little-known work published in the early 1920s. The view of the Queen from 'below stairs', and her attitude towards entertaining and diet, is taken from the memoirs of M. Gabriel Tschumi, *Royal Chef*, published in 1954. M. Tschumi joined the royal kitchen staff at Windsor in the reign of Queen Victoria, later served both King Edward VII and King George V, and was chef to Queen Mary at Marlborough House from 1948 to 1952.

[10]

It would have been impossible to write the life of Queen Mary without reliance on James Pope-Hennessy's 658-page volume on her published in 1959 – one of the finest biographies of the twentieth century.

Twenty years have passed since I first began collecting material for this book. I have talked to many people, some sadly now dead, of her work in various fields of interest, and to them all I owe my gratitude.

I have tried to show that Queen Mary was unique in her style, her dignity and her loyalty, and to explain how she held the firm grip that she did on the affections of both her own generation and those younger than herself. Time has allowed new light to fall on a woman who was a part of the national scene, and I feel that the opportunity has arrived to be able to walk close by the real Queen Mary through the years when the world changed more quickly than it had ever done before.

DAVID DUFF

CHRONOLOGY

1866 Francis, Duke of Teck, married Princess Mary Adelaide of Cambridge.

1867 Their daughter Mary (May), born (later to become Queen Mary).

1868 Adolphus of Teck born.

1870 Francis of Teck born.

1874 Alexander of Teck born.

1891 Prince Albert Victor, Duke of Clarence, engaged to Mary (May).

1892 Prince Albert Victor died.

1893 George, Duke of York, married to Mary (May).

1894 Mary and George's first baby, David (later to become Duke of Windsor), born.

1895 Albert (Bertie, later to become George VI) born.

1897 Mary (Countess of Harewood) born.
Mary Adelaide, Duchess of Teck, mother of the future Queen Mary, died.

1900 Henry (Duke of Gloucester) born.
Francis, Duke of Teck, died.

1901 Queen Victoria died and was succeeded by King Edward VII.
World tour of George and Mary.
George and Mary created Prince and Princess of Wales.

1902 Coronation of Edward VII.
George (Duke of Kent) born.

1904 George and Mary make official visit to Vienna.

1905 Prince John born.
George and Mary visit India.

1906 George and Mary in Madrid for the wedding of Princess Ena of Battenberg to King Alfonso of Spain.
George and Mary at Coronation of the King and Queen of Norway.

1910 Death of Edward VII.
Prince Francis of Teck (Mary's brother) died.

1911 Coronation of King George V and Queen Mary.
David invested as Prince of Wales at Caernarvon.
King George and Queen Mary attend Delhi Durbar.
King George and Queen Mary visit Berlin for the wedding of the Kaiser's daughter.

1914 State Visit to Paris.
First World War began.

1915 King George injured in fall from horse in France.

1917 Teck name changed to Cambridge. Adolphus, Duke of Teck, became Marquess of Cambridge.
Alexander of Teck became the Earl of Athlone.

1918   King George and Queen Mary celebrate the Silver Jubilee of their
       marriage.
       Armistice Day.

1919   Prince John died.

1920   Albert (Bertie) created Duke of York.

1922   Wedding of Princess Mary to Viscount Lascelles.
       State Visit to Belgium.

1923   Wedding of the Duke of York to Lady Elizabeth Bowes-Lyon.
       State Visit to Italy.

1925   For the sake of the King's health, King George and Queen Mary make
       Mediterranean cruise.
       Death of Queen Alexandra.

1926   Birth of Princess Elizabeth of York.
       The General Strike.
       King and Queen move into Sandringham House.

1928   King George's serious illness.

1929   National Thanksgiving Service at St. Paul's for his recovery.

1930   Birth of Princess Margaret Rose of York.

1932   The King made first Christmas broadcast.

1935   Silver Jubilee of the reign of King George V and Queen Mary.

1936   Death of George V and accession of Edward VIII.
       Abdication of Edward VIII, who became Duke of Windsor.
       Accession of King George VI and Queen Elizabeth.

1937   Queen Mary at the Coronation of King George VI and Queen
       Elizabeth.

1939   King and Queen tour Canada and U.S.A.
       Queen Mary involved in car accident.
       Second World War began.
       Queen Mary moved to Badminton, Gloucestershire.

1942   Queen Mary at the confirmation of Princess Elizabeth at Windsor.

1945   End of the war.
       Queen Mary's return to Marlborough House.
       Queen Mary visited by Duke of Windsor.

1947   Wedding of Princess Elizabeth to Prince Philip, Duke of Edinburgh.

1948   Birth of Prince Charles.

1949   First illness of the King.

1950   Carpet made by Queen Mary produced £35,354 for the Exchequer.
       Birth of Princess Anne.

1951   Queen Mary at the Festival of Britain.
       The King underwent serious operation.

1952   Death of King George VI and accession of Queen Elizabeth II.
       Decline in the health of Queen Mary.

1953   Death of Queen Mary.
       Coronation of Queen Elizabeth II.

The Royal House of Württemberg, and the House of Cambridge Queen Mary's paternal and maternal families

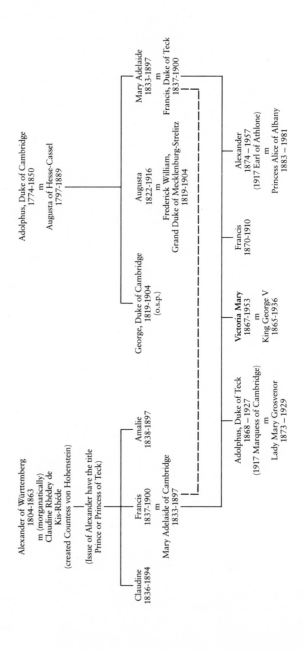

Adolphus, Duke of Cambridge
1774-1850
m
Augusta of Hesse-Cassel
1797-1889

Alexander of Württemberg
1804-1863
m (morganatically)
Claudine Rhédey de
Kis-Rhéde
(created Countess von Hohenstein)

(Issue of Alexander have the title
Prince or Princess of Teck)

Claudine
1836-1894

Francis
1837-1900
m
Mary Adelaide of Cambridge
1833-1897

Amalie
1838-1897

George, Duke of Cambridge
1819-1904
(o.s.p.)

Augusta
1822-1916
m
Frederick William,
Grand Duke of Mecklenburg-Strelitz
1819-1904

Mary Adelaide
1833-1897
m
Francis, Duke of Teck
1837-1900

Adolphus, Duke of Teck
1868 – 1927
(1917 Marquess of Cambridge)
m
Lady Mary Grosvenor
1873 – 1929

Victoria Mary
1867-1953
m
King George V
1865-1936

Francis
1870-1910

Alexander
1874 – 1957
(1917 Earl of Athlone)
m
Princess Alice of Albany
1883 – 1981

The Family of King George V and Queen Mary

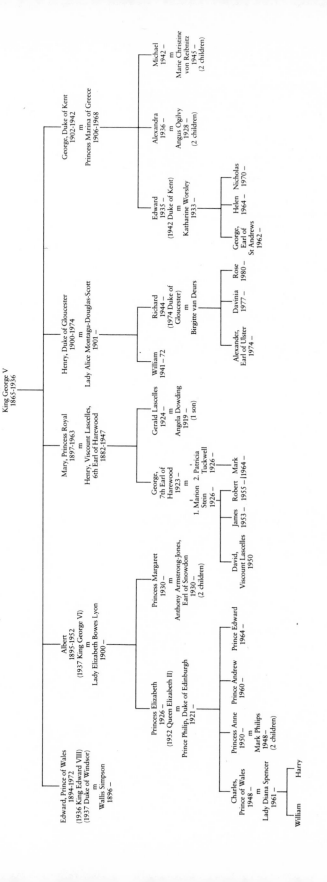

To distinguish her from her mother, Mary, Duchess of Teck, and also because she was commonly so known in her younger days, the subject of this biography is referred to as 'May' until the time when she became Queen, and thereafter as 'Queen Mary'.

CHAPTER I

In the Beginning

QUEEN MARY was woven inextricably into the three major crises in the personal life of the royal family during the nineteenth and twentieth centuries. The first was in 1817, when Princess Charlotte, the only direct heir to George III in the second generation, died in childbirth. As a result of the scramble engaged in by the King's sons to produce an heir, her mother was born. But for the tragic death of the young Princess, there would have been no Queen Mary. The second came in 1892, when Prince Albert Victor, Duke of Clarence, eldest son of the Prince of Wales, afterwards Edward VII, died of pneumonia. He was engaged to be married to Mary, then Princess 'May' of Teck. The third came in 1936, when Edward VIII abdicated the throne. Mary was his mother.

To understand the background story of Queen Mary it is necessary to examine the first crisis. Its repercussions deeply affected her early days.

In 1817, the British monarchy was in a parlous state. King George III was considered to be mad. He was not mad as we understand the meaning of the word today, but was the victim of physical suffering so great that the focus of his brain was upset. That he imagined that he was married to someone else was probably only the surfacing of a wish. Queen Charlotte was neither beautiful nor a good nurse – when he was ill she worried so much that her stays wrapped twice around her and she locked her bedroom door to keep him out. For the last six years of her life she never laid eyes on her husband. The poor King suffered from porphyria. For him there was no alleviation of the pain by drugs, and the contemporary treatment for the subsequent mental derangement was beating into submission and the strait-waistcoat.[1]

His eldest son, George, Prince of Wales, acted for him as Prince Regent. He was married to Caroline of Brunswick, a woman of little physical beauty or attraction. It was an arranged union, and when George first saw the bride who had been selected for him, he swore and called for a brandy. He spent the wedding night prostrate in the hearth in a drunken stupor. But duty was done and a daughter, Charlotte, was born. George then separated from Caroline and war between them was declared. Poor Charlotte had an unhappy and upsetting childhood and grew up to be a most rebellious young lady. In 1813, her father tried to marry her to Prince William of Orange, a vacuous individual nicknamed 'The Frog'. Charlotte refused and threw a tantrum. On the rebound she fell in love with an ambitious young man named Prince Leopold of Saxe-Coburg, in London with the Allied sovereigns to celebrate the victory over the French. Leopold was after power and money: the Regent spotted this, took a dislike to the young man and dubbed him *le Marquis Peu à Peu*. But Leopold played his cards well, ingratiated himself with the right people, and married Charlotte in the Grand Crimson saloon at Carlton House on 2 May 1816.

It was announced that a child was due in the autumn of 1817. Charlotte became so immense that it was thought that she would have twins. She was taken ill on 3 November, but it was not until two days later that her son was born dead and a fortnight overdue. Charlotte became ice cold and suffered a haemorrhage. The *accoucheur*, Sir Richard Croft, plied her with hot wine and brandy. The treatment was wrong. The next two hours, said a doctor who was present, 'were like a hurricane'.[2] Then Charlotte died. Shortly afterwards, Sir Richard Croft put pistols to either side of his head and blew his brains out.

On the day after the Princess's death, the sons of George III began their planning to produce an heir. The unseemly haste caused the popular satirist, Peter Pindar, to write:

> Yoics! the R- - -l Sport's begun
> I' faith but it is glorious fun

For hot and hard each R- - -l pair
Are at it hunting for the Heir.

George, the Prince Regent, fifty-five, was not considered to be a serious contender owing to the acrimonious relationship he had with his wife. In addition the doctors were of the opinion that his mode of living made it doubtful whether he could ever be a father again.

Frederick, Duke of York, fifty-four, was married to the Princess Royal of Prussia. He was childless, and his wife did not hold the premier place in his affections. The eccentric lady was living alone at Oatlands Park, Weybridge, and her interest was centred on a pack of forty dogs and a collection of parrots and monkeys.

William, Duke of Clarence, fifty-two, had a large family, the illegitimate offspring of Mrs Jordan, the actress. In the eyes of the law he was still a bachelor. He was a favourite to win the race.

Edward, Duke of Kent, fifty, a soldier and a martinet, had lived for twenty-seven years with a charming French woman, Julie de St Laurent. Whether there were offspring of the union has remained a mystery from that day to this. There has been an army of people claiming to be descendants, but no concrete proof has emerged. Edward was ever in a financial crisis, and in 1817 was living with Julie in Ghent for reason of economy. He at once announced that he was prepared to separate from his faithful companion – at a price. He wanted £25,000 a year for the sacrifice,[3] but did not get it. His brothers called him Joseph Surface. Reward or not, he was determined to sire an heir.

Ernest, Duke of Cumberland, forty-six, was married to a German widow, Frederica of Solms-Braunfels. He was an unpleasant and detested man and his wife was little better. It was rumoured that she had murdered two husbands, while he, it was said, had cut the throat of his valet. They lived mostly in Berlin and the royal family would not speak to them. But being married, they had a flying start.

Augustus, Duke of Sussex, forty-four, was the unambitious one and not interested in the race. He was living with Lady

Cecilia Underwood* and had no intention of changing ladies.

Adolphus, Duke of Cambridge, was a bachelor and unencumbered by mistress or bastards. He was Governor-General of Hanover. George III's favourite son, it was generally hoped that he would provide the next monarch.

Weddings took place quickly. William of Clarence married Adelaide of Saxe-Meiningen: Edward of Kent married Mary Louisa Victoria, the widowed Princess of Leiningen and sister to Prince Leopold of Saxe-Coburg; and Adolphus of Cambridge wooed and won Augusta of Hesse-Cassel, a union which turned out to be a love-match.

Britain seethed with excitement as news was awaited of the arrival of the first baby. There was not long to wait, for the spring of 1819 witnessed the arrival of a crop of princes and princesses. The Cambridges won by a nose. On 26 March, they had a son, George. The very next day, the Duchess of Clarence had a daughter, but the baby lived only for a few hours. On 24 May, a daughter, Victoria, was born to the Duchess of Kent. The Cumberlands were close behind, a son, also named George, being born three days later. The position then was that Victoria of Kent was first in line to the throne, but doomed to be an only child as her father died in 1820.

George III also died in 1820, and the Regent succeeded him as George IV. The marriage race continued. In the same year the Clarences had a daughter, Elizabeth, thus displacing Victoria of Kent. But Elizabeth lived for only a year. The Cambridge family was enlarged in 1822 by the birth of a daughter, Augusta.†

When the Duke of Clarence succeeded George IV in 1830 and became William IV, he decided that his two young nephews, George of Cambridge and George of Hanover, both living in Germany, should be brought up in the British way of life and arranged that they reside with him and his wife, Queen Adelaide.

The King had ideas that one of the boys would become the husband of Victoria of Kent. George of Cambridge was favoured. His cousin, George of Cumberland, suffered from poor

* Afterwards Duchess of Inverness.
† Afterwards Grand Duchess of Mecklenburg-Strelitz.

health and the legacy of a general dislike of his parents. His chances finally disappeared when, in playing with a chain, he swung it into his eye and became blind. George of Cambridge was the blue-eyed boy of Queen Adelaide, who, having lost two children of her own, looked upon him as if he were her son.

In 1833, George's father, Adolphus, by this time Viceroy of Hanover, pulled a surprise. He became the father of a second daughter, Mary Adelaide – the final arrival in the marriage race. Mary Adelaide was destined to become the mother of Queen Mary.

When William IV died in 1837, his successor, Princess Victoria of Kent, was prohibited, by Salic Law, from becoming Queen of Hanover. Ernest, Duke of Cumberland, became King there and Britain heaved a sigh of relief to be rid of him. The Cambridges returned to England and settled at Cambridge Cottage, Kew, a house on the south side of Kew Green which had been bequeathed to the Duke by his father; their London house was Cambridge House, Piccadilly, later to become the Naval and Military Club.

Duke Adolphus, now in his sixties, was more like a grandfather than a father to his young daughter, Mary Adelaide, whom he adored. He was deaf and a difficult man to talk to as he tended to repeat himself three times. A lady-in-waiting to the Queen made note of a conversation she had with him after dinner at Windsor:

> Where do you habitually reside, Ma'am? Oh, Hagley – you did live there. I see, I see – your son lately married – how long? A few months? I understand. Now where do you mean to live? At Richmond for the winter? Oh, I see. Where have you been since your son's marriage? Leamington? Why to Leamington? Oh, your brother – I understand! Your brother Captain Spencer! I remember – I perfectly recollect. A naval man, I believe. Yes, I saw him in 1825 at your father's in the Isle of Wight. Yes, yes, I know – Frederick Spencer, to be sure! Your father-in-law, Mr Poyntz? No, surely not so, Ma'am. Oh, his father-in-law? Oh, I see, I see . . .[4]

Not even the sanctity of the church silenced him. On being instructed to pray, he would say loudly, 'Certainly'. When the

vicar, in recounting the story of Zacchaeus, announced, 'Behold
the half of my goods I give to the poor,' the Duke exploded,
'No! No! Can't do that; that's too much for any man – no
objection to a tenth.' On the congregation being asked to pray
for rain, the Duke interjected, 'Yes, yes, quite right, quite right.
But it will never rain till the wind changes.' The ordeal of taking
a service proved too much for the curate and he resigned.[5]

The Cambridges looked to the future with equanimity, for
they took it for granted that their son George would marry
Victoria of Kent, thus increasing their status and ensuring their
financial stability: the latter was an important consideration, as,
like his brothers, Adolphus was always hard-pressed for money.
They overlooked two points. The first was that other suitors
were being groomed for the role of husband of the Queen, for
the prize in honour and income was great. The second was that
young George might not fancy his cousin Victoria and might
refuse to do as he was bid.

In fact plans to capture Victoria were being hatched in all
the palaces of Europe. As Lord Palmerston wrote, 'There seems
to be a flood of German princes pouring over us; the Duke of
Brunswick, the Prince of Solms, two Dukes of Württemberg,
and the Prince of Reuss-Loebenstein-Gera have all been seized
with a sudden desire to see England.'[6] There were others. The
Prince of Orange arrived with his two sons. From Copenhagen
came Prince Christian, nephew of the King of Denmark, who
made such progress that for a time many considered that he
would prove the lucky one. Both France and Portugal produced
candidates. But behind the scenes the mastermind moved the
pieces about the chessboard. Prince Leopold of Saxe-Coburg,
widower of Princess Charlotte and uncle of Queen Victoria,
who had become King of the Belgians in 1831, was determined
that his nephew Albert, second son of the Duke of Saxe-Coburg,
should win the prize. The trouble was that Albert was a weakling,
suffering from croop and gastric trouble. Also he actively disliked
girls. When first produced before Victoria, he made a poor
impression, as he was suffering from seasickness after a rough
Channel crossing. He could not dance, fell over on the floor and
dozed off to sleep at ten o'clock. Leopold decided that he should

be given a course of training to toughen him up and appointed a German doctor, Baron Stockmar, as his mentor.

Meanwhile George of Cambridge was way out in the lead. He opened all state balls with Victoria and had the backing of the Conservative Party and the Established Church. But when Victoria became Queen and he reached man's estate, a change came over George. He developed into a flirt, with a taste for flamboyant women, just as had his uncles, the sons of George III. He saw little romance in the short Queen, plump fore and aft, who fixed her protruding eyes upon him with an 'I want' look. She ate fast, cramming food into her mouth, and was a glutton for soup. She picked up bones in her fingers and gnawed them. She was far from George's ideal of femininity. When he was invited to spend a weekend alone with Victoria at Windsor in 1838, he decided that the danger was becoming too great. He bolted. Having entered the army, he arranged to be posted to Gibraltar. He then took a long leave, exploring the Mediterranean and visiting relatives in Germany. Victoria guessed the reason for his absence and was furious. When her uncle Leopold produced a transformed Albert, she clutched at him. On hearing news of the engagement, George returned to England. The Queen summoned him to Windsor and dressed him down. He was unrepentant.

On the wedding day of Victoria and Albert, 10 February 1840, the Duchess of Sunderland gave a full dress party. At it George met a lovely actress from Drury Lane named Louisa Fairbrother. He fell wildly in love and set up home with her in Queen Street, Mayfair. A curtain fell over the handsome soldier-prince who had been groomed as Consort. The Queen never mentioned his name and the stock of the Cambridges fell. The bitterness between the families became acute and reached explosion point when the penniless Prince Albert from Saxe-Coburg was given precedence over the surviving sons of King George III.

Little Mary Adelaide spent her childhood days at Kew and money was short. Conversation round the meal table concentrated on the wrongs which had been done to the Cambridges, the wickedness of the Saxe-Coburgs, and the magic of the letters

'HRH'. That magic was to stay with Mary Adelaide all her life, and was passed on to her only daughter.

Queen Victoria exacerbated the uneasy relationship. Prepared to believe anything bad of Prince George, she gave credence to the rumour that he was about to have a child by Lady Augusta Somerset, daughter of the Duke of Beaufort. Thus the rumour gained ground and the Duke and Duchess took the matter up with Victoria direct and with such fervour that she and Prince Albert were forced to retract. In fact George was living in blissful contentment with Louisa Fairbrother, now known as Mrs FitzGeorge. He had three sons by her and married her in 1847.

The Cambridges fared better in their relationship with ruling houses on the Continent. In 1842, the Duchess's niece, Louise, married Prince Christian of Schleswig-Holstein-Sonderburg-Glucksburg, who a few years earlier had been foremost in the chase to marry Queen Victoria. Christian was destined to become King of Denmark, and the union was of the utmost importance to the Cambridges. The following year Augusta, Mary Adelaide's elder sister, married the son and heir of the Grand Duke of Mecklenburg-Strelitz.

In 1850, Duke Adolphus died, leaving only £30,000 to his family, a sum which was considered next to destitution. One solution was that seventeen-year-old Mary Adelaide should find a husband of wealth and standing. Queen Victoria, ever intrigued by matchmaking, joined in the hunt.

The problem with Mary Adelaide was her size. She was huge. The American Minister put her down as being all of eighteen stone, and the poundage increased with the years. She was known as 'Fat Mary' or 'Mary the Mountain'. Lord Granville described her as being too big to fit into St George's Chapel, Windsor,[7] and Lord Clarendon forecast that no prince 'would venture upon so vast an undertaking'.[8] King Leopold of the Belgians summed her up as being 'grown out of compass' and Queen Victoria, herself fast making weight, deplored the *Embonpoint*. On the dance-floor she was regarded as a menace, and a girl who collided with her in the Lancers was sent spinning across the floor. Finding a horse for her to ride, and a saddle to fit her, were problems. Springs groaned when she entered a carriage.

This was sad as, but for her size, Mary would have been beautiful. She was tall, with ash-blonde, wavy hair. She had dark blue eyes and a good complexion, and she moved with a natural grace. The root of her trouble lay in her immense appetite and love of food. When she said 'cream' she rolled the 'r' and lingered on the word. When asked out to meals, hostesses were embarrassed by the demand for further helpings and the consequent length of the repast. She would criticize the cooking. On being served with wild boar's head with Cambridge sauce, she commented, 'The sauce which we have here is wrongly made. A real Cambridge sauce is made of nothing more than red currant jelly, red wine and the hottest possible English mustard, which must all be stirred together as long as possible. But this sauce is made up of raspberry jelly, port, orange peel and the mildest mustard.'[9]

Apart from the disadvantages of size and appetite, Mary Adelaide posed other problems in the matrimonial field. Perhaps because of an inferiority complex over her measurements, she behaved in the most extraordinary manner when possible suitors were produced for her at a dance. She would completely ignore the candidate for her hand and flirt openly with other partners. Her loud, Hanoverian guffaw would echo across the floor and the husband-elect would beat a hasty retreat. She thus won herself the reputation of being a coquette, and the future Queen Louise of Denmark warned her daughter Alexandra, soon to become Princess of Wales, that if *she* behaved like that she would get her face smacked.[10]

Another difficulty for Mary Adelaide was that her suitors were restricted to the royal blood: members of the British aristocracy were not to be considered. This came hard on her, as she fell in love with Lord Skelmersdale, but was warned off. Thus she was understandably riled when, some years later, Queen Victoria allowed her own daughter, Louise, to marry the Marquess of Lorne and her granddaughter, Louise of Wales, to wed the Duke of Fife.

At the relevant time the choice of royal suitors was poor indeed, and the rulers of countries who put forward candidates did so in the hope of strengthening ties with Britain. Foremost in this attempt was Emperor Napoleon III of France, who wished to scale the social ladder by coupling himself to the family of Queen Victoria. It was he who, for his own ends, put a stop to the chances of the Prince of Orange, known as 'the Orange Boy' or 'Citron'. Napoleon feared a connection with the Dutch, and foiled the romance by the simple trick of ensnaring 'the Orange Boy' with a strumpet named Elizabeth Cookson as he made his way towards London. In the event this proved fortunate, as 'the Orange Boy' was a rake and a drunkard who ended his short life as a *roué* in Paris.

Napoleon then put forward his objectionable cousin, Napoleon Josef, son of ex-King Jerome, ever smarting that he was not the ruler of France. But Mary Adelaide had heard of his reputation and character and put her heavy foot down firmly upon the idea. She did the same when an offer came from King Victor Emmanuel of Sardinia. He was another of the same ilk and had shocked Empress Eugenie of France by telling her that he liked the ladies of Paris because they wore no knickers. His religion was given as the excuse for turning him down; the Duchess of Cambridge was convinced that her daughter's mind would be poisoned by the Jesuits if she went to Sardinia. Empress Eugenie then produced Prince Oscar of Sweden. He came to London, took one look at 'Mary the Mountain' and in silence returned to his own country.

Many other suitors came and went. They included Prince William of Baden, the Duke of Brunswick, the Duke of Saxe-Meiningen, Prince Waldemar of Holstein and Prince Nicholas of Nassau. In 1859, Princess Mary Adelaide confided in Lord Clarendon that she had made up her mind 'to be a *jolly old maid*'.[11]

Queen Victoria became impatient with 'Fat Mary' and lost interest in her matrimonial affairs. At the same age she had been the mother of five children. Her impatience turned into annoyance when Prince Albert died in 1861 and the country was plunged into black-edged gloom: Mary Adelaide was the exception in the royal circle and continued to be 'a *jolly* old maid' – much too jolly for the Queen's liking. But her chances of getting a husband brightened two years later when her cousin, Princess Alexandra of Denmark,* married Albert Edward ('Bertie'), Prince of Wales. Bertie and Alexandra were determined to find a husband for Mary Adelaide and the search was on once more.

Bertie found the answer in Hanover in 1864. There he met an officer in the Austrian army whom he thought would fill the bill, in fact just the sort of chap who would enliven his dinner parties at Sandringham. He was handsome, tall and well built. His hair was so black that in the lamplight it shone as dark blue. Below his high forehead were beautiful and kindly eyes. Beneath his waxed moustache was a little imperial, the small tufted beard popularized by Napoleon. In Vienna he was known as *der schöne Uhlan*, the beautiful young man; in truth he was a prince right out of a Strauss operetta. His name was Prince Francis of Teck. His disadvantages were that he was of a lower rank than Mary Adelaide, only a serene highness, was four years younger than her and had no money. But the urgency of finding a husband for 'Fat Mary' had become so tense that these points were overlooked. Bertie was ever a man to make decisions on the spot and let the future care for itself.

Francis of Teck's father was Duke Alexander of Württemberg, who would have succeeded to the throne there had he not married outside the Austrian royal family, the Hungarian beauty Countess Claudia Rhèdey, and thus lost his right. Claudia, created Countess Hohenstein, had three children, of whom Francis was the second. When he was only three, tragedy struck. His mother, on horseback, was watching a review of Austrian cavalry. Her mount took fright and bolted straight into the path of a galloping squadron. She was trampled to death.

The Emperor Francis Joseph and the Empress Elizabeth of Austria were deeply shocked by the tragic death of Countess Claudia and made a pet of young Francis; when he became of age he was commissioned into the Imperial Gendarmerie. He

* Eldest daughter of Prince Christian of Glucksburg, afterwards King Christian IX of Denmark, and Louise, daughter of Landgrave William of Hesse.

was ever conscious of his junior rank owing to his father's marriage, and hampered by the lack of money. It was in 1860 that his interest was aroused in things British. Empress Elizabeth was ill and Queen Victoria lent her the royal yacht, *Victoria and Albert*, in which to travel to Madeira to recuperate. Prince Francis was a member of the Empress's suite. He was duly impressed with the royal yacht and the obvious power of Britain. When the Prince of Wales suggested to him in 1865 that he visit England and inspect Princess Mary Adelaide, he jumped at the chance. By this time her brother, George, Duke of Cambridge, had become Commander-in-Chief, and Francis, therefore, being a military man, had high hopes of a sinecure.

Plans for their future together were kept secret from Mary Adelaide, although the Duchess of Cambridge, George and her sister Augusta were in the know. They were all of the opinion that Mary Adelaide was daily becoming more fractious and difficult to handle and they reckoned it would be best to take her by surprise in case she pulled her 'coquette' act. They looked upon Francis as her last chance.

Francis was the guest of the Prince of Wales at Sandringham. He was taken to see Queen Victoria at Osborne and passed the test with flying colours. There were three reasons for this. Firstly, Victoria was susceptible to handsome men. Secondly, she considered it wrong that Francis should have been barred from succession in Württemberg. She was many years ahead of her time in her attitude towards morganatic marriages: in her own words, 'In England if a King chose a peasant girl she would be Queen just as much as any Princess.'[12] Thirdly, he was dark-haired and dark-eyed, and this was of vital importance to her. Every word that Albert had spoken was still echoing in her memory, and he had stressed that, 'We must have some strong dark blood in the family.' In his opinion constant fair hair and blue eyes made the blood lymphatic. That was why when Alice, the Queen's second daughter, had her first child in 1863, the chosen wet nurse was a dark-eyed Irish girl of peasant stock, who had to be bathed before being put into service. Francis of Teck appeared to Victoria to be just the kind of husband Albert would have chosen for Mary Adelaide.

Francis came to England again in 1866 and visited Cambridge Cottage, Kew. Mary Adelaide was bowled over by his outward attractions and events moved fast. On 6 April, they became engaged during a stroll in the Rhododendron Walk in Kew Gardens. Augusta was informed by telegraph. She replied, 'Who would have thought it possible, and in so short a time too! To me it is like a dream! I see her as you say, "rushing about like an emancipated schoolgirl" . . .'[13]

No time was lost in tying the knot. The couple were married on 12 June in the little church on Kew Green. A vast crowd gathered as Queen Victoria was there and it was rare for her to emerge from her mourning gloom. She allotted to the newlyweds the apartments in Kensington Palace that her mother and she had lived in when she was a child. Redecoration began.

All the interested parties had been so eager to see 'Fat Mary' wed that many of the troubles that were to face the couple in married life – and they were endless – had been overlooked. Suddenly a major worry loomed ahead – what would be the fate of Mary Adelaide when the time came for her to have a child? They had not long to wait as by the winter the signs of her first pregnancy were obvious. In those days it was considered most unusual, and highly dangerous, for a woman to have her first child at the age of thirty-three. Girls who reached their twentieth birthdays without being attached would joke about becoming old maids. If they were still unmarried by twenty-five, they were considered to be 'on the shelf'. The Queen's eldest daughter, 'Vicky', the Princess Royal, had become engaged at fourteen and was married to Prince Frederick William of Prussia soon after her eighteenth birthday. The second daughter, Alice, was nineteen when she married Prince Louis of Hesse, and the third, Helena, became Princess Christian of Schleswig-Holstein at the same age. In addition, Mary Adelaide's size was seen as a grave risk. She became enormous, leading to the forecast that she would have twins. It was feared that she would share the same tragic fate as Princess Charlotte. It was therefore in some trepidation that George, Duke of Cambridge, drove from Queen Street to Kensington Palace on the evening of 26 May 1867. There he waited in the room next door to that in which the

Duchess of Kent had given birth to the future Queen Victoria in 1819. Francis had taken station beside his wife – an unusual occurrence in those days. George later wrote in his diary, 'Dear Mary was confined at one minute before twelve o'clock. Everything passed off wonderfully well and we have to be most grateful for God's mercy in this respect.'[14]

Queen Mary was born.

CHAPTER II

Growing Up

QUEEN VICTORIA, 21 JUNE 1867: 'At half past five drove in the open carriage and four from Buckingham Palace, through the densely crowded Park to Kensington Palace, to see dear Mary Teck. It seemed so strange to drive into the old courtyard and to get out at the door, the very knockers of which were old friends. My dear old home, how many memories it evoked walking through the well-known rooms! Franz* received me at the door, and we went up to the top of the house, where I lived the last two years; and here, in the former bedroom, in which Mama and I slept, I found dear Mary, Aunt Cambridge, and the baby – a very fine one, with pretty little features and a quantity of hair . . . I am to be one of the godparents.'[1]

A month later, the baby was christened by the Archbishop of Canterbury. The names given were Victoria Mary Augusta Louise Olga Pauline Claudine Agnes. In the family she was known as 'May', after the month in which she was born. The name stuck, and she was to be known as Princess May until she became Queen.

May was not long alone in the nursery, three brothers joining her. Adolphus ('Dolly') arrived on 13 August 1868, Francis ('Frank') on 9 January 1870 and Alexander ('Alge') on 14 April 1874. May and Dolly were fair-haired, Frank and Alge dark. They were all strong children and good looking – when she was five May christened her brothers 'the beauty boys'. Dolly was her favourite. History repeated itself when her turn came to be a mother: her family consisted of one girl and five boys. Her

* Francis.

[31]

great-granddaughter, Elizabeth II, has one girl and three boys.

By the time the Teck family was complete, the Queen had lost interest in the arrival of royal babies. She announced that she was no more interested in their coming than she was in the breeding habits of the rabbits in Windsor Park.[2] There was an element of jealousy in her bitter comment. At heart she wanted to be the mother, the star. As she said at the confinement of Princess Alice, 'Oh, if it could be I who was to wear that shift, that it could be I who was to undergo the trial, that I could be giving another child to Albert.'[3]

The lack of interest affected the relevant families deeply, for the fountain of those two essentials, status and power, played at Windsor Castle. Queen Victoria ran a close second to God, and she was an awe-inspiring figure to the inmates of nurseries. If the sun of her goodwill shone, then life was easier and much more pleasant. Mary Adelaide and Francis of Teck assessed the situation wrongly from the start. They made error after error and jeopardized their own future. It was a case of mistaken values.

No sooner were they married than the couple began a campaign to obtain higher rank – above all Francis wanted to become a royal highness. The first step was for him to become a duke. Lord Clarendon, the Foreign Secretary, was approached, and he talked with the Queen. She was dead set against the idea, pointing out that it would lead to endless problems, putting him above the relations of Queen Adelaide and the descendants of the Duchess of Kent. In particular she gave the example of Prince Ernest of Leiningen, one of the Duchess's grandsons. As a result Francis refused to attend any function at which Prince Ernest was present. Other relations joined in the row and Francis became exceedingly unpopular. But he struggled on and in 1871, King Carl of Württemberg granted him the coveted rank of Duke, but of Teck, not Württemberg. Francis wanted the latter, as Teck was only a minor house. He considered that he had been insulted.

To counteract the lack of honours for her husband, Mary Adelaide plugged her royal image as the granddaughter of George III. While the Queen hid away in her mourning seclusion, her cousin appeared frequently in the streets on her way to any function at which she had been asked to preside. She was always smiling and waved graciously to the crowds. Fat royalties who smile have ever been popular, and the point was taken by Queen Victoria. What annoyed her in particular was that the Tecks were using the same liveries as herself for their servants, and that their carriages were identical to those in which she travelled. She ordered an enquiry, demanding to know why their coachmen and footmen were in livery of scarlet and dark blue and their carriages painted chocolate brown. The answer came back that the servants' waistcoats were black, the Württemberg livery, and not blue, and that the crowns on the carriages were different. The Queen was not amused.

Nor did Francis obtain the military sinecure he had expected, his brother-in-law merely bestowing upon him the colonelcy of the Post Office Volunteers. This was tantamount to a rebuff. Yet George of Cambridge had grounds, for, from a military viewpoint, it was a serious time for Britain and there was no room in the army for decorative figures. Trouble was looming in India, Turkey and Egypt, while in Germany Bismarck was laying the foundations of the German Empire. The Schleswig-Holstein war of 1864 had crumpled Denmark. Two years later the Frankfurt Diet voted that the Duchies of Schleswig and Holstein should become a separate state. This was in direct opposition to Bismarck's wishes, but he saw in the decision a chance to put an end to Austrian influence. Hanover, Hesse and by the Rhine, and Saxe-Coburg, all with strong ties with Britain, backed the Diet and Austria. Bismarck marched. On 3 July 1866 the bloody name of Königgratz was written into history, the needle musket of the Prussians inflicting forty-five thousand casualties on the Austrians. Overrun, King George of Hanover lost his throne: Saxe-Coburg and Hesse sacrificed much of their independence and were impoverished by the cost of war. The humbling of Austria hit Francis hard, but he continued to press for a military appointment.

At last, he was given a chance. He was posted to a staff job in the Egyptian war of 1882. It was not a success, the glamour of the Austrian Imperial Gendarmerie contrasting strongly with the rigours of the British army in action. Francis became involved in a row when he accused his batman of stealing his kit[4] and on his return to England he announced that in future he would only fight with German soldiers. Queen Victoria, who was very proud of the prowess of her son Arthur, Duke of Connaught, in the same campaign, commented that Francis had done absolutely nothing. There were to be no more chances.

Mary Adelaide, on the other hand, was well liked by leading statesmen and soldiers. She was guaranteed to make a party live, despite her strong views, freely expressed, on international affairs. Her aggressive attitude over the Russo-Turkish war of 1877 earned her the title of 'Queen of the Jingoes'. She was a particular friend of Disraeli, Lord Beaconsfield. She was sitting next to him at dinner one evening at the time that the Russians were threatening Constantinople and the British fleet was at the Dardanelles. She asked the Prime Minister what he was waiting for. With an air of anxiety Beaconsfield looked round the table and then whispered, 'For the potatoes, Madam.'[5]

Although rank counted high in the Tecks' estimation, there was an even greater problem: money. This it was that blackened their lives, and those of their children. In the event it was only in her babyhood, in the sumptuous apartments at Kensington Palace, that May was free of the curse of it. By the age of seven it had infiltrated her thoughts and become the dominating theme. The lack of finance and the resulting problems were with her every minute until she married at the age of twenty-six. It penetrated her very being, and to it she attributed the early deaths of her mother and father. It broke her confidence, made her shy and tongue-tied. She put on a brave face, but the nightmare of it, and the constant strain, affected her permanently. Even as Queen of Great Britain and Empress of India, it still haunted her. Tragically, in her last years, the nightmare was resurrected. Where suffering has been, the echo long remains. There were to be other dreads in her life – an innate fear of thunder, a horror of illness and mutilation – but the fear of lack of money overrode them all.

The Tecks began married life on less than £8000 a year. Parliament had granted Mary Adelaide £5000 and the Duchess of Cambridge weighed in with £2000. To set up the apartments in Kensington Palace to the standard in which they expected to live, £8000 was borrowed from Miss Coutts, of the banking family. In a few years the loans from the same lady had risen to over £50,000, while the Duchess of Cambridge somehow managed to raise £60,000 to keep the Teck family going.[6] They were spending more than twice their income.

Mary Adelaide had inherited the trait of her 'wicked uncles', the sons of George III. Money had no meaning for her, and she believed that the British public should support its royals. Although she was generous beyond her means in the field of charity, her main extravagance was entertaining. The hospitality of Kensington Palace was generous to a degree and ever open to visitors. It became a favourite headquarters for visiting royalties from the Continent, who regarded the British purse as bottomless. Dinner parties were lavish. Exotic dishes were conjured up and the ingredients obtained regardless of cost. Clad in an apron, Mary Adelaide supervised every detail of the menu, while Francis watched over the silver-laden table. A multitude of servants attended to every wish. Up and up went the amounts due to the shops which supplied the repasts, and no accounts were settled.

Help from relations did not materialize. Mary Adelaide considered that her brother George, Duke of Cambridge, should come to the rescue, but this proved fruitless for a number of reasons. Firstly, George had two establishments to run, his own and that of his wife, Mrs FitzGeorge, in Queen Street. He also had three boys to educate. Secondly, he had another female attachment in the person of a Mrs Beauclerk. George had always had a liking for the ladies and he was besotted with Mrs Beauclerk, to the fury of his wife. On being requested by his sister for a loan, he informed her that Mrs Beauclerk absorbed 'all that he could give'.[7] Thirdly, the Tecks were apt to criticize and make snide remarks about George's involvements, and these came to his ears. In any case Francis, starved of a military appointment, regarded George as his 'mortal enemy'. There was little hope in that direction.

Mary Adelaide's sister, Augusta, Grand Duchess of

Mecklenburg-Strelitz, was a delightful woman, intelligent and intensely British, and was regarded by May as a second mother. But Augusta was well known as the biggest miser in Europe. She would not even have rubber tyres fitted to her carriage wheels, choosing to be bumped about on the cobble stones of Neu Strelitz rather than go to the expense.

Bertie, Prince of Wales, was married to Mary Adelaide's cousin, Alexandra of Denmark. The two women were the closest of friends and loved one another deeply. But Bertie was in no position to help as he was himself yearly 'in the red' to the tune of £30,000, most of this going on maintaining Sandringham, that 'voracious white elephant' as Edward VIII was later to call it.

This left the Tecks with only one direction in which to turn – Windsor Castle. It was surely, they considered, up to the Queen to so arrange matters that there were no scandals in the royal family. It was certainly in her power to do so, but she did not. If Prince Albert had lived, matters would doubtless have been ordered differently, but Albert was dead and in his shadow walked John Brown, the Queen's 'particular gillie' and her personal servant. Indirectly, it was upon John Brown that the onus lay for the plight of the Tecks and the plague which cursed Princess May.

Throughout her life Queen Victoria absorbed the character and the ways of the man of the moment. During her first years as Queen she was dominated by Lord Melbourne, her Prime Minister. Evening after evening they were closeted together, and from him she learned worldly wisdom and how to rule. Although he was forty years older than she, there was undoubtedly a degree of sexual attraction: when she attended Ascot, cries of 'Mrs Melbourne' came from the stand.

Melbourne was perhaps the best influence on Victoria, but his power was obliterated when Albert arrived on the scene. Albert taught his wife 'oneness' – the divine right of being whom she was. He also taught her efficiency, how to work hard and a smattering of the arts. He was careful with money, but he showed her how to make it. When he died there was a void. In her efforts to fill it, Victoria demanded the frequent presence of her daughters. Two of them, Vicky and Alice,* were married and lived in Germany and found the demands wearing and almost impossible to fulfil. Their attempts to cheer up their mother were met with the reply that it was all very well for them to talk: they had companionship, while she had only an old red dressing-gown to grasp at night. When a clergyman suggested that she should look upon Jesus Christ as her husband, she commented that that was what she called real twaddle.[8]

The answer came in 1864. Alice and Sir Henry Ponsonby, the Queen's Private Secretary, who had both noticed that Victoria seemed content only when with her gillie at Balmoral, put their heads together, and Brown appeared at Osborne. There were no more demands for the presence of the elder daughters. But there was another change: there were no more presents or financial aid. This hit Alice hard, as the Hesse family had been reduced to poverty after their lands had been overrun by the Prussians in 1866. Alice began to wonder if she had been wise about Brown. When, on a rare visit to England, she asked if her husband might be given a horse from the royal stables, her mother made no reply, concentrating on the food on her plate. Later she was told that pearls did not grow on the bushes at Windsor.

The public also noted Victoria's meanness and, in the revolutionary outbursts of 1871, criticism of her income on the one hand and expenditure on the other became bitter. It came to a climax with the publication of a malignant tract entitled, 'Tracts for the Times, No. 1: What does She do with it?'[9] The writer argued that the Queen was amassing a vast private fortune, estimated to be as much as £5,000,000, that she had no right to this money as it came from the Civil List, and that unspent amounts should be returned to the public exchequer at the end of the year. Feelings were exacerbated by the republican speeches of Sir Charles Dilke.

But the main reason for what had happened was that the Queen had absorbed John Brown's attitude to money. Brought up on a small farm on Deeside, he thought in terms of bawbees*

* Princess Alice married Prince Louis of Hesse and by the Rhine in 1862.
* Informal Scottish word for halfpenny.

and was canny to a degree. Queen Victoria ceased to buy clothes, wearing skirts until they were frayed. The silversmith who called regularly at Windsor for orders found that suddenly there were none: he adopted the ruse of asking Brown to expensive lunches, which improved matters. When she visited big houses in Scotland, she gave parting presents of ghastly fairground pottery representing Windsor Castle and the like. The Queen treasured the small gifts which Brown gave her. One was an egg cup, a souvenir of a seaside resort, and this she used daily. Early morning tea was rationed to one lump of sugar and there were newspaper squares in the lavatories.

Unfortunately for the Tecks, this attack of meanness and Brown's rule coincided with the period when they most needed financial help, to set up their homes and to educate their children. Mary Adelaide was an expert wheedler, but she met her match in Queen Victoria. There was a positive 'no' to financial aid. When she was asked for £1200 to keep the most vociferous of the Teck creditors at bay, she refused, saying that if she gave it she would set a precedent and 'once done it will be asked for again and again'.[10]

But Mary Adelaide had one success. She managed to get permission to have the White Lodge, a grace and favour residence in Richmond Park, as a rural retreat. It was a struggle but at length the Queen gave in to the plea that the Teck children needed a country home. The Queen also hoped that her cousin would spend less on entertaining when away from the heart of London. As regards the children, there were grounds for the move: as an infant, May had nearly died from an illness contracted from the smell of the Round Pond, Kensington Gardens, which in those days was little more than a sewer.

The Queen's hope that by granting the White Lodge to the Tecks she would curtail the Tecks' spending was to prove groundless. While retaining the apartments at Kensington Palace in the same sumptuous style, they simultaneously set about converting the White Lodge into a most desirable country residence. The house was shabby, the last incumbents having been Bertie, Prince of Wales, and his tutor, who had been incarcerated there in 1858 in an attempt – which did not succeed

– to inculcate some learning into the head of the heir. The state of repair did not suit the Tecks at all, but they soon altered that and in 1870 an army of decorators and gardeners was put to work.

In two directions Francis was gifted – interior decoration and gardening. Having no full-time occupation, he exploited these gifts to the full. The rooms of the White Lodge were transformed: out went the ottomans and the heavy tables, the eastern rugs and portraits of distant relatives. The walls were papered in light shades of blue and green and the new furniture arranged and rearranged until perfection had been reached. Van-loads of lilacs, syringas and roses arrived for the garden, and by 1875 everything was complete. All that was then required was the settlement of the bill.

May loved the White Lodge and the illnesses which had plagued her in London disappeared. By the age of eight she was alarmingly tall, but, the Queen noted, 'very plain'. She had a little room of her own, 'top of the staircase on right' as she described it. There she would sit darning her brothers' socks, for she soon played the part of a second mother to them. Mary Adelaide rarely appeared on the scene before two in the afternoon and then was soon off in her carriage to keep London appointments.

The Tecks adopted a practical and sensible attitude towards the upbringing of their children. Mary Adelaide told Mrs Dalrymple,* 'A child has enough to do to learn obedience and attend her lessons and to *grow*, without many parties and late hours, which take the freshness of girlhood away, and its brightness and beauty. Then children become intolerable. There are too many grown-up children today.'[12] Francis was averse to sport for women and had precise ideas of the conduct befitting a lady: he insisted that May wore gloves even when in the garden. An old servant at the White Lodge recalled, 'The Duke of Teck did not believe in no rough, horse games for women, he didn't. It wasn't no golf that produced our Princess.'[13] And May never did show much interest in sport. But she had a pony,

* An old family friend.

and the same man remembered her cantering down the Queen's Walk: 'Such a figure! Fine, full of health, not athletic in the horsey sense.'

Francis was apt to be short-tempered with his sons and shout at them, but May was his pet, and he hers. He called her 'dearest pussy'. When he was away she would send him pressed violets. She was happiest when wandering in the park, picking wild flowers and learning about trees. That was where she was invariably to be found when her studies with her Hanoverian governess were over.

Her mother insisted that she became aware of the living conditions of the poor. She was despatched with food to needy families, and instructed to stay there to watch them eat it. She was a frequent visitor to the Royal Cambridge Asylum, a home for old women which had been named after her grandfather, and there distributed vegetables and flowers from the garden of the White Lodge to the seventy inmates.

From infancy she was intensely shy and, at the sight of a stranger, would burst into tears and hide herself in her mother's voluminous skirt. At fourteen her teeth chattered with fright when she was told to do a solo turn at dancing class. Her tendency to introversion increased when other children made snide remarks about her mother's fatness, as on the occasion when Mary Adelaide had to be provided with two chairs to sit and watch the dancing lessons. One simply was not enough.

Queen Victoria's children were too old to be companions of the Tecks, and the only royal family of a like age in England was that of the Wales. This consisted of Albert Victor (Eddy),* George,** Louise,*** Victoria and Maud.† To the Queen's dismay they were physically puny, all having been born prematurely. But they were wild, and very conscious that they were the children of the Prince of Wales. Isolated in their own kingdom of Sandringham in Norfolk, they considered that they had been poured direct from the salt cellar of God. Their mother spoiled them and their father was determined that they should not be subjected to the reign of terror which had blighted his boyhood.

* Duke of Clarence. ** George V. *** Duchess of Fife. † Queen of Norway.

They saw little of their grandmother, who would have put them in their place, for the Queen went seldom to Norfolk – too flat: she liked the hills and the lochs. Also Bertie abhorred John Brown and refused to accord him the treatment upon which his mother insisted.

These little terrors teased May unmercifully and gave her an inferiority complex. They were for ever plugging their rank, poking fun at her mother's figure and pointing at May's 'Württemberg hands', which were on the stubby side. She did not like their wild games and mischief. They would slide down the stairs on tin trays and on one occasion took a pony upstairs to Princess Alexandra's bedroom.

Although the two mothers were bosom friends, Mary Adelaide did not get on well with Bertie; it was an uneasy relationship. He would make bitter jokes about her and then smile disarmingly. He had inherited the trait from the Saxe-Coburgs: Prince Albert was the same. He would roar with laughter if a visitor slipped on a mat and ended on his backside. As a boy he had put a frog in a girl's bed and filled another's coat pocket with custard. Bertie was worse. Mary Adelaide could not abide the tormenting of his stooge, Christopher Sykes: Bertie would burn the palms of Sykes's hands with his cigar end and pour brandy over his head.[14] Mary Adelaide was a kind-natured, hearty woman and the treatment revolted her.

May retreated further inside herself. She was at a bazaar in Kew Gardens with Louise, Victoria and Maud. She sold a fan and the purchaser asked her to autograph it. 'With pleasure,' she said, blushing, 'but aren't you mistaking me for one of my cousins of Wales? I am only May of Teck.'[15]

There were no holidays for the Teck children, in the accepted sense of the word. They relied on invitations from friends and acquaintances. One summer they visited the stately homes in the Dukeries of Nottinghamshire. Several times they went to Hopetoun* near Edinburgh. There lawns stretched a mile long towards a sandy beach and the children had endless fun collecting shells and sea-anemones. There was also a heated swimming

* Home of 6th Earl of Hopetoun, whose son became 1st Marquess of Linlithgow.

bath, in which May would splash and laze through the afternoons. This she adored. The Hope children were fascinated by
the Tecks' huge appetites, and particularly their mother's. While
they longed to get back to their games on the beach, Mary
Adelaide would prolong meals by as much as three hours as
she devoured helping after helping.

Every few years the Tecks visited Germany and Austria,
staying with relations at Rumpenheim on the Main, Neu Strelitz
(with the Grand Duchess Augusta), Württemberg and Vienna.
May did not much enjoy Germany, being, like her aunt Augusta,
intensely British at heart. She once struck her chest and exclaimed, 'I am British through and through,' which was in
contrast with Prince Albert who had stressed that he was
German through and through, and ever would remain so. But
she got the chance of seeing Germany before the rule of Bismarck
became absolute and the country was modernized. She travelled
in special saloon coaches on the railroads, sailed the rivers and
lakes in the pretentious royal barges, and experienced the
old-world tradition and customs of grand-ducal castles. It was
a journey back through time, and it instilled in her a respect for
history and impressed upon her that European royalty operated
like a trade union, and very much a closed shop.

Some of these journeys were long hauls indeed, such as that
from Württemberg in the south of Germany to Neu Strelitz in
the far north-east. They took the train from Stuttgart to Frankfurt and there changed to the Berlin express. On arrival a post
coach was waiting to carry them on to Fürstenberg on the
borders of Strelitz. There they were met by the Grand-ducal
carriage, drawn by six black horses. They then travelled in state,
with an outrider, two postilions liveried in black and scarlet, a
coachman and footman hanging on as best they could. The
carriage journey alone took eight hours.

Schloss Rumpenheim, which stood by the river Main opposite Hanau, was the headquarters of the Hesse-Cassel family
and often on the Tecks' visiting list. Rebuilt by Princess Mary
(daughter of Britain's George II) who had married the Landgrave
of Hesse-Cassel, the charming castle had been left by her son to
his six children on the condition that they and their families

should gather there biennially. This they did – to the consternation of European leaders, who imagined they were hatching
all sorts of plans. In particular did this apply to Bismarck, for
after his wars of 1864 and 1866, the houses of Hanover, Hesse,
Denmark and Württemberg bore a deadly hatred for everything
Prussian.

The Continental travels were marred for her by her father's
temper. Once back on his own stamping ground, Francis would
become intolerable, feeling more deeply than ever the loss of
the kingship which should have been his. On occasion it was
necessary for the journey to be broken by overnight stops at
hotels. On arrival Francis would stage a scene over the rooms
given to his party. But that was nothing to the row that he raised
when he got the bill in the morning.

It was at Neu Strelitz in 1873 that the seventy-six-year-old
Duchess of Cambridge suffered a stroke which left her paralysed.
She was brought back to England and installed in St James's
Palace. It was her grandmother's case which instilled into May
a lasting horror of illness. The Duchess, even in middle-age, was
not an attractive woman. Thick, black eyebrows dominated a
coarse-skinned face. She plastered her hair with black pomade.
She was large and she was severe. The stroke exaggerated her
handicaps and the Teck children dreaded visiting her. They were
given 'stingy' teas and were ordered to stand before her and sing
'God Save the Queen'. Then they were told to sit and be quiet
and look at albums. Strokes were not understood in those days
and the treatment was often wrong; certain it is that the sight
of her grandmother terrified May. The old Duchess lived on for
sixteen years, annually becoming more decrepit. She was so bent
that it was necessary to kneel on the floor to speak to her. She
went bald and kept her wig on a stand beside her. One visitor,
Princess Marie of Battenberg,[*16] was disconcerted, for 'her
absolutely bald head looked like a very big egg'.

Another problem about visiting the old Duchess was the
presence of her lady-in-waiting, Lady Geraldine Somerset, a
waspish woman with a strong preference for men. She adored

* Earl Mountbatten's aunt.

George of Cambridge – an unrequited love – and was kind to Francis and his sons. But towards Mary Adelaide and May she held a diabolical hate, the cause of which was hard to trace. This lady kept two diaries, one for the Duchess of Cambridge and one, in secret, for herself, a habit not uncommon among court officials of the nineteenth century. To its pages she confided the wrongdoings of Mary Adelaide and May. She was probably the only enemy in the life of the future Queen Mary.

The time came for the boys to go to school and, with floods of tears, they drove away. Dolly was May's favourite and she wrote to him daily, telling of her doings. She did not write to Frank: he was mischievous and cheeky. He never changed. When the two went on to Wellington, Frank surpassed himself by throwing the headmaster over a hedge, a feat of physical strength which earned him expulsion. He moved on to Cheltenham. His exploit did not please Queen Victoria, as Prince Albert had been deeply interested in the founding of Wellington College, introducing Teutonic methods of teaching with an army tradition and laying down rules which were designed to convert the British public schoolboy into an angel. When Alge's turn came, he was sent to Eton.

The loneliness of the White Lodge without the boys, the additional burden of the school fees and the ever-mounting household debts corroded the Tecks' marital relationship. He chain-smoked and shouted at his wife in public. At length he announced that his marriage had been engineered by the Cambridges and that he would much rather have wed the daughter of a rich industrialist.

Higher and higher climbed the debts and in 1880, the Duchess of Cambridge was forced to take over the education of the children. Yet Mary Adelaide still refused to take matters seriously or alter her ways. She was even apt to joke about the position. At the close of a charity meeting, a charity of which Mr Barker, the Kensington storekeeper, had been a generous supporter, she turned towards him, smiled, and then said to the audience, 'And now I must propose a special vote of thanks to Mr Barker, to whom we all owe so much.'

As the debt situation drew towards its climax, endless family meetings were held to decide what must be done. It was at length agreed that the Tecks should retire to the Continent, to retrench and keep clear of their creditors. A sum of money was raised by their German relations, guaranteed against the will of the Duchess of Cambridge and administered by a trustee. The Kensington Palace apartments were to be given up and the White Lodge put on a care-and-maintenance basis. It was the debts to the shops which had brought about this final step.

Mary Adelaide, who was in the process of again redecorating the White Lodge, fumed and took the train to Osborne. The timing was unfortunate for her, as John Brown had just died and the Queen was in low spirits. Mary Adelaide raved on about her rich brother who refused to help, about her miserly sister, and insisted that she was good value to the British public. All to no avail. On 6 June 1883, she wrote to a friend, 'I do my best to keep up my spirits and make myself pleasant, for alas! a great trial is before me. On Saturday next we are going up to Kensington Palace to wind up there, and break up the beautiful, happy home that has sheltered us for the last *sixteen* years, and in which all our children were born. You can guess the wrench it will be to us ...'[17] There followed a public auction at Kensington at which the Teck household possessions were sold: it turned out to be a most public occasion and the press gave it ample coverage.

At half past seven on the evening of Saturday, 15 September 1883, there gathered on the Continental departure platform at Victoria Station a sombre group of royalties: the Duke of Cambridge, humming and haaing in his usual manner; Augusta, Grand Duchess of Mecklenburg-Strelitz, in floods of tears; Lady Geraldine Somerset, representing the old Duchess of Cambridge; the Duke and Duchess of Teck, their daughter May and their sons. They stood there saying their goodbyes beside the train which was to take them to Paris via Newhaven and Dieppe. It was a silent farewell, even Mary Adelaide being subdued as she attempted to comfort her sister. It had been feared that Francis would stage one of his scenes, but he stood silent and apart as if in a trance. May snuggled deep into her long coat and sheltered in the shadows which the gas lights threw. This was disgrace, and she knew it. Even her identity had gone, for the Tecks were travelling as Counts and Countesses of Hohenstein.

They took their seats in the saloon coach. At 7.50 the whistle blew. Lady Geraldine said, 'There was no sound at all but the screeching of the engine.' The Tecks were going into exile.

CHAPTER III

Exile

THIS EXILE had a deep effect on May, altering not only her adolescent years but lasting on through the rest of her life. It was the humiliation which hurt. Unavoidably, it downgraded her parents in her estimation. To date, she had taken them for granted, as children do, but now she had reached an age when she could think for herself and she realized that she was under a handicap in life. Her contemporaries were completing their education and beginning to think of parties and 'coming out' and boyfriends, while May found herself backward in learning, totally unfitted for the ballroom and obviously without the financial background necessary for launching her into the social round. The bad temper of her father and the erratic behaviour of her mother, which evoked criticism and sniggers, destroyed her faith in herself. Always there was the thought that her parents' morganatic marriage reduced her to second rate among those with whom she should have moved with ease and equality. Her brothers being younger than herself, she was held back in sophistication, causing her to be treated as younger than she really was. Yet she had to play the part of 'little mother', mending their socks and tears in their clothes. She arrived in Europe somewhat bewildered, an errand boy for her mother, a placator of her father, living in a strange new world far removed from the garden at White Lodge and the woods of Richmond Park.

Her mother adopted a very different attitude towards the enforced exile. Once the Channel was crossed, she regained her natural aplomb. Not for her a silent and incognito retreat to the second-floor rooms of the Hotel Paoli in Florence. Once again she was the daughter of the Viceroy of Hanover, niece of the

King of Great Britain and fifth in line to the throne. She was irrepressible, somewhat to the embarrassment of her family.

The first weeks of exile were spent in delightful surroundings – a villa belonging to the Württemberg family on the Swiss shore of Lake Constance. An added advantage was that it was free. For a month, May and her brothers enjoyed themselves by the smooth water of the Bodensee. Then the time came for the journey to Florence and for the older boys to return to school in England. Sadly, May saw them off.

Mary Adelaide soon disposed of the incognito of Countess of Hohenstein and travelled in state. To her delight, Prefects met the party at the stations at which they halted. The highlight was an invitation to break the journey and dine with King Humbert of Italy. Mary Adelaide kept a detailed diary and after her experience at Monza she wrote:

> Dressed in red and black gown for the dinner, and about seven Francis and I reached the station, where one of the King's gentlemen received us and took us to the special train. We entered the royal saloon, which was handsomely fitted up and in twenty minutes reached Monza, where the King met us, and drove with us to the Palace just outside the town. We passed up a flight of steps and through a grand hall to a vestibule, or large *Saal*, in which we found the Queen – handsome and very pleasing – and all the company assembled. The Prince of Naples, a nice little fellow of fourteen, appeared for a few minutes before dinner, which was served in an adjoining large room. I sat between the King and Ministro della Casa, Conte Visone, and got on very pleasantly . . . Afterwards we adjourned to a small saloon, and I sat on a sofa talking to the Queen till summoned to depart. She embraced me repeatedly at parting.[1]

Thus inflated, the Teck ménage arrived at Florence. Here came contrast. The Hotel Paoli, in which rooms had been reserved for them, advertised that it catered for English tastes. The first shock was the wallpaper, '*huge* patterns and *glaring* colours and *hideous* contrasts.'[2] The second was that there were other guests on the same floor. To have strangers in their midst was intolerable to the Teck way of thinking, and they ordered that the relevant rooms should be kept empty. But when Francis received his account at the end of the month, he discovered that he was being charged for these rooms and there followed one of the uncontrollable fits of temper which were becoming more and more frequent in his life.

At first May did not like Florence, pining as she was for the wood and parkland surrounding the White Lodge, Richmond, and the Arno seemed small and brown after the gleaming Thames. From her window she looked down on a street wider at the bottom than it was at the top, and so narrow that two carriages could not pass. At dusk funeral processions wound along it, 'the body lying on an open bier (no coffin), surrounded by white-robed and hooded men, their faces, all but their eyes, concealed by white hoods, carrying torches'.[3] These depressed and haunted her. Her shyness was increased by hotel life. Her experience of hotels was limited to occasional overnight stops on journeys and she had never stayed in one before. And she had never before dined in a restaurant, open to the public gaze. She wrote to her brother Dolly, now back at school in England, that Florence was dull beyond words, that the houses were uncomfortably arranged and dirty and that the people all smelled of garlic. Her father noticed her melancholy and shared her feelings. He wrote to a friend in London that the only comfort in being without a home and a wanderer in foreign lands was that of being away from those whose want of heart, instead of preventing a scandal, increased it by word of mouth. He added that he had no intercourse with 'the enemy's camp', and by that he meant the Cambridge family, on whom he put the blame for all his troubles.

On the other hand Mary Adelaide was in her element. There was plenty of scope for social activities and she was quick to make the most of it, assisted by King Humbert, who lent her his royal box at the opera. There was a considerable Russian colony in Florence and in the autumn came an influx of those British who preferred warmth and music to the hunting fields of the shires and the draughts of the stately homes – authors, artists, poets, sculptors and academics. Ouida* cold be seen driving out

* Pseudonym of Maria de la Ramée, English novelist, author of *Under Two Flags*, etc.

[49]

in her carriage, and the painter Thaddeus Jones* enlivened the parties. They brought with them a relaxation of standards: *ménages à trois* became part of marital life. Word got back to London that Mary had been seen at a party where a society hostess was engaged in playing cards with her first husband, her second husband and her lover. Life there was in startling contrast to that at Windsor, and Queen Victoria disapproved. She wrote to her cousin regretting her choice of Florence as a place of retrenchment, it being a town of attractions and expense. It was not that she feared Mary Adelaide would give way to moral temptation – the very idea would have convulsed her – but she feared the possible financial outlay and the effect on sixteen-year-old May. She had grounds for her fears, for at Christmas she heard from the Cambridge trustees that Mary Adelaide had already spent £2000. Despite reprimand, she waltzed on. Her rooms were heavy with the scent of violets and roses, she hired carriages in which to parade in the Cascine, she gave dinner parties in the style of those she had staged at Kensington Palace, she ordered new gowns and sparkled with her splendid diamonds and tiara which she had resolutely refused to sell.

It was not until the New Year that May came to appreciate, and love, Florence. The change came about through a switch in staff. Her governess, Fraülein Gutman, was insular, stern and disapproving of both the Italian way of life and the culture. Aunt Augusta, Grand Duchess of Mecklenburg-Strelitz, who kept a watchful eye on the Teck children, decided that she must go. This coincided with the views of May and Alge. Ten-year-old Alge had expressed his opinion most forcibly when he pushed his sister's governess into a fountain. Mary Adelaide found Fraülein Gutman no companion and became tart with her. One afternoon, the Duchess asked her to fetch the biscuits which she would find in a hair-box in the bedroom. The German lady commented that she would not eat biscuits which were kept in such a place. At which Mary Adelaide snapped, 'If a Princess of Great Britain and Ireland can eat biscuits out of a hair-box, I

---

* Henry Thaddeus Jones settled in Florence in 1881. He later achieved great success as a portrait painter.

presume that the daughter of a Dresden dentist can.'[4] So the governess departed, without regrets on either side. In her place came an Italian mistress and teachers of French, music and drawing. May blossomed at once. Selected girls of her own age were brought in to share her studies, and expeditions began to galleries, concerts, the theatre and places of historic interest.

May read books about Florence and its art, studying in advance the scene of her next expedition. She wandered in the church of San Lorenzo, drinking in the wonders of Brunelleschi's interior. She read the life of Andrea del Sarto before visiting the cloisters of the Recouets in the Via Cavour. In the entrance hall of the Duomo she saw the portrait of Sir John Hawkwood, the Essex soldier of fortune who reached France as an archer of Edward III and put his sword at the service of Florence, helping to defeat her enemies, and wrote in her diary of his magnificent burial place, made at his own direction and adorned with frescoes by Uccello. She was a tireless walker and led her small party through the Pitti Palace and up the hill to the Boboli Gardens to savour the panorama of Florence. May had found herself.

On the night of 5 March 1884, disaster struck the Teck family. Duke Francis had a severe stroke. His left arm and leg were paralysed and his mouth was left crooked. His talking was confused. His wife could not come to terms with the shock. She put the illness down to sunstroke or a chill and took comfort from the more optimistic remarks of the doctor, convincing herself that Francis would be completely cured in three or four weeks. Frankly, she did not want to become deeply involved. She was still in her forties and was enjoying a continuous social whirl. Her husband was four years younger than she was and she could not bring herself to believe that he would be an invalid for the rest of his life, conveniently choosing to forget that Prince Albert, the Consort, had died at the age of forty-two. The oculist, who came later in the day, warned her of the seriousness of the illness, but she would not listen.

Upon May, who was only sixteen, fell the burden of his nursing. She shrank from illness, a result of paying visits to her grandmother after her stroke. But she had to attend to her father every hour of the day, and nearly a week passed before she could find time to write to Dolly and give him the news. The crisis had one notable effect on May. She, like her brothers, had inherited her father's temper. In future she determined to keep her emotions strictly under control and not to allow her father's quirks to upset her. It was a ruling which she was to adhere to for the rest of her life and one which showed at the time of the abdication of Edward VIII.

It was clear that the outbursts of rage contributed to the stroke. The trials of having no occupation and the constant worry over lack of money coupled with the final degradation of exile had proved too much for his volatile temperament. Although the seriousness of the situation was glossed over in Florence, it certainly was not in London and Mecklenburg-Strelitz. Grand Duchess Augusta attributed the attack solely to Francis's excited state and his violence. The Duchess of Cambridge was of the opinion that it was the result of a stand-up row between Mary Adelaide and her husband. The Duke of Cambridge dismissed Mary's sunstroke theory as rubbish, recognizing the symptoms of a regular stroke.[5] Travellers returning from Italy increased their fears. The British Ambassador, Sir James Hudson, gave a 'deplorable account', saying that Francis was now an old man, that the stroke had been a very severe one and that his memory had gone.[6]

Mary Adelaide remained undismayed. On 20 March, she wrote in her diary, 'Francis walked about the passages and into his sitting room for the first time since his illness. Hurrah! I dressed in grey satin and wheatears for the Artists' micareme fête at their club, Circular Artistico, to which at ten o'clock the Monsons, Colnaghis, and Edgar accompanied May and me. The rooms were most artistically decorated by the artists themselves. The grand centre room had sun and moon transparencies, and was hung with stuffs . . .' etc., etc. It was clear where her interests lay. Soon she had Francis going out to dinner parties and taking part in expeditions. When his words became confused, she excused him with the explanation that his 'brains were loose in his head'. His treatment was the complete opposite to that which should have been applied to a convalescing stroke case.

Francis's illness temporarily interfered with a long-cherished plan of Mary Adelaide's – she wanted a house of her own where she could entertain and return the hospitality she had received. She was lucky in her planning, for she was offered a house free of rent. It was called I Cedri and lay on the left bank of the River Arno at Bagno a Ripoli, some four miles from Florence. The owner was Miss Bianca Light, sister of Major Light, President of the English Club in Florence, and Miss Light's only stipulation was that she should be allowed to occupy her own apartment there when she felt so inclined.

The Villa I Cedri was originally a fifteenth-century building, with a flat, tiled roof. As its name implies, it was rich in cedar trees, but the garden was in the English fashion and full of daffodils and narcissi, violets and hyacinths. There was an uninterrupted view of the river, and an old mill and a farmhouse in the grounds. The Duke's illness was not long allowed to prevent the move and by 3 April, the Teck family were installed.

To May it was heaven and a great relief to be away from the narrow city streets. In a wide straw hat she wandered among the flowers, strolled down to the river, sketched the old farmhouse and chatted with the peasants. The change was also appreciated by her mother, who adored the garden. But her chief satisfaction came from the financial aspect. Urged by London to economize, she was now able to reply that she was living rent free and no longer having to settle the accounts of Signor Paoli. But, unbalanced as she was in matters monetary, she convinced herself that she was now free to spend in other directions. Of course, she must have a carriage, to reach her friends in Florence. Alterations had to be made to the drive to cope with guests' vehicles. And the backlog of hospitality must be caught up with without delay. And it was. In fact, she was no better off than she had been before.

The twenty-sixth of May was Princess May's seventeenth birthday. It is time to look at this maturing young lady. She was five feet seven inches tall, with an erect figure, tightly corsetted, and beautiful legs – which were hidden, rather to her sadness, then and always. Her hair was a mixture of light brown and yellow and shone gold in the sunlight. Her eyes were piercing blue and her complexion was described as 'wild rose'. Her mouth twitched when she was amused but she seldom laughed in public as she considered, quite wrongly, that she had a vulgar laugh. She thought herself too like Queen Charlotte, wife of George III, ever to be beautiful. The picture of her was somewhat spoiled by her hairdos. She wore her hair dressed tight with braid, with an artificial fringe, called a 'bang', on her forehead. This was her mother's idea and Mary Adelaide had little idea of dress or fashion. Her own conception of being smart was to robe herself in a tent of rich satin or velvet, of striking colours, drench herself with the scent of hot-house flowers and crown the ensemble with tiara and diamonds. In May's wardrobe no attempt was made to follow prevailing fashion, nor any effort made to convert her into an enticement to men. She was a thoroughly personable young woman, popular with everyone, but considered staid and somewhat prim.

Her mother turned up trumps for the great occasion of her birthday, giving her carbuncle and diamond earrings and two bracelets with pearl clasps. But there were few other gifts except trinkets from the staff and a few tokens from Florentine friends. From England came nothing but a miserly £2 from grandmother Cambridge. May considered that she was lucky that it was not thirty shillings. Now this was strange, for seventeenth birthdays were always treated as milestones in the royal circle and the occasion for particular presents. Nothing came from Queen Victoria, the Prince and Princess of Wales or the Duke of Cambridge. There was a reason behind this. The relations at home considered that by this time May should have been confirmed, but this important event in her life had not yet taken place. This was because Mary Adelaide was of the opinion that her daughter, as a great-granddaughter of King George III, should be confirmed at the Chapel Royal, St James, and not in obscurity in Florence. Queen Victoria, the old Duchess of Cambridge and Uncle George, Duke of Cambridge, did not agree. They knew full well that if the Teck family were to return to London for the event, it would be used as an excuse for a permanent return and that Mary Adelaide would stage an occasion which would involve a great deal of money and a great deal of fuss. Having made her views clear, Mary Adelaide adopted a cunning ploy: she refused to answer letters on the subject. This suited her, as she was so busy entertaining at I Cedri that she had little time for writing letters: she used the abrupt and expensive telegraph system instead. Even Queen Victoria could not obtain replies. She was unaccustomed to such treatment, and said so. Mary Adelaide countered with a telegram: 'Gracious letter received. Answer follows.' The Queen went so far as to arrange for the Bishop of Gibraltar, a pawn in her game, to travel to Florence and conduct the service, but Mary Adelaide circumvented that. So, in her eighteenth year, May remained unconfirmed.

Mary Adelaide was never content to be in one place for long and by mid-summer she was thinking of a holiday. Using the excuse that the heat of I Cedri was too great for Francis's health, still far from stable, she asked her mother for a loan. The Duchess of Cambridge offered £200 provided the Tecks went to Schloss Rumpenheim on the Main, the family home of the Hesses, where relations could keep an eye on expenditure. This was not at all the kind of vacation that Mary Adelaide had in mind – she wanted a spa. When she refused to go to Rumpenheim, the Duchess withdrew her offer: by now she had come to regard her daughter as a delinquent. With or without financial support, Mary Adelaide decided that she would have the kind of holiday she wanted, and on 2 July the Teck family set out for Seelisberg on Lake Lucerne. There Francis was to take the water-cure, including a course of rubbing and *Heil-Gymnastick*.[7]

The party stayed at the Hotel Sonnenberg, which was crammed with German tourists who tramped the uncarpeted corridors the night through. They were not the kind of people with whom the Tecks were accustomed to mix, and urgent messages were sent to friends in Florence to join them and leaven the mixture. They made expeditions into the mountains, but there was difficulty in finding an alpenstock which would support Mary Adelaide: she had a nasty fall when one snapped under her. They went up the Rigi to see the sunset of one day and the dawn of another, resting for the intervening hours at an hotel at Vitznau. May's comment was, 'Horrid hotel and rude people.'

It was decided to move on. Their next target was the Württemberg relations on the Bodensee. Here they discovered that the hotel into which they had booked was a 'pot house', but the Württembergs were in residence at the Villa Seefeld and there the Tecks spent most of their time. They sailed and fished and in the evenings played cards and charades, life being somewhat rough as Dolly and Frank were on holiday from school. May noted that their voices had become gruff and wondered why.

One evening, at the instigation of the older boys, an attempt was made at table-turning. The object of the experiment was a massive mahogany dining-table which, in the normal course of events, would have taken six men to lift. But in due course the table began what a guest described as 'a jumping progress round the room'.[8] Owing to her size, Mary Adelaide was slow in taking evasive action and the table 'jumped' on her, knocked her flat and pinned her to the floor. The spell having broken, it took twelve men, women and children to free her.

On the further shore of the lake was Schloss Friedrichshafen, where lived King Carl I and Queen Olga of Württemberg. King Carl was odd: the Empress Frederick of Germany described him as being not 'all there'. It was left to his Queen to keep the court running. The Tecks were bidden to make a state visit and to introduce their children, an ordeal for Francis, who considered that it was he who should be King. The visit was exceedingly formal and proved something of a strain, but it gave May the chance of seeing German court life as it used to be. She remembered details of that afternoon until there was no one left alive to recall the etiquette of Friedrichshafen.

The Tecks' next halting place also had strong royal connections. An invitation was accepted to stay with the Hanover family at Gmunden, and on 10 September they entrained for the palace lying by Traun See lake in Austria. It was in violent contrast with the visit to Friedrichshafen. Ernest, Duke of Cumberland, was their host. He was the son of blind King George of Hanover, who had lost his throne in the war of 1866. In turn, King George was the son of the dreaded Ernest, Duke of Cumberland, son of George III, who had succeeded to the throne of Hanover when Victoria became Queen of Great Britain, thus displacing Mary Adelaide's father as Viceroy.

Ernest had poor shoulders, a long neck, was bald and wore strong spectacles. He had the reputation of being the ugliest man in Europe, but he was kind-hearted and May was very attached to her 'Uncle Ernst'. He had complicated the royal family network by marrying Princess Thyra of Denmark, younger sister of Princess Alexandra of Wales. Thyra's other sister was Marie Feodorovna, wife of Emperor Alexander III of Russia. Her brother was King George of the Hellenes, who had married Grand Duchess Olga of Russia, and they were also guests at Gmunden, with their four wild sons. Queen Victoria disapproved of the Gmunden establishment, which she referred to as 'the Royal Mob'. And not without reason, for all the offspring of King Christian IX and Queen Louise of Denmark were well known for their pranks and roystering, and the Russians were just as bad. They were all masters at making rude noises and if they saw anyone trying to write a letter or a diary they would howl in unison. Apple-pie beds were a common feature of life and it was wise to check a door to ensure that a bucket of water was not balanced upon it. Outings on the lake usually ended in someone being submerged and mountain expeditions were fraught with danger. The result was that May's studies were nonexistent. Yet she became familiar with a wide spread of European royalty which was to stand her in good stead in later years. In particular she became the close friend and confidant of Queen Olga of Greece, and this was to prove a friendship which affected her eventual choice of a husband.

Mary Adelaide's itch for being on the move was still not satisfied, and after two months at Gmunden the family moved on to Graz and then, for two days, to Venice, where May commented that her father did not like the rooms and staged one of his 'scenes'. Money and invitations being exhausted, the Tecks returned to the Villa I Cedri at the end of November.

Meanwhile, at home, discussions were afoot as to the future of the Tecks. George, Duke of Cambridge, was persistent in the view that there was no point in keeping them abroad any longer.

May was not receiving a proper education and young Alge was not being educated at all. Traipsing round Europe was obviously bad for Francis's health. Financially, there was no advantage in their absence as Mary Adelaide was spending more than she would be able to do at home, where an eye could be kept on her. Queen Victoria, thinking of May's confirmation, was agreeable to the return of the 'delinquents', but considered that they should foresake White Lodge, Richmond, and be content with an apartment in Kensington Palace. Mary Adelaide turned down this idea flat: it was White Lodge that she wanted. The old Duchess of Cambridge proved the stumbling block to the Teck return: she was now very old and did not want the peace of her life at St James's Palace disturbed. But in April 1885, she relented and a message was despatched to I Cedri that the exiles might return.

The Cambridges, who considered that they were behaving magnanimously, were in for a shock. Mary Adelaide fired back, announcing that she could not possibly leave for at least six weeks owing to prior engagements. Even then she would need a house in London as White Lodge was not ready for occupation. In the event it was not until the evening of 24 May that the Tecks joined the night express from Florence. They spent the next day in Paris, where the opportunity was taken to visit the Louvre. May wrote, 'I admired the Rubenses and some of the Murillos immensely. The rooms are beautiful . . . We lunched with Lord Lyons (the British Ambassador), who was kindness itself . . . We left Paris at eight, and our crossing was so-so, rather a swell.'[9] She never was a good sailor.

At six o'clock next morning they stepped on to the platform at Victoria station. It was May's eighteenth birthday.

CHAPTER IV

Debutante

THE TECKS arrived back in London with no home to go to. Once again Baroness Burdett-Coutts, of the well-known banking family, came to their rescue and they found themselves in a little house in Chester Square. May wrote to a friend in Italy:

> We came to this tiny nutshell which can only contain Mama, Alge and myself and seven servants, Papa staying elsewhere. The advantage is that it has been lent us by Baroness Coutts' sister, the disadvantage is that the drawing room contains nine cases of stuffed birds, hideous prints of ancestors, etc. which we can't get rid of as there's no room to store them in . . . We breakfasted at Marlborough House and then came here . . . I am not going out much here as the charming family (the Wales) don't think it good for me, I am so young you see! Only eighteen.

At that age she considered herself grown-up and objected to being treated as a child and referred to as 'the chick' by her mother. Fortunately by the end of July she was back at the White Lodge and free to roam once more about Richmond Park.

Mary Adelaide soon came to blows with her relations over the status of her daughter. She wanted to take May to a court concert, but was told that she could not as May had neither been confirmed nor presented to the Queen. So steps were taken to put matters to rights.

The debutante days of the girls of the late nineteenth century were taken for granted as being the happiest of their lives and no effort or expense was spared in making them so. But for May they were not, all the fates seeming to conspire against her. She had not been through the preliminaries of confirmation and presentation. Her family had no money. Her father was ill and, although he had his good days, he was gradually deteriorating. Her grandmother, the Duchess of Cambridge, was eighty-eight, chairbound and exceedingly awkward. Her mother was out of favour with the royal family. May herself had only been educated on a scrappy basis, was inherently shy and had no experience either of court life or the high-life of society over which Bertie, Prince of Wales, reigned. In addition, a death disrupted her programme. Two days before the first dance was staged for her, Francis's father, Duke Alexander of Württemberg, died and she was restricted by a lengthy period of mourning. Often she wished that she was back at I Cedri. 'Oh! how happy those days were – I sometimes long to go back there,' she wrote to a friend in Florence. She was also lonely, for her constant companion, her young brother Alge, was sent to Eton and Dolly and Frank passed through Sandhurst and joined their regiments. Dolly was posted to India and she missed him most of all.

May was confirmed on 1 August 1885 at the Chapel Royal, St James, by the Bishop of St Albans. The day was not without its ructions. The chairborne Duchess of Cambridge wished the ceremony to take place before her, in her own room, but Mary Adelaide was insistent on the chapel. George of Cambridge was in a towering rage as the carriage which he had sent to Richmond to pick up the party had been kept waiting for two hours by his sister. It was unpunctuality such as this that instilled into May the importance of keeping to a programme to a minute: she was never late.

But for the first time in her life she received valuable presents. The Queen gave her a diamond butterfly brooch and an inscribed white ivory prayer book. The Prince of Wales produced a beaten gold bracelet, the Duchess of Cambridge some beautiful diamond stars and George of Cambridge a clasp containing the hair of George III and Queen Charlotte. Her mother gave her a diamond bracelet and diamond and pearl earrings, and her father a brooch.

The next step was presentation to the Queen. This took place in a Drawing Room at Buckingham Palace in March of the following year. May stood between her mother and the Princess of Wales in the semi-circle of princesses and royal duchesses

H.S.H. Francis, Duke of Teck

H.R.H. Mary Adelaide, Duchess of Teck

Princess May on her father's knee, with her mother
in the garden of Kensington Palace

Princess May of Teck in her 'teens

Prince George as a young man

Princess May at the age of 19

beside the throne. Being only a Serene Highness, May was getting preferential treatment which she would never have received at a German court, but Queen Victoria did not put much store by the handicap of being the child of a morganatic marriage. She was early impressed by May and noted her potential and good looks. On a number of occasions she asked her to stay at Windsor, on one occasion commenting that May was 'in great looks'[1] and on another that 'May Teck looked very pretty.'[2]

May and Queen Victoria were two of a kind and, when roused, May had the same capacity as the Queen for being outright. Her *bête noire*, Lady Geraldine Somerset, was for ever picking fault with both her ('May in a *hideous* bonnet') and her parents. May wrote to her aunt Aunt Augusta, who was her confidant and ally, of the action she had taken:

> After Papa's illness she wrote me one of her rudest letters, you know her style, complaining in very insolent terms of Mama. I do not think she ought to be allowed to write and speak to us children about Mama and Papa in the way she does . . . for it makes it very unpleasant. I have written to her about it and given her a bit of my mind and I daresay she will be frantic and complain of me to Uncle George, but I don't care . . .[3]

May began to play her part in state functions and in January 1886 was present at the opening of Parliament. She witnessed the laying of the foundation stone of Tower Bridge by the Prince of Wales and was with Queen Victoria at the opening of the Colonial and Indian Exhibition and of the People's Palace in the East End of London. The greatest excitement of her debutante days came with the Golden Jubilee of 1887. The Cambridges had their own little procession of three carriages, May sharing one with her three brothers. Mary Adelaide received a boisterous reception from the crowds, who loved her. She had a way of turning up her plump, smiling face as she waved, and this was much appreciated by those in upstairs windows. When it was all over, May wrote to a young friend in Baltimore, USA, 'We have all been so overworked this year that we are nearly dead. I really cannot describe all the fêtes. The excitement here in London was something not to be imagined, and I believe it was this that kept us all up through that fatiguing time when we were on the go from morning till night – *sans relâche.*'4

In the social field May preferred visits to country houses to parties and balls. At the latter a degree of forwardness and some bright remarks were called for, and May was never any good at small talk. Her shyness was a big drawback. Mary Adelaide had many friends and invitations to visit stately homes poured in. The Tecks went to Rufford, Ashridge, Welbeck, Thoresby, Hardwicke, Ford Castle, Alnwick, Clumber, the Grange in Hampshire and many houses in Scotland. For May, the journeys were a thrill: the entries in her diary demonstrate her powers of observation of the countryside. Servants and porters cared for every detail regarding luggage, and luncheon baskets, foot-warmers and rugs made travelling comfortable. There was so much to study in the architecture and the furniture of the houses which she visited, and there were lovely gardens and parks in which to roam. There was music in the evenings, Mary Adelaide being in much demand as she had a most pleasing voice.

The families the Tecks visited were in contrast with those patronized by the Prince of Wales, who liked to gamble and frequent the bowling alley until the early hours of the morning. Corridor-creeping was a pastime unknown to May. Her favourite place was Hatfield: 'Really quite the nicest house I have ever stayed in. The house is beautiful, and everything so well arranged. We were a party of forty. The ball was delightful, and we enjoyed ourselves thoroughly.'5

But there was one weekend visit which May did not relish, and that was to Sandringham House, Norfolk, the home of the Prince of Wales. Firstly, her mother did not get on well with Bertie. He was forever teasing her and making jokes about her weight, and Mary Adelaide did not like it. Secondly, Sandringham house-parties were highly organized and ran to a tight schedule. While Alexandra, Princess of Wales, was kindness itself as a hostess, Bertie had his own way of doing things and one had to conform. Thirdly, the Wales girls had grown up to become difficult young ladies. All three – Louise, Victoria (Toria) and Maud (Harry) – suffered from poor health, and neuralgia, fevers, abscesses, influenza and cysts succeeded one another with regular monotony. This was not their fault, but an inherited weakness which also afflicted their brothers, Albert Victor and George. All the children of Bertie and Alexandra (Alix) had been born prematurely. Their father's blood was rhesus positive, their mother's rhesus negative, the consequences of which were not understood in those days. Queen Victoria could not fathom it and dubbed them a 'puny lot'. It indeed seemed strange that while Bertie and Alix were full of high spirits, brimming with energy and able to dance all night, their offspring were lethargic and backward. The girls had scarcely been educated and May found it hard to find common interests. Yet Louise, Victoria and Maud were full of their own importance, for on the Norfolk estate they were queens of all they surveyed. And they were Royal Highnesses, while May was only Serene, and they let her know it. They also had, in common with all the descendants of King Christian IX of Denmark, a liking for practical jokes and making fun of people. May tried to write a letter. She ended, 'Silly Harry has just made this blot I am so sorry – Louise, Toria and Maud are making such a row I cannot write any more.'[6]

One day she overheard Victoria tell a male guest that he was to sit next to May at dinner. She apologized for this, saying that May had nothing to say for herself and was a bore. This made May even more tongue-tied than usual. What she needed was encouragement. Even her mother took the wrong line, apologizing for her daughter and urging her to brighten up.

May was not starved of Continental travel, visiting St Moritz annually with her mother and staying at the Hotel Victoria. Good, clean fun was the order of the day, a favourite after-dinner game being 'Mrs McGullicudy's family', which was a contrast indeed with the idea of fun at Sandringham. Half the guests left the room, half stayed put. Those outside were called in one by one to guess a word which the 'McGullicudy family' acted. One evening Sir Charles and Lady Wyndham were participants in the game. Lady Wyndham failed to guess the word and her husband ribbed her, 'I thought you had more intelligence than that.' 'Only an idiot would think of a word like that,' answered his wife. 'Really,' laughed Sir Charles, 'it was Her Royal Highness's suggestion.'[7]

Lady Wyndham recalled the occasion when she was in a

party which set out to climb a glacier. She had no idea of the ordeal before her, was soon exhausted and the heels came off her shoes, whilst far ahead was the seemingly tireless, lithe figure of Princess May. 'She simply went on and on.' Her ladyship returned to the hotel and collapsed in a chair. May was spry and sound in both legs at dinner. Lady Wyndham asked her how she had managed it. 'Oh,' replied May, 'I had a hot bath and then it seemed as if nothing had happened.'[8]

One morning in 1888, May made a shock discovery. In her own words, spoken half a century later, she said, 'I suddenly discovered that I was not educated.'[9] The reason behind the discovery was the arrival at the White Lodge of a governess-companion. Her name was Mademoiselle Hélène Bricka, but she was known simply as Mlle Bricka. She was tall and dark and ugly, with a mottled complexion. She wore a *toupé*, about which the Teck boys teased her. She was French Alsatian, widely travelled and spoke English, French and German fluently. She had studied modern history and social problems, was radically minded and no respecter of royalty. She treated May as if she were a child and swamped her field of intelligence. 'Bricka' had a fiery temper but May soon learned to master this, and the two became bosom friends and so remained until the governess's death during the First World War.

May's plan was to improve her education by reading for six hours a day, every day of the week, regardless of other engagements – the only exception being when she was bidden to Sandringham where reading was impossible. May, when Queen, said, 'I tried not to let anything interfere with my reading. Somehow I managed to get six hours out of every day.'[10] Bricka and she devoured Meredith, Carlyle, Froude and George Eliot, specializing in British history but interchanging that with the talked-about new books of the day. It was here that May came across a habit of her mother's which she found most irritating. Mary Adelaide read only spasmodically and in a narrow field, but she found it an advantage to be able to air her views on new books at the dinner table. So May would be quizzed about the highlights and paragraphs of special interest and then, in the evening, from her place at the dinner table, she would hear her mother discoursing learnedly about the latest best-seller, quoting points which May had given her that morning. Thus, through her studies, May became more widely read than any of her contemporaries. It was strange that she was to marry a man who did not like reading. When King George V told John Buchan (Lord Tweedsmuir) how much he enjoyed his books, his wife remarked, 'The King does not get much time for reading, and when he does I'm afraid he reads the most awful rubbish.'[11] But then George was one of the Sandringham tribe who had made reading impossible for May.

As she progressed through her fifties, Mary Adelaide became increasingly involved in charitable works; they became an obsession. Although an expert at organizing, she was no business-woman, and the White Lodge was covered with the confetti of unanswered letters. Staffing was largely the trouble. Inside the house were a groom of the chambers, a butler, an under-butler, two footmen, a steward and his assistant, four dressers, a cook, a kitchen-maid, a scullery-maid, four housemaids and three laundry-maids – but no secretary or lady-in-waiting for Mary Adelaide. The answer was that May was called upon to fill the gap, a big strain on a girl who was trying to read for six hours a day.

The most important of the charities was the London Needlework Guild, and the piles of gift parcels made the White Lodge look like a jumble sale. Mary Adelaide was forever urging her friends to send more, without contemplating the work involved in sorting them. Thus May, on her knees, would have to make sense of hastily packed parcels, trying to match up stockings and shoes. Even the Prince of Wales was ensnared. On the second occasion he included a curt note, saying that he hoped that this time Francis (still ill but alert enough to know a bargain when he saw it) would not extract the better of the suits for himself.

In those days, obtaining places in charity homes and hospitals depended on the recommendation of the powerful and letters had to be sent to the governors asking for vacancies for old ladies in rest homes and treatment for ill people in hospitals. Mary Adelaide was inundated with the names of the needy and the burden of writing the letters fell on May.

The plight of the poor of London in the cold winters at the

end of the 1880s was appalling and Mary Adelaide campaigned vigorously for something to be done. Her chief enemy was the 'sweating system', by which cheap labour was exploited. On ordering a new pair of shoes for May, she demanded of the maker how much he paid his workers. When she found out, she pronounced that no more orders would come from her unless the wages were improved. They were. May never forgot this and throughout her life watched the welfare of her workers.

In 1888, the House of Lords appointed a Select Committee to enquire into the 'sweating system' in the East End of London. 'Over a period of eight or nine months, the committee sat, examining some two hundred-odd sweated workers, who trekked from the Mile End Road, Whitechapel and Bethnal Green to give evidence before the lords of their starvation wages, the horrible length of their average working days and those of their children, who worked with them, revealing in their course a story of disease, destitution and sheer human misery which made the lords shudder in their judgement seats, and on one notable occasion, moved them to such an extremity that they rose from their seats and, 'with due and proper escort, made a personal tour of the wretched hovels of the East End'.[12]

Mary Adelaide and May took an intense interest. The chairman of the committee, Lord Dunraven, was a friend and a neighbour of the Tecks and he enlightened them on the unreported details. In the event little but suggestions for sanitary improvements emerged from the committee's report, but May learned much of blue books* and like literature and her charitable work as Queen was largely founded on this experience.

Another duty which occupied much of May's time was frequent visits to her grandmother, the Duchess of Cambridge, at St James's Palace. These visits were somewhat of an ordeal, the Duchess being so bent that May had to sit on the floor to talk to her. One obsession ruled the old lady's life, and that was May's marriage. She was forever producing new candidates, some entirely unsuitable and some already married. Her mind was beginning to wander and she relied on the *Almanach de*

---

* Official reports of Parliament on the Privy Council.

Gotha,* regardless of the point that the last thing May wanted was to be tied to a small Continental court. The Duchess pushed the cause of the Grand Duke Michael of Russia (whom her family considered absolutely wrong and an enemy of Britain), the Prince of Anhalt and the Prince of Naples. May had seen the last named in Florence but, on seeing him again, dismissed him as being too short and not beautiful to behold. The position as regards an alliance with a leading royal house was summed up by the Crown Princess of Germany, wife of the future Emperor William II. She condemned (to the fury of Queen Victoria) a union with her brother, the Duke of Schleswig-Holstein, as a *mésalliance* and one that she would not dream of encouraging. The truth was that May was not royal enough to be selected by senior princes, and not rich enough to marry into the British aristocracy, who, owing to the fall in prices of wheat and land, were feeling the pinch. In addition it must be appreciated that she was not a man's girl. She was unemotional, too withdrawn and too occupied with her family's problems and her own education. Her relations feared that she would be like her mother, who had not married until she was thirty-three.

In the early months of 1889, the Duchess of Cambridge's health declined further. She died suddenly on 6 April. Only the Princess of Wales, who was at Marlborough House, was able to reach the deathbed in time. George of Cambridge was inspecting troops in Ireland and Mary Adelaide was immersed in a hot bath at the White Lodge. May had a traumatic time breaking the news to her mother, extracting her from the bath and driving up to St James's Palace.

Although the Duchess was nearing her ninety-second birthday and her death was not unexpected, her passing was deeply felt as she was the last of the Georgians, having been born in the eighteenth century. Queen Victoria wrote to her cousin George, 'It is a sad and solemn feeling that there is no one above us any longer, and that *we* are now the *only old ones left*.'[13] She attended the funeral at Kew, the first time that she had attended such a service in England.

---

* An animal directory to the aristocracies of Europe.

It was during this sad time that the Queen spotted what she thought and hoped was the answer to an awkward situation. Her eldest grandson by the Prince and Princess of Wales, Albert Victor (Eddy), next in line of succession after his father, was sorely in need of a wife. In fact he needed more than a wife – he needed a guide, a secretary and a support. The Queen watched May dealing with all the troubles of her grandmother's death, noted her quiet demeanour and her efficiency, and said to herself, May is the solution.

Eddy was indeed a problem. He was a five-month child, having been born in January 1864 although he was not expected until April. A puny child, he was entirely dependent on his mother, brightening when she was near, and she saw an appealing side to him which others did not. He was backward in learning, as, to a lesser extent, was his younger brother George. Both were undisciplined, interrupted grown-ups in conversation, played havoc with stately games of croquet and used bad language picked up in the stables. Queen Victoria wished the boys to go to Wellington College, in which the Prince Consort had taken such a lively interest. She was told that this was not feasible, and that they were going to join the *Britannia* training ship at Dartmouth. She objected, writing, 'The very rough sort of life to which boys are exposed on board ship is the very thing not calculated to make a refined and amiable Prince, who in after years (if God spares him) is to ascend the throne. It would give him a very one-sided view of life which is not desirable . . .'[14] She was then told that if Eddy went to a public school, he would be dubbed a dunce. Well then, answered the Queen, why not send the elder boy to *Britannia* and the younger to Wellington? She had to be told the truth: Eddy and George could not be parted as if they were, Eddy would go to pieces. This was the first example of weakness in the premature children of the Prince and Princess of Wales, a weakness which spread to the grandchildren. Thus George V became dependent on May, Edward VIII on Mrs Wallis Simpson.

In due course the boys, as naval cadets, were sent round the world in HMS *Bacchante*. It appeared a strange decision to many thus to despatch the two sons of the Prince of Wales, heirs

to the throne after him. If they were drowned in a mishap at sea
— as they nearly were in a gale off the west coast of Australia —
the next in line would be Louise of Wales, a hypochondriac and
shy. Louise married the Duke of Fife in 1889. Next year she had
a son, born dead.

At the ages of eighteen and seventeen, the boys came safely
home. George opted to stay in the navy, while a band of tutors
descended on Sandringham in an effort to instil enough learning
into Eddy's head to enable him to attend Cambridge University
and then enter the army. One of the tutors reported, 'He hardly
knows the meaning of the words *to read*.'[15] But he was sent to
Trinity College. Strange rumours began to float about regarding
his goings-on there. Then *Punch* produced a cartoon of his life
at college. Eddy was shown on a balcony, two undergraduates
looking up at him. One says, 'Isn't it beautiful?' The other adds,
'Too lovely to look at.'[16] The inference was obvious.

In a rage Bertie descended upon Cambridge and took his son
away. He was shortly afterwards gazetted a lieutenant in the
10th Hussars. But the army could do nothing with him. Popular
enough as he was with his fellow officers, he was completely
lethargic, condemned his General as a 'lunatic' and rebelled against
the rigours of cavalry routine. In 1889 came scandal. It was
revealed that men in high society were visiting a homosexual
brothel off Tottenham Court Road: among the names listed was
that of Prince Eddy. Rumours continued that he often frequented
such clubs and there was known as 'Victoria'. Eddy was despatched to stay with relations on the Continent and then sent
to India. On his way home he sampled the pleasures traditionally
enjoyed by Eastern princes. The climax came when the magazine
Truth[17] published an imaginary interview with him about his
Indian tour. He was asked of his impressions of the country.
The answer attributed to him was:

> You ask me what impressed me most
> Whilst Hindustan I travelled o'er?
> My answer is, A certain man
> I came across at Shuttadore.

The character in question was revealed to be a laundryman at Shuttadore. The jibe about 'Shut that door' was to live in the public's mind for a century, as were other sins. Eddy was suspected of being the murderer Jack the Ripper and the rumour would not die, despite the fact that he had obviously neither the brains, the skill, nor the fire.

Something had to be done and quickly. Eddy was created Duke of Clarence and Avondale and it was decreed that in future he was to be known strictly as Albert Victor. The ruling came from Windsor that he must be married off without delay. Under considerable pressure from his father, the Prince of Wales, Albert Victor turned his eyes to the ladies. Margaret, daughter of the Empress Frederick of Germany and sister of Kaiser William, was produced but turned down because she was too 'horsey'. But it remains a point of interest to speculate on what would have happened in 1914 if the British King had been married to the Kaiser's sister. Another candidate was Hélène Louise Henrietta, daughter of the Comte de Paris, head of the French royal house. This was impossible on religious grounds. Albert Victor switched his attentions to Lady Sybil St Clair Erskine, who kept his letters but gave her heart elsewhere.

The next head to be prepared for the block was that of Princess May of Teck. The 'chief' executioner staging the scene was none other than Queen Victoria. In view of the foregoing, it is worth considering how she could have contemplated such a fate for a girl for whom she had great admiration and who was a blood relation.

Not for want of trying, Queen Victoria knew little about sex. This was for the simple reason that there was no one to tell her. Her father had died when she was an infant. She was not on good terms with her mother. Albert, although of high fertility, was not interested in matters sexual, certainly not considering it a subject for conversation. The household and royal advisers could hardly be expected to call a spade a spade when conversing with the formidable Queen. Yet her curiosity was obvious. When her two eldest sons strayed, she insisted on dredging up all the 'sordid details'. But she did not learn much. She did her own study. One afternoon when she was believed to be mourning

Albert in solitude at Balmoral, it was discovered that she was deep in a lurid book entitled *The Confessions of a Priest*.

For all that, she remained a tyro on the matter of perversion and sexual oddities. If she had known anything of homosexuality, she would scarcely have encouraged the marriage of Grand Duke Ernest of Hesse and the Rhine to his cousin, Princess Victoria Melita of Edinburgh. 'No boy was safe,' said fiery Victoria Melita, 'from the stable hands to the kitchen help. He slept quite openly with them all.'[18] The Queen knew Ernest better than she did Albert Victor, for his mother, Princess Alice, had died when he was young and the Queen had had a considerable say in his upbringing, yet she never guessed – and was never told. On the distaff side she knew nothing. When the draft of a bill allowing sexual intercourse between consenting males and consenting females was sent to her for approval, she crossed out 'consenting females' and wrote in the margin, 'Impossible.'

The Prince and Princess of Wales were divided in their opinions as to the future of their eldest son. Bertie, with good reason, wanted him out of the way and suggested that he be sent off on a lengthy tour of the Empire, on a slow ship which took as long as possible between halting places. He was himself involved in so much trouble that he did not relish the problems of others. He was head over heels in love with Lady 'Daisy' Brooke, afterwards Countess of Warwick, and was engaged in furious conflict with her former lover, Lord Charles Beresford. He was deeply concerned in the Tranby Croft baccarat affair, in which Sir William Gordon-Cumming was accused of cheating: he was now planning to take the matter to court. Kaiser William, with whom he was at loggerheads, was due to make a state visit to Britain and doubtless would have some unpleasant remarks to make both about the Tranby Croft affair and Albert Victor – as he did. So Bertie was fully occupied and had no time for the vagaries of a recalcitrant son.

For her part, Alexandra wished to have her Eddy at home, where she could keep an eye on him. It reached a stage where she could no longer discuss the matter with her husband and she disappeared to Denmark. Neither objected to May as a bride for Albert Victor, though they were apt to regard her as a makeshift, being a 'poor relation'.

Queen Victoria did not wish Albert Victor to go on a colonial tour – he had already been round the world and visited India. Why not let him go to Europe, of which he knew nothing, and make himself known to the courts there and learn something of diplomacy? He could then marry May in the spring of 1892. She planned rigorously and in detail. More and more often May appeared at court balls and functions and invitations came to her to visit the best houses. Then, in October 1891, she was bidden to Balmoral. It was in the nature of a final inspection and May passed with flying colours. The Queen wrote to the Empress Frederick, 'May is a particularly nice girl, so quiet and yet cheerful and so very carefully brought up and so sensible. She is grown very pretty.'

By now everyone but the parties concerned seemed to know all about the proposed alliance. The Tecks took it for granted that it would come off. Mary Adelaide and her husband were in a tizzy of delight and George of Cambridge was ill advised enough to chat about it to Lady Geraldine Somerset, who had her own acid comments to make. Lips were kept tight shut while May was around. Albert Victor was not apprised of the situation until the end of November, his father issuing the appropriate instructions. His son agreed, as he was wont to do when faced with any issue.

An invitation came to May and her parents to stay for five days at Luton Hoo, the pretentious house in Bedfordshire rented by the Danish Minister, Mr de Falbe, and his rich wife. The de Falbes were close friends of the Princess of Wales and therefore *persona grata* with the royal family. The Princess instructed Eddy that he was also invited and was to attend. On Wednesday, 2 December, May and the chosen guests left by special train for Luton. The names of the travellers read like an extract from *Debrett*. Eddy was, of course, among them and in lively form.

On Thursday there was a shoot and May lunched with the men in the fields and later walked with them. In the evening there was a county ball and Luton Hoo was *en fête*. Madame de Falbe loved heat and May commented that the rooms were like a hothouse. The hostess also liked exotic flowers and their scents wafted over the dance floor. There were romantic places for sitting out. The conservatory was rich in palms and camellias and from a wicker wheelbarrow trailed begonias and sweet geraniums. Gaily coloured birds sang from their cages. There was also Mme de Falbe's own boudoir, reserved for special guests.

Now Eddy had been instructed that he was not to propose to May until she was asked to Sandringham after Christmas. Luton Hoo was to be used as a 'warm-up lap'. But he was a man who was propelled by the flow of adrenalin and there was everything there that night to make the adrenalin flow. The strains of *The Blue Danube* lifted the feet of the dancing couples, the heat and the smell of flowers went to his head. He was dancing with May. Rumours may have reached her that something was afoot; everyone was complimenting her on her dress and Mary Adelaide was stoking up the excitement. Eddy took May by the hand and led her into the boudoir. There he proposed to her. In her own words, 'To my great surprise Eddy proposed to me in Mme de Falbe's boudoir – Of course I said Yes! We are both very happy. Kept it secret from everybody but Mama and Papa.'

Later, in her bedroom, she danced round the bed singing, 'Fancy it being poor little me . . .'[19] For the first time in her life she did not know the floor from the ceiling. She could have danced all night.

It was her first experience of love and Eddy was an experienced wooer. The touch of his hand, the lilting music, the smell of the flowers had gone to her head like wine. There was also the elixir of realizing that she, a morganatic Princess, had won the outstanding prize – the heir direct after his father. There would be no more financial crises, no more patronization. One of her mother and father's dreams had come true and she rejoiced in their happiness. News of Eddy's aberration had been carefully kept from her and there were no clouds in her sky as she fell asleep. There was much to dream about – the wedding in the Chapel Royal; a home of her own; overseas tours to India, Canada and Australia. It was the happiest night of her life.

CHAPTER V

Married

MAY HAD her dream days. Congratulations poured in from all over Europe and the Empire and the engagement photographs were taken. Eddy went to Windsor to give Queen Victoria the news and to ask for her blessing. She had just been to see the Empress Eugenie: 'Heard on returning that Eddy was there and wished to see me. I suspected something at once. He came in and said, "I have some good news to tell you! I am engaged to May Teck." . . . I was quite delighted. God bless them both! . . . I had much wished for this marriage, thinking her so suitable.'[1]

On 7 December, the day on which the engagement was publicly announced, May returned to London. At St Pancras she received her first taste of acclamation. The crowds were out in force and struggling to get a glimpse of the future bride. May was accustomed to cheers and applause, for her mother was popular and always well received, but this was something different, louder and more enthusiastic, and the cheers were aimed at her and her alone. There was a grand lunch at Marlborough House and then, in the evening, came a signal honour. Queen Victoria made one of her rare visits to London, to offer her congratulations: 'Marlborough House was all brightness and joy. Alix and the girls were in, Bertie arriving a little later . . . We took tea, and then Mary arrived with May, all smiles and looking very bright. Mary was *très émue* in talking of it all, and of the kindness shown by everyone. Franz also came in for a little and seemed much agitated.'[2]

The next morning Victoria received a letter from Kaiser William of Germany:

Dearest Grandmama,
What happy and interesting news! Eddy is engaged! I congratu-
late you with all my heart . . . He is indeed a lucky creature,
and may look forward to a happy life! For a handsomer and
more accomplished young Princess is rarely to be found. I
saw much of her last year, and I must say, '*Sie gefiel mir
ausnehmend gut.*' I am sure the country at large will ring with
joy, and merry will this Christmas be for you and the whole
of the United Kingdom.[3]

The wedding was fixed for 27 February 1892 at St George's
Chapel, Windsor. The couple's London headquarters was to be
the apartments at St James's Palace, until recently occupied by
the Duchess of Cambridge, and May paid a fleeting visit and
chose new wallpaper.

The dream continued, keeping the adrenalin flowing through
Eddy's brain. Adrenalin was also a necessity for May, apt by
nature to be lymphatic. Throughout her life she sparkled only
at moments of high excitement: her first engagement; the
assassination attempt on King Alfonso and Queen Ena of Spain
after their wedding in Madrid in 1906; the Delhi Durbar and
the festivities in India in 1911; the balls in Berlin given in honour
of the marriage of the Kaiser's daughter in 1913. Now the
couple's days were full of thrill and excitement, enriched by
the cheers and the clapping. Together they went to *Cavalleria
Rusticana* at the Shaftesbury theatre, to *The Pantomime Re-
hearsal* at the Court and to see 'Modern Venice' at Olympia,
where they shared a gondola. They stayed with the Queen at
Windsor and then Eddy was a guest at the White Lodge. The
Tecks were invited to Sandringham after Christmas.

But behind the scenes all was not so serene. There were those
who did not approve of the marriage and those who doubted if
the result would be happy and successful. Empress Frederick of
Germany was put out because one of her daughters had not
been chosen. The same applied to her sister Helena (Princess
Christian of Schleswig-Holstein), who had an unmarried
daughter, Helena Victoria, who was known as 'the Snipe' owing
to her long nose. Another of the Queen's daughters, Louise,
Marchioness of Lorne, whose marriage had been unfortunate,

uttered some of the 'bitchy' comments for which she was well known. Aunt Augusta of Mecklenburg-Strelitz, Mary Adelaide's elder sister, was annoyed because she had not been consulted. She wrote:

> Was it premeditated going to Luton Hoo, came it on there by chance? and do they care for each other? It is an immense position for poor May and has ever been your heart's desire, but it is a serious, great undertaking for poor May, and to fill a Queen of England's position in present times, a serious matter . . . What does poor Franz say? does he *cry* or *swear*? perhaps both! I hope it won't be too much for his head.[4]

Francis was indeed a problem, the shock having upset his stroke-ridden brain. Queen Victoria had noticed this when she visited London.

Kaiser William, despite his kind letter, was in a fury. He was informed that he would not be invited to the wedding, partly due to the aversion of Alexandra, Princess of Wales, to Germans.

But for May, the signs that all was not to be bright and beautiful in the months ahead came from an unexpected quarter – none other than her future father-in-law, the Prince of Wales. Bertie, who had managed to put on a cheerful face when the engagement was announced, was in the worst of humours. Disaster after disaster had fallen upon him. There had been a serious fire at Sandringham. George, his second son, had had typhoid and was still convalescent. His wife had disappeared abroad with his daughters and only returned when the news was telegraphed of George's illness. Worst of all was the row blowing up regarding Lord Charles Beresford and Lady Daisy Brooke. Lord Charles and Lady Daisy had been lovers. When Charles returned to his wife and a child was born, Daisy sent him an angry and stupid letter accusing him of infidelity with his own wife. The letter was intercepted by Lady Beresford, who put it in the hands of a leading society lawyer. Then Bertie and Daisy became lovers and she persuaded him to try and get the letter back, which he failed to do. In a temper he refused to invite Lady Beresford to Marlborough House, which was the equivalent of social ostracism. Charles threatened to punch Bertie on the nose. Then Lady Beresford's sister wrote a pamphlet called *The River* which told the story of Bertie's affair with Daisy: it circulated in all the best drawing rooms. Still Lady Beresford received no invitations. Lord Charles threatened that if he did not receive an apology from the Prince, he would make all the details public. The Queen and the Prime Minister, Lord Salisbury, were involved and it was not until 24 December that the row was partially patched up. A letter of apology was sent and accepted and Lady Brooke excluded from court circles for a while, but the settlement was so long delayed that Bertie was unable to spend Christmas at Sandringham, and that made him furious.

During his periods of bad temper Bertie spoke to May on a number of occasions in a way which caused her to rethink her position. He was continually urging her 'to keep Eddy up to the mark', to see that his clothes were right and that he spoke to the right people. 'May, please see that Eddy does this or that.' He referred to his heir as 'collars and cuffs' and poked fun at him. May began to wonder if she was being engaged as a governess or secretary. Prodded in this manner, she now saw weaknesses in her fiancé which had been hidden from her in her first engagement days. Deeply worried, she approached her mother and said, 'Mama, do you *really* think I can take this thing on?'[5] The world fell about Mary Adelaide's ears. After years of scraping, just when all her difficulties had seemed to be over, everything that she had planned for and dreamed of was to be snatched away. 'Of course you can,' she snapped back. 'If I can put up with your father for twenty-five years, you can handle the Heir Presumptive of Great Britain.' So May had no alternative but to continue on her agreed path.

It was a grim Christmas for Britain. An influenza epidemic was raging and the obituary columns were long. Among the casualties was Prince Victor of Hohenlohe-Langenburg,* the Queen's nephew. The Prince of Wales and his heir attended the funeral, and the festivities arranged for Eddy's twenty-eighth birthday on 8 January – a ball and a lawn-meet of the hunt – were cancelled due to court mourning.

---

* Better known in the art world as Count Gleichen.

A mantle of icy, yellow fog enveloped London and East Anglia was shrouded; there was a serious railway accident at Beccles. May developed a heavy cold but was able to leave for Norfolk with her parents on 4 January. The lake at Sandringham was frozen hard enough for skating. Inside the house illness abounded. The Princess of Wales was snuffling and Princess Victoria was in bed with influenza, which had also claimed three senior members of the household. Prince George was weak after his attack of typhoid. Yet Bertie insisted on having his fun and a shoot was arranged for the seventh. Eddy was next to show signs of a cold, caught as he shivered by the graveside of Prince Victor, but no excuse was accepted for his not joining the guns. As he went off down the drive he turned, waved and smiled at his mother, who was watching him from a window.

May lunched with the men and spotted immediately that Eddy was unwell. She persuaded him to return with her to Sandringham House: there his brother George took his temperature and packed him off to bed. May sat with him in his small bedroom, which had a bay window and was cold. It was so small that when he put out his hands, Eddy could touch the mantelpiece with one and the windowsill with the other.

Next day was his birthday. He tottered downstairs to see his presents, but then had to retire to his room and missed his birthday dinner and the entertainment – a ventriloquist and a banjo player – laid on to celebrate the occasion. There were so many cases of influenza in the house that no one took Eddy's illness seriously; all the guests were quaffing quinine. The Princess of Wales telegraphed the Queen, 'Poor Eddy got influenza, cannot dine, so tiresome.'

Next day Dr Manby, the local practitioner, diagnosed inflammation of the lungs. Two specialists, Doctors Laking* and Broadbent,** were sent for. May and George were allowed to peer at the patient over a screen. Two nurses took charge. Constant telegrams were sent to Windsor. Queen Victoria panicked and suggested that she hurry to Norfolk. But there

---

* Physician-in-Ordinary to the Prince of Wales; afterwards Sir Francis Laking.
** Dr Broadbent was subsequently knighted.

were those at Sandringham who well remembered the disturbance she had created when she made the same journey in 1871 when Bertie nearly died of typhoid, and dreaded the royal arrival. For once Bertie was firm with his mother and answered, 'There could be no question of your coming here.'[6]

By the twelfth, Eddy was delirious. He shouted and raved, and strong language echoed along the corridors of Sandringham. He called out many names, those of Lord Salisbury and Lord Randolph Churchill among them. Some he cursed roundly, for others he expressed feelings of great love. Queen Victoria was among the latter. Constantly came the sad call of 'Hélène, Hélène' – the daughter of the Comte de Paris with whom he had been in love. His lips were livid and his fingernails were blue. May peeped over the screen, but her name he did not call.

Queen Victoria dreaded the fourteenth, for on that day in December the Prince Consort and her daughter Alice had died and Bertie had all but succumbed to typhoid. At three o'clock in the morning the death struggle began. Everyone was roused: Princess Victoria came from her sick bed and even Francis of Teck, who was scarcely *compos mentis*, was summoned. They crowded into the tiny bedroom. The Princess of Wales held the hand of her dying son, fanning his brow and smiling bravely at him. The Domestic Chaplain, fittingly clad, intoned the prayers for the dying. Kneeling round the bed were George, Dr Laking, Dr Manby and two nurses. Victoria, Maud and May shared chairs. Grouped by the door were the Prince of Wales, the Duke and Duchess of Fife, Dr Broadbent and the Duke and Duchess of Teck. For six hours they kept their vigil, although all hope had gone. Some were never to recover from the shock. It hastened the deaths of Mary Adelaide and Francis and the memory remained with May for the rest of her life. Alexandra of Wales was so close to her son in spirit that she said afterwards she felt it was she who was dying.

At 9.35 on that morning of 14 January 1892, Prince Albert Victor, Duke of Clarence and Avondale, died. The flowers piled high upon him and his mother decreed that no single item in his room was to be touched – the soap to lie on the washstand, the jug to remain unemptied, his personal possessions to stay where he had last put them. Dry-eyed, May stumbled back to her room. She was just May of Teck again, waking from a dream that had begun with delirious excitement and ended in a soul-shattering nightmare.

Then came anticlimax, poor May being caught up in a row she wished to be spared. The Princess of Wales wanted Eddy to be buried at Sandringham, beside his brother Alexander John, who had died in infancy. The Queen decreed otherwise, insisting on a state funeral at Windsor. Alexandra had no alternative but to agree, but she expressed her desire that no women should be present. This clashed with the determination of other members of the royal family to witness such an important occasion, and it brought to the fore the animosity which existed between the two sections of the family, the so-called 'Sandringham set' headed by the Prince of Wales, and the 'Osborne' or 'German set', which included the Empress Frederick, Princess Helena and Princess Beatrice, wife of Prince Henry of Battenberg. There were many reasons for the animosity, one being Bertie's feeling that his mother did not confide in him enough and another being Alexandra's aversion to Germans. The ladies of the 'Osborne set' prepared to move on Windsor. The Queen, warned of the danger of catching influenza, agreed not to attend the funeral and to move out, handing over the castle to the Prince of Wales, his household and the mourners from Norfolk.

Meanwhile, on the fifteenth, Eddy's body was moved to the local church of St Mary Magdalene. On Sunday, the seventeenth, a service was held there. At the foot of the coffin lay a wreath in the form of a harp with broken strings, a token to May from the ladies of Ireland. Three days later, the coffin was taken to Wolferton station on its way to Windsor, May following in a carriage, the blinds of which were closely drawn. At the journey's end minute-guns boomed from the Long Walk and the bell of St George's tolled.

It was half past three when the procession entered the chapel, wherein were packed representatives of the royalty of Europe and the institutions of Britain. The most heart-stirring moment in the service came when the Duke of Teck handed to the Prince of Wales a replica of the bridal wreath of orange blossom

May had been scheduled to carry. It was laid upon the coffin. Alexandra hid herself from view in the shadows of the Queen's Closet.

When the service was over, the ladies of the 'Osborne set' discovered that they could not open the door of their closet and came to the conclusion that they had been purposely locked in. Princess Beatrice complained officially and the equerry to the Prince of Wales sent back the following message:

> The Prince of Wales desires me to say that – the harem of princesses was *not* locked into the . . . pew closet but the door got jammed, and adds that they were none of them wanted at all. No ladies were to attend, and the Princess of Wales especially requested privacy – and to avoid meeting her Osborne relations. So they all came. If Princess Beatrice was annoyed it cannot be helped and she must get over it – as she likes.[7]

Thus was this tragic afternoon fraught with feud. There were other difficulties. As the same equerry, Sir Arthur Ellis, commented, 'In every – even the saddest – occurrence of life there arises a comic side – a gleam of absurdity, which helps one to bear the gloom.'[8] The resident staff at Windsor had their own way of doing things, laid down by the Prince Consort. Windsor was completely strange to the invading force from Sandringham, most of whom had never been inside the castle. Sent out with messages, they became lost in the maze of ill-lit corridors. Those sent to find them suffered the same fate. There were accidental intrusions into bedrooms. There were wry smiles over the 'one lump per cup' sugar ration and the newspaper squares in the lavatory.

Two days later, May and her family returned through the fog to the White Lodge. In a note she confided to a friend that she could neither read nor write. This was her first meeting with death and the experience had shattered her. A further trial was her father, who wandered round the house muttering, 'It must be a Cesarewitch [Tsarevitch]!' So May knew that another bridegroom was already being thought of, but she did not guess that it was Eddy's brother, George, who was being widely talked about for her.

In the second week of February, the Tecks were invited to Osborne, the Queen commenting that May looked like 'a crushed flower'. From there she went on her own to stay with the Wales family at Compton Place, Eastbourne, lent by the Duke of Devonshire. She was there on 27 February, the day on which she should have been married. She was presented with the *rivière* of diamonds which the Prince and Princess of Wales had intended as their wedding present, and the beautiful dressing bag which Eddy had ordered. Bertie was pale and aged, Alexandra shrouded in black. George was there, talking endlessly of his 'darling boy', as he called Eddy. It was a sad nine days that May spent there.

Mary Adelaide decided that her family needed a holiday and a rich friend, Lady Wolverton, provided her with a villa at Cannes. They were there from March until May. The Wales had had the same idea and rented an apartment at Cap Martin. The Prince of Wales and George paid a number of visits to the Tecks at Cannes and tongues began to wag. Rumour of an engagement appeared in the press.

From Cannes the Tecks moved to Stuttgart and there stayed with their Württemberg relations. May appeared reluctant to return home and it was not until July that she reached the White Lodge. Meantime George had been created Duke of York. Another pointer as to what was afoot was that Bachelors' Cottage at Sandringham, built to take the overflow of guests, was renamed York Cottage.

At the head of the planning was Queen Victoria, determined that there should be heirs to the house of Albert and herself. Most of her relations agreed that May was the right girl for George, an exception, strangely enough considering his past love life, being the Duke of Cambridge, who regarded the idea as 'unfeeling and horrible'. The Queen silenced him with the unexpected comment, 'You know May never was in love with poor Eddy.'[9] The idea spread that this had been an arranged affair and that May had really always wanted to marry George.

George was in contrast with Eddy. Physically he was shorter and had more colour. He was a typical, bearded naval officer and, when on form, was full of chaff. He was ambitious and his hobbies were shooting and stamp collecting. He had never contemplated the thought of being King, his outlook being similar to that of his own second son, also George, in after years. Now shattered by his brother's death and weak after the attack of typhoid, he showed no signs of preparing himself for kingship. So inactive and aimless was he that a member of his father's household sent a memorandum to Windsor, pointing out that his way of life was no preparation for things to come. He was an ageing man at twenty-seven. After taking part in naval manoeuvres he commented, 'I hope that I shall never be in any other manoeuvres . . . Hate the whole thing.'

In the field of romance his experience was strictly limited. He had had a slight affair with his cousin, Marie of Edinburgh,* daughter of his uncle Alfred, Duke of Edinburgh. He had kissed her once and was simple enough to consider this grounds for marriage. But Marie's mother, a Russian, had different ideas and married her off to the Crown Prince of Romania. Apart from a scandalous report in the press that George had married a girl in Malta, a report which subsequently led to a libel case, there had been no stains on George's escutcheon.

The real stumbling block on the road to George's marriage was his mother, the tie between them being as close as had been her tie with Eddy. He was her 'Georgie boy' and she his darling 'Motherdear'. Robbed of Eddy, Alexandra had no intention of losing George. Even if he were to marry, she was determined not to lose her hold. Thus it appeared that if a bride was forced upon George, she would get but half of a man.

George's attitude to May was completely platonic. To him, she remained Eddy's girl, now one of the family. He liked to reminisce with her and to play bezique. His letters to her were reserved, one ending, 'Goodbye, dear "Miss May" . . . ever your very loving old cousin Georgie.' And 'devoted cousin' was how May replied. He revolted at the very idea of encroaching on Eddy's preserves. This feeling was kept alive by Alexandra. For the anniversary of the engagement day at Luton Hoo, the Tecks were guests at Sandringham. She led the way to Eddy's bedroom.

---

* Afterwards Queen Marie of Romania.

There a fire burned in the grate, flowers were everywhere, a Union Jack lay on the bed and water had been poured into the basin. May looked at the hairbrushes neatly laid out, the soap in its dish, and felt no urge to repeat the experience.

Bertie and Alexandra were not enthusiastic about George's marriage to May. Firstly, they felt that it was somewhat of a slight on the memory of Eddy. Secondly, they were smarting under what they considered the insult of Marie of Edinburgh being married to the Crown Prince of Romania in preference to George. But the pressure from Windsor was strong and in the New Year they agreed to the marriage. Yet Alexandra was set on having her 'Georgie boy' to herself for one more time and in March took him to Italy and Greece. It was at the court in Athens that George finally made up his mind, his mentor being Queen Olga of Greece, a particular friend of his. She said to him, 'I'm sure, tootsums, that she will make you happy, they say she has such a sweet disposition and is so *equal*, and *that* in itself is a great blessing, because nothing can be more disagreeable in everyday life than a person who is in high spirits today and low tomorrow.'[10]

At Malta Alexandra and George parted, he making his way home alone, for she could not bear the thought of being in England when the engagement was announced. Arriving in London, George found that plans had been carefully laid. He was directed to stay with his sister Louise, Duchess of Fife, who lived at East Sheen Lodge, handy for the White Lodge. On 3 May, a lovely, sunny day, Mary Adelaide and Francis tactfully went off on separate errands, leaving May alone in the White Lodge. She went to the Fifes for tea, on the excuse of seeing Louise's new baby, Maud. George was there. After tea was over, Louise said, 'Now, Georgie, don't you think you ought to take May into the garden to look at the frogs in the pond?'[11] It was typical Wales sense of humour, but it provided the necessary excuse. It was a repeat of the engagement moment of the Prince and Princess of Wales, who had been propelled into a grotto.

George, knowing that the moment was at hand, looked down at the frogs and put the question. May said Yes. They drove off to the White Lodge to tell the Duke and Duchess, who had returned to await them. The evening was spent in telegraphing. Now telegraphing was Mary Adelaide's delight and she despatched messages not only to all her relations but to all her friends as well, instructing them to keep the news quiet until it appeared in the newspapers. As she telegraphed through the public post office, this was pointless. Fortunately the Queen knew her cousin and gave permission for the news to be published immediately. The announcement gave certain newspapers the chance to resurrect the rumour that George had been married in Malta. But the relief of having his marital future settled had quietened him and he managed to laugh at the story. 'I say, May,' he quipped, 'we can't get married after all. I hear that I have already got a wife and three children.'

Yet May and George were, both mentally and physically, incapable of playing the role of lovers. They never held hands, exchanged glances or whispered asides. They behaved as an old married couple might when romance has flown away. Lady Geraldine Somerset commented, 'It is clear there is not even any pretence at love-making. May is radiant at her position and abundantly satisfied, but placid and cold as always; the Duke of York apparently nonchalant and indifferent.' The sad part was that both realized their failing. She wrote to him, 'I am very sorry that I am still so shy with you. I tried not to be so the other day, but alas failed. I was angry with myself! It is so stupid to be so stiff together and really there is nothing I would not tell you, except that I *love* you more than anybody in the world, and this I cannot tell you myself, so I write it to relieve my feelings.' He wrote to her, 'Thank God we both understand each other, and I really think it unnecessary for me to tell you how deep my love for you, my darling, is and I feel it growing stronger and stronger every time I see you – although I may appear shy and cold . . .'

The wedding was fixed for 6 July at the Chapel Royal, St James, and there was a great deal to arrange in eight weeks. Of priority was May's trousseau. She still had the outfit prepared for her marrage to Eddy, but fashion and sentiment demanded another one. Her Aunt Augusta contributed £1000 for this, although there was much speculation as to where the rest came from, the trousseau including no less than forty outdoor suits, five tea-gowns and fifteen ball dresses. But at least now there was ample security, for the presents to George and May were valued at £300,000. They went on show to the public, the proceeds for seeing them going to charity.

The Tecks were invited to stay at Buckingham Palace for the wedding, Queen Victoria joining them there on the fifth. The heat, she said, was 'quite awful'. London was *en fête*. In the afternoon, the Prince and Princess of Wales gave a Garden Party at Marlborough House, to which five thousand guests were invited. In the evening there was a dinner in the Supper-room of the palace. Except for the Lord Steward and the Lord Chamberlain, all present were royals, one of the biggest assemblies of all time. The Queen wrote, 'I sat between the King of Denmark, who led me in, and the Cesarewitch, who is charming. His great likeness to George leads to no end of funny mistakes, the one being taken for the other!'[12] In fact the likeness was so close that Tsarevitch Nicholas received congratulations on his wedding on more than one occasion.

London was packed. A contemporary press report ran:

> Throughout the evening preceding the wedding day, countless throngs flocked to the line of the route, some on foot, some in carriages, and many more in large hired conveyances to see the decorations, rendering the streets well-nigh impassable till nearly midnight. No intending passenger who desired to obtain a seat on the roof of any of the omnibuses journeying between Liverpool Street and the West End had a chance of outside accommodation, except in the case of those who were fortunate enough to start from the termini. Private carriages innumerable swelled the ranks of the vehicles plying for business purposes; waggonettes, which were easily filled, even at the charges of sixpence and a shilling a head, ran between the Great Eastern terminus and Piccadilly, and they all had, perforce, to move so slowly that the occupants were able to enjoy an ample view of the beautiful and costly decorations which adorned the City.[13]

The sixth was a summer's day such as one can only have in England. The scene was unforgettable, the tapestry of the gaily dressed crowds lying like a carpet beneath the green parasols of the plane trees which lined the route. What better description of the day can be given than that of an eye-witness – none other than Queen Victoria herself:

The great day, so anxiously looked forward to, was very bright and fine, but overpoweringly hot. To describe this day fully would be impossible. It was really (on a smaller scale) like the Jubilee; and the crowds, the loyalty and enthusiasm were immense . . . While I was dressing, Mary (herself very handsome) brought in May, who looked very sweet. Her dress was very simple, of white satin with a silver design of roses, shamrocks, thistles and orange flowers, interwoven. On her head she had a small wreath of orange flowers, myrtle, and white heather surmounted by the diamond necklace I gave her, which can also be worn as a diadem, and her mother's wedding veil . . . At a quarter to twelve I left, driving with Mary Teck, in the new State Glass Coach with four creams, amidst a flourish of trumpets . . . All along the route, which was wonderfully kept, there were very fine decorations and enormous crowds, who cheered tremendously and were in the best of humour. It took us about forty minutes going up Constitution Hill and down Piccadilly and St James's Street.

I was the first to arrive and enter the Chapel, which was not intended, but which I was glad of, as I saw all the processions, which were very striking and dignified . . . My children all took up their places behind and beyond me, close to the altar. The Queen of Denmark came in with her grandson the Cesarewitch, and dear Alix (looking very pale) with her father. The Bridegroom's procession followed rapidly, being supported by his father and uncle Affie,* all in naval uniform. They had to wait a very short time, when the Bride appeared, followed by her ten dear bridesmaids, Victoria, Maud,** Ducky, Sandra, Baby B.,*** Thora,† Daisy, Patsy,†† Alice Battenberg††† and Ena,†* the four little ones looking very sweet. May was supported by her father and her brother Dolly. George gave his answers very distinctly, while May, though quite self-possessed, spoke very low . . . I could not but remember

* Duke of Edinburgh. ** Princesses, of Wales. *** Princesses Victoria Melita, Alexandra and Beatrice of Edinburgh. † Princess Helena Victoria of Schleswig-Holstein. †† Princesses Margaret and Patricia of Connaught. ††† Afterwards Princess Andrew of Greece, mother of Prince Philip. †* Daughter of Prince and Princess Henry of Battenberg; afterwards Queen Victoria Eugenia of Spain.

that I had stood where May did fifty-three years ago, and dear Vicky thirty-five years ago, and that the dear ones, who stood where Georgie did, were gone from us! May these dear children's happiness last longer! The Archbishop gave an excellent address. The guns fired, but were hardly heard, when the dear couple were declared man and wife. After the last hymn and the benediction, they came forward to kiss my hand, and I embraced them affectionately, so did their grandparents and parents. Then they left the Chapel together, followed by the bridesmaids and supporters. We drove back amidst the same tremendous cheering. Mary had been a little upset, but was very brave.

We got home before everyone else . . . Very soon the Bride and Bridegroom arrived, and I stepped out on the balcony with them, taking her by the hand, which produced another great outburst of cheering . . . The King and Queen of Denmark and all the Royalties having arrived, the signing of the register began, after which we received the Ambassadors and Ambassadresses, and the family Ministers, *viz.* Belgium, Portugal, Denmark and Roumania. All this took some time, and we got rather late to luncheon, which was served in the large dining room at seven small tables . . . When luncheon was over, which was not till shortly before four, went into the Blue-room, whilst the Bride and Bridegroom, Bertie and Alix and the bridesmaids went to be photographed. Then went to my room to see the young couple go away . . . Dear May came in looking very pretty in her dress of white poplin edged with gold, and a pretty little toque with roses. Was rolled over to the Middle-room looking down the Mall, and found all the family assembled there. Wished the young couple affectionately goodbye. Mary was a little upset, and poor Franz very much so. They drove off amidst great cheering, and were going through the City to Liverpool Street Station *en route* for Sandringham . . .[14]

Their train left at twenty-five past six and the little Norfolk station of Wolferton was reached before half past eight. The road to Sandringham was gay with Venetian masts and triumphal arches and the village people and the staff were out in force. So George and Mary came to York Cottage. As they drove up, the island on the lake, the rustic bridge, the boathouse and the trees around were illuminated by hundreds of hanging lamps and Japanese lanterns. Both were tired out, grey with the dust churned up by the carriage wheels on the dry and sandy roads. They stepped into their new home.

It was a strange choice for a honeymoon. As York Cottage was to be their home, it was in fact not a honeymoon at all in the accepted sense. Queen Victoria disapproved, considering the choice to be both sad and unlucky. But it was George's wish: Sandringham was the place that he loved best of all. He knew every inch of the grounds and he had known the men who worked the estate since schooldays – in fact he felt really at home. But it was not right for May. She needed to have the adrenalin running. All day she had been, for her at least, at a fever pitch of excitement. London had given her a reception such as had not been seen since the Jubilee. The guests gathered at Buckingham Palace were probably the most distinguished collection ever to meet there. The weather had been perfect. Suddenly the adrenalin ceased to flow. What she craved for was a long train to carry her to Italy, a royal yacht to take her to the Mediterranean. What she dreamed of was to be in a world alone with George, away from the chaff and bossiness of the Wales family, away from the ghost of Eddy, away from the stern regime of Queen Victoria and the demands of her mother, somewhere where there was music and beauty, mountains and lakes. She was the kind of woman who became entranced as she wandered round an historic building or listened to the opera. She would have liked to go to I Cedri, its garden a bouquet of summer flowers, the River Arno flowing on the edge of the slope. She would have liked to sketch the old mill there and sit reading in the sunshine. She was no sportswoman, and now she found herself on an estate where sport was predominant.

York Cottage was a maze of narrow passages and small rooms dark from the laurels which grew without. She gazed at the decoration and the furniture and was appalled. George had had full charge of its preparation, his mother wanting no part in it. His answer had been to call in 'the man from Maples' and an architect friend with like ideas to his own. The result was a cross between the lower decks of a warship, a boys' preparatory school and an hotel at Eastbourne. It was dark, rigid, meticulous and showed no trace of taste. One of the few things May had

[89]

learned from her father was the art of interior decoration.
With little else to do he had spent whole days arranging and
rearranging the furniture in Kensington Palace and the White
Lodge. He was brilliant with colours. Now, looking about her,
May saw no colour scheme at all.

She shrivelled up inside herself. The shock was such that she
could not help but show it. George noticed and wondered why:
to him the house was perfection. She sat by the window of her
separate bedroom, looking out over the lights towards 'the Big
House' where a candle burned in Eddy's room. Above, the sky
turned inky black as great thunder clouds came in from the sea;
May dreaded thunder and lightning. She pondered on many
things. What now would happen to her mother, robbed of her
secretary, guide and companion? What effect would the busy
day and the separation have on the upset brain of her father?
What kind of a life would she have at the hands of her in-laws?
Would she ever have a life of her own, or would she be looked
upon as a poor relation and at the beck and call of those who
lived at Sandringham House? Would she, with George, be able
to satisfy her craving for learning and the arts? Would she be
able to stand up to the sexual side of marriage and the indignities
and personal intrusion of having babies?

CHAPTER VI

The Opening Door

MAY'S PERIOD OF CHILDBEARING covered some of the greater years of change the world has ever known. Her first baby arrived in 1894, when the 'safety bicycle' had just been marketed and it was still forbidden to ride them in Hyde Park. Electric light, mains water and drainage were luxuries and many people had never seen a motor car. The army and the navy had changed little since the Crimean War and balloons were the only means of becoming airborne. By the time her last child had arrived in 1905 modern conveniences had reached the better-off urban areas. The Wright Brothers had flown the first power-propelled aeroplane, airships droned in the sky, landaulets had taken the place of broughams before the doors of the stately homes and petrol-driven buses rattled through the streets of London. The army had been revolutionized by the Boer War and the navy was building submarines and Dreadnoughts. Marconi had sent the first wireless messages. The whole world had altered in little over a decade.

May also experienced a great deal of change during the time that her children were arriving. On the death of Queen Victoria she was promoted from Duchess of York to Princess of Wales. Both her parents had died, as had her uncle, George, Duke of Cambridge. Two of her brothers had married. She had been round the world. But she was a Victorian until she was thirty-three and she remained one, clinging in outlook, dress and character to the century that was gone, encouraged by her husband who was forever fighting a rearguard action to protect it.

When George and May married there were many ribald jokes cracked in London clubs about what would happen during the honeymoon days – the couple had appeared so indifferent to one another. Thus the question was asked, would Britain get an heir to the throne? Queen Victoria's belief that if a young couple were pushed together into a bedroom, the natural would occur, proved right. There was little sign of courtship. May would be lying in bed in her separate room when the door began to open. Then a beard would appear in the gap, followed by two expressionless eyes. 'Oh, it's only you,' she would say with relief. The door kept on opening through the years, long after she would have preferred it to stay shut.

The first child was born on 23 June 1894 and christened Edward Albert Christian George Andrew Patrick David, known in the family as David.* There were some black looks from Queen Victoria because his first name was not Albert. Eighteen months later, a second son arrived. He had the misfortune to make his appearance on 14 December, the anniversary date of the death of Prince Albert, known in the family as 'Mausoleum Day' and spent by Queen Victoria in the deepest gloom. To counteract the effect on her, the baby was named Albert – 'Bertie'** for short. On 25 April 1897, the sequence of boys was broken by the advent of Victoria Mary, always known as Mary.*** In the last year of Queen Victoria's reign a third boy was born and christened Henry.**** It was then that May considered that she had done enough. She wrote to her Aunt Augusta, 'I think I have done my duty and may now *stop*, as having babies is highly distasteful to me . . .'[1] But still the door opened. George***** appeared on 20 December 1902 and, belatedly, John on 12 July 1905. It soon became apparent that there was something wrong with John – he proved to be an epileptic. Thereafter the door remained closed. May was thirty-eight.

Although May always disliked the business of child-bearing, her worst experience was the first. Having no sisters or close girlfriends, she had no idea how to cope. Her husband knew nothing at all and her extrovert mother and mother-in-law were

---

* Afterwards Edward VIII and Duke of Windsor.
** Afterwards Duke of York and King George VI. *** Afterwards Princess Royal, Countess of Harewood. ****Afterwards Duke of Gloucester. *****Afterwards Duke of Kent.

May and George at the
time of their wedding.
George is in the uniform
of a captain in the
Royal Navy

May and George, then Duke and Duchess of York, in a group photograph taken
at the Royal Residence at Coburg on the afternoon of the wedding of Princess
Alexandra of Saxe-Coburg, daughter of Alfred, Duke of Saxe-Coburg, second
son of Queen Victoria, and Prince Ernest of Hohenlohe-Langenburg in April 1896

The Duke and Duchess of York with Queen Victoria at Osborne House, Isle of Wight

of little help. In any case May did not wish to talk about it. The Empress Frederick of Germany tried and was rebuffed. 'She does not wish it remarked or mentioned,' she reported. And the spotlight of public interest was full upon her, just as, in after years, it was to fall upon Diana, Princess of Wales, for if she gave birth to a son he would one day be King.

The place where the birth would occur was the subject of endless discussion. Buckingham Palace was suggested, but dismissed by May as attracting too much publicity. York House, the London headquarters of the Yorks, which once had housed the old Duchess of Cambridge and had been assigned as the home of May and Eddy, was ruled out on the same grounds. May was averse to York Cottage, Sandringham, for good reason. While there she was under the thumb of Alexandra and her daughters. They were forever descending on the cottage, often at breakfast time and always with a pack of dogs, demanding that Georgie and May come up to the 'Big House' to play games or go on an outing. May did not relish such invasions at a time when all she wanted was privacy. So she made what proved to be a mistake and plumped for the White Lodge, Richmond, there supposing that she would be out of the limelight. She overlooked the activities of her mother.

May's marriage had had a disastrous effect on Mary Adelaide. She had relied on her quiet and unassuming daughter for everything – the running of the house, the care of money, the overseeing of her multiple charitable activities. Suddenly she found herself all alone, with a husband who was deteriorating fast as a result of Eddy's death and May's marriage. When May was in London hardly a day passed without a visitation from her mother. She would arrive for lunch and stay for dinner. Although May could cope with her parents, George most certainly could not. He was irritated by Mary Adelaide's unpunctuality. He objected to her suddenly bursting in upon them unannounced. He was at a loss as to how to treat Francis. He complained often to May, but was not the kind of man who could put the fat Duchess in her place.

The Yorks moved into the White Lodge on 4 June and stayed there for six trying weeks. The baby was due in the middle of the month, but was late. Queen Victoria became worried and impatient. So did May. Each morning, to her horror, she looked out of the window to see large numbers of people gathered beyond the gates, hoping for a glimpse of her or to be the first to learn the news. On the evening of the twenty-third a son was born. Alexandra was there. She cradled the baby in her arms and whispered, 'My first happiness since Eddy died.'[2] Queen Victoria was not far behind: 'We went by rail to Richmond and drove from there. Great crowds in the town. Mary gave us tea, and then I went to see the baby, a fine, strong-looking child. I saw Dr Williams in the drawing room. He did not wish me to see May, but said she was extremely well.'[3]

In fact May's nerves had been shattered by the birth and she was suffering from post-natal depression. A holiday was indicated and off she went with her mother to the Hotel Victoria, St Moritz. In those days the fashionable season at the now top skiing resort was the summer and May met many of the people she had known on previous visits. She walked, played games and soon recovered her equilibrium. Sad as he was to lose May, George left the White Lodge with a sigh of relief and took himself to the more amenable atmosphere of Cowes. From there he wrote to May, 'I assure you I wouldn't go through the six weeks I spent at White Lodge again for anything . . .'[4] May took the hint and Mary Adelaide was not invited to see her next child until he was a month old, and she was abroad at the time of his christening.

Meantime, May was much occupied with family affairs. Firstly, her eldest brother Dolly became engaged to Lady Margaret Grosvenor, daughter of the first Duke of Westminster. Dolly was fair, extremely handsome, and a captain in the 1st Life Guards. They were married at Eaton Hall, Cheshire, on 12 December 1894. May was delighted at her brother's match. Queen Victoria had hoped that Dolly would select either Victoria or Maud of Wales, but once again these two eligible young ladies were ignored. The Queen satisfied herself with the consideration that he had married into big money, always a high priority with her, particularly in the case of the Tecks.

But the one who objected strongly to the wedding was Duke

Francis, who was obsessed with the royal connection. He had hoped that his heir would marry the daughter of the King of Württemberg and he ranted and raved when he learned that Dolly was engaged to the daughter of a first duke. He was accordingly most unpleasant. Mlle Bricka, May's companion, commented that he was impossible. If Margaret had been a German princess, however junior, he would have been delighted and found her charming. As it was the White Lodge household had to suffer his temper.

George was not impressed with Dolly's match and preferred to stay at Sandringham and shoot rather than attend the wedding. It needed some pressure from his wife to make him change his mind. That he did showed the power that May had over him. She wrote to Meg (Margaret), 'I assure you I am so excited I hardly know what to do.'

There followed two family experiences which deepened May's character. The first was separation from her husband. The two of them had become so close that being apart had a deep effect. Their parting came about through the death of Emperor Alexander III of Russia, who was married to Dagmar, sister of the Princess of Wales. The Tsarevitch Nicholas, who succeeded as Emperor and who had been a guest-of-honour at May's wedding, had become engaged in the spring to Alicky, youngest daughter of the late Princess Alice and therefore a granddaughter of Queen Victoria. Alicky, a spoilt and petulant young lady, had been chosen as a bride for Eddy but had turned him down flat. Having a homosexual brother of her own, she was more aware of the hazards than May, and anyway she was in love with Nicholas.

On receipt of the telegram telling of the illness of the Emperor, the Prince and Princess of Wales set out immediately for the Crimea via Vienna. They arrived too late, but were faced with the ordeal of travelling in the black-draped funeral train on its long haul from the Crimea to St Petersburg. At every station there were funeral services – thirty-nine in all. Whiling away the days in a gloomy railway carriage did not suit Bertie at all – but for the death he would have been shooting in his beloved fields at Sandringham.

[95]

On the other hand the departure suited May and George well. For the first time since their marriage they were alone at Sandringham and there were none of the summonses from 'Motherdear' to come up to the 'Big House' and play games. George had the shooting to himself. Then a telegram shattered their peace. It bid George to report to St Petersburg as soon as possible. He was too obedient a son to argue. May said goodbye to him at Wolferton station and then wrote to him, 'That saying "Goodbye" this morning was awful, and I did it so badly too . . .' George was equally miserable and wrote from St Petersburg, 'I really think I should get ill if I had to be away from you for a long time.' This was a most revealing statement. It showed clearly that not only had he fallen deeply in love, but that he was now dependent on May, and, in fact, he was to remain so for the rest of his life. George was a pallbearer at the funeral and it was his duty to kiss the lips of the deceased and the Holy picture grasped in the stiff hand. A witness, Lord Carrington, said, 'As he lay uncovered in his coffin, his face looked a dreadful colour and the smell was awful.'[5]

May's second son, Albert, known as Bertie, arrived on 14 December at York Cottage, where the remainder of her children were also born. The birth was normal but precedent was upset because there was no home secretary present. He had taken a calculated risk but arrived some hours after the baby was born. His own arrival having been unsupervised may have influenced Bertie, when he became George VI, to request that the historic duty be waived when Prince Charles was born in 1948.

May's next problem was concerned with her brother Francis (Frank). Frank was indeed a problem, and had been ever since he was expelled from Wellington. Like his brothers, he was a soldier: handsome, witty, he was always well turned out but unfortunately did not pay his tailors. From his mother he had inherited a profligacy with money; it was difficult to spot from where he had obtained his other weaknesses. In violent contrast with his father, he considered royalty to be funny. He referred to his sister and brother-in-law as 'Master and Mistress York'; May he nicknamed 'the head nurse'. He refused to take seriously 'Mausoleum Day' (the *in memoriam* occasions for Prince Albert) or the gloomy family gatherings held on the anniversaries of the death of the Duchess of Cambridge. His great weakness was horse racing. He loved betting and when he learned that May and George had attended Newmarket, suggested that he send his sister a betting book for Christmas.

Frank was most amusing and appealed to the Wales Princesses, Victoria and Maud, one of whom it was hoped he would marry. But Frank's attentions were otherwise engaged. He was entangled with a married woman much older than himself and she ran his life. His collapse came while he was stationed in Ireland. He went to the Punchestown races and there placed a bet of £10,000 when all he possessed was the coins in his pocket. The horse lost. As was usual in the Teck family, May was called in to sort out the mess. Somehow she managed to collect the money, but obviously something had to be done about Frank and he was posted to India, a place he described as being the nearest place to hell.

May was mentally defeated by her brother: she just could not understand him, as, later, she was to fail to understand the behaviour of her eldest son. His chaffing letters to her were unintelligible. She had been brought up to respect the throne above all, and here was Frank poking fun at the Queen and all the things that she held sacred. He was in complete contrast with Dolly and Alge, with both of whom she got on very well. Hers was a simple nature, her values clear-cut, and she could not see the point in creating trouble. She had had enough bitter experiences with her mother and father. She had always been lost at dinner parties where the talk was smart and innuendoes the signal for laughter. She could talk on specific subjects but was at sea when it came to chatter for chatter's sake. George's simple navy humour she could appreciate, but Frank might have come from another world.

Her brother's aberrations therefore had little effect on May, although they widened her experience of life. She lacked her mother's buoyant sense of humour, and clearly took after her father in that respect. She set her standard for royalty and there was no excuse for not conforming. But, strangely, she showed in a very different light in another family trouble.

May's Aunt Augusta, Grand Duchess of Mecklenburg-Strelitz, a very sensible old lady and her niece's friend and mentor until she died in 1916 at the age of ninety-four, had a granddaughter named Marie. Duchess Marie and her sister and two brothers were brought up under very stern and formal conditions in the parental Palais at Strelitz. Court procedure was rigid and inflexible. One of the odd regulations, passed down through the years, was that only footmen were allowed to carry the lamps: it was against 'union' rules for the maids to touch them. So, every evening, a young footman entered the bedroom of nineteen-year-old Duchess Marie. He took advantage of the situation and slipped into bed with her. In due season it was noticed that Marie was pregnant and the Strelitz family reeled under the shock. Ignorant of how to deal with such an unheard-of situation, they mismanaged it drastically. The footman was discharged on the grounds that he had been stealing. This meant that he could not obtain further employment and accordingly he consulted a solicitor. The story reached the press and all Europe was agog.

The British royal family was, in general, much more sympathetic towards Marie than were her German relatives. Queen Victoria, who was always intrigued by the details of a scandal, had a long and understanding talk with the Grand Duchess Augusta. After a chat with May, the Prince of Wales, working on the principle that 'There but for the grace of God go I,' campaigned on the side of the girl. But it was May who set the magnificent example. She hurried out to Strelitz to see if she could help and went so far as to drive around in public with the unfortunate Marie. In a letter home, she complained that the whole affair had been mismanaged and that it would have been simple to send Marie to some quiet place far away on the grounds of ill-health, and then no one would have been the wiser.

It was strange indeed that May, who had no experience at all of the seamier side of sex, should be the champion of her cousin in her time of trouble. One might have expected her to withdraw and regard the affair as unintelligible. But she faced the problem squarely, brushing aside the excuses that Marie had been drugged or hypnotized: it was clear that the footman had paid more than one visit to her bed. Maybe she was looking back in time and recalling other slips. George III had slept with Hannah Lightfoot and had a son by her; the vagaries of his legitimate sons were beyond count; even her own uncle, George of Cambridge, had lived in sin with an actress, had children by her, and, when married to her, had looked elsewhere for love. There was precedent in plenty, yet her attitude revealed the deep sense of charity in her, and her loyalty to her friends. May came out of that affair very well.

But illness she could not understand: in the young she regarded it as a waste of time.[6] But now she had to turn her hand to it, as her mother's health was failing. Mary Adelaide, in her sixties, refused to grow old. She continued on her social round and never let up on her charitable work. But her heart could not cope with her great weight and she began to suffer from fainting fits. May took her to St Moritz to recuperate. It was to prove Mary Adelaide's last Continental jaunt.

May's attitude to ill-health was common among the women of her day, an attitude founded on that of Queen Victoria. To the Queen, death was the only excuse accepted for not being present at dinner. She had shown a remarkable lack of sympathy with her youngest son, Leopold, Duke of Albany, who suffered from haemophilia and died young. She had not been able to understand Prince Albert's last illness, commenting that he was fussing as all men did. She attributed his death to a lack of spunk, a crude expression used by staid old ladies of the time. That Bertie recovered from typhoid ten years later she considered was because he had more spunk – the will to live. Illness, therefore, to the medically ignorant Victorians, was regarded as a state which came over people before they died of old age. Otherwise it was unnecessary and a waste of time.

May never understood her father's illness. He was expected to carry out the role of parent at family functions, such as marriages and funerals, despite the fact that by 1895 he was apt to break out into unexpected fits of laughter for no reason and at other times talked absolute balderdash. To May, neither her mother nor her father were old enough to be seriously ill. Queen

Victoria was fifteen and more years older and she did her mighty job singlehanded; George, Duke of Cambridge, of a like age, was only now reluctantly retiring from the position of Commander-in-Chief, after forty years' service.

In the pre-drug age remedies were restricted and simple. There was castor oil for constipation, quinine for influenza, smelling salts for dizziness and fainting and mysterious powders for undiagnosed diseases. 'Faith' was the big factor in effecting a cure and most women put that faith in some patent medicine or food: in the glossy magazines, the Empress Frederick of Germany and other royalties expressed their belief in a patent food, such advertisements attracting many followers. May believed in rest, fresh air and walking, and a plain diet. When her own children were ill, she prescribed stewed plums and rice pudding. She never came to terms with the fact that the children and grandchildren of the Prince and Princess of Wales were puny. She prided herself that she came from a long-lived family and could never understand why the Wales' offspring – Louise, Victoria, George V and Maud – all died in the 1930s, while she was still spry and full of energy.

So Mary Adelaide continued on her wayward way, the White Lodge packed with bundles for jumble sales.

On 25 April 1897, May had her third child – a girl, to George's great delight. She was named Victoria Mary, but called Mary after her maternal grandmother. By this time, young David was old enough to enquire where the sister came from. He was told that she was a little angel who had flown in through the window and had her wings cut off. As May recovered, the news came from the White Lodge that Mary Adelaide had undergone a serious emergency operation. Despite the danger of her heart failing, she recovered quickly and wrote to May that she was on a diet of roast lamb, boiled mutton, roast chicken and asparagus. She was present at the Queen's garden party in a wheelchair. There was no restraining her.

Came the summer of Queen Victoria's Jubilee. On the evening of 22 June 1897, May wrote in her diary, 'A never-to-be-forgotten day. No one ever, I believe, has met with such an ovation as was given to me, passing through those six miles of streets . . .'[7] But also never had such an ovation been given to a mere princess, for it was Mary Adelaide's day. She climbed from her wheelchair into her carriage and was cheered all the way to St Paul's and back, a tribute both to her courage and the work that she had done in the field of charity.

Buckingham Palace swarmed with visiting royalties like a beehive: among the visitors was the Grand Duchess Augusta, who commented that in the chaotic conditions there, 'only May keeps her head on her shoulders alright'.[8]

At the end of October, May travelled to the White Lodge to see her mother. The house was full of packages and sacks and she spent the day sorting out their contents for the benefit of the Needlework Guild. The next day Mary Adelaide was unwell and the doctors decided that a second emergency operation was necessary. This took place at midnight and three hours later the heart of the Duchess of Teck ceased to beat.[9]

Her death led to Duke Francis's complete breakdown. He was despatched to his Württemberg relations, but they found that he was too difficult a case with which to cope and he was returned to the White Lodge. A strange reaction was that he could no longer bear to see his children, the sight of them bringing on paroxysms of temper and shouting. May never saw him for months on end. He was cared for by a doctor and two male nurses, his wild laughter echoing through the garden which he had tended for so long. Rotting away in loneliness, a prisoner in Richmond Park, he was to die on 27 January 1900.

CHAPTER VII

※※

The End of an Era

THE CLOSING YEARS of the nineteenth century were sad for May and George. On the international scene there was trouble all over the world. Military expeditions were needed to repress disorder on the Indian frontier. The campaign of British and Egyptian troops finally crushed the long drawn-out rebellion in the Sudan at the battle of Omdurman in 1898, but the occupation of the town of Fashoda on the Upper Nile by the French led to bitterness between Britain and France, and Queen Victoria had to give up her holidays on the Riviera, so tense was the feeling. There was revolution in Greece and an attempt was made on the life of King George of the Hellenes, brother of the Princess of Wales. Anarchists stalked Europe. The beautiful Empress Elizabeth of Austria died at Geneva, a dagger deep in her back. An attempt at assassination was made on the Prince and Princess of Wales, a bullet passing between their heads as they sat in a compartment at Brussels station. On 11 October 1899, the Boer War began.

On the personal side, May was grieving for her mother and permanently worried over the sad state of her father. Her three brothers were all serving in South Africa. There were upsets in her husband's family and she had to take the strain of these. The marriages of three of his cousins* were on the rocks. Of his other cousins, Prince Alfred of Edinburgh died from riotous living, and Prince Christian Victor of Schleswig-Holstein died while serving in the Boer War. Both his uncle Alfred, Duke of

---

* The Grand Duke and Duchess of Hesse and the Rhine, and Princess Marie Louise of Anhalt.

Edinburgh and of Saxe-Coburg and Gotha, and his aunt the Empress Frederick of Germany, were dying of cancer. His grandmother, Queen Louise of Denmark, passed away. In addition there was the stress and extra work caused by the Boer War – troops to review, charities to organize.

The health of Queen Victoria was another permanent worry. Now almost sightless and immobile, her handicaps made life hard for her advisers and relations. Yet the Queen retained her shrewdness and remarkable memory and she would not hand over the reins of power. She relied on her youngest daughter, Princess Beatrice, and that lady was not up to the job, being more interested in fêtes and bazaars. The Queen's Assistant Secretary, Sir Frederick Ponsonby, commented, 'Apart from the most hideous mistakes that occur, there is the danger of the Queen's letting go almost entirely the control of things which should be kept under the immediate supervision of the Sovereign.'[1]

Fortunately May and George were on hand and gradually they began to take over some of the load which had been borne by Princes Beatrice alone. The more the Queen saw of May, the more she liked her and put her trust in her. She wrote from Balmoral in September 1897, 'Took leave with much regret of Georgie and May, who are leaving first thing tomorrow morning. Every time I see them I love and like them more and respect them greatly. Thank God! Georgie has got such an excellent, useful and good wife!'[2] The result was that May was summoned more and more often. In 1898, she spent a month at Osborne, eight days at Windsor and a week at Balmoral, as well as answering calls to see the Queen at Buckingham Palace. In 1899, her duties increased and she received the signal honour being invited to accompany the Queen on her holiday (her last) to the south of France, staying at the Hotel Regina at Cimiez. This was somewhat of an ordeal owing to the anti-British feeling in France caused by the Fashoda affair, but the Queen's popularity overcame this – 'not a hiss or a boo', May wrote back to George.

It was in this year that May became pregnant for the fourth time. On 31 March 1900, she gave birth to a son, who was

called Henry.* Kaiser William was a godfather and he wrote to
Queen Victoria:

> Most beloved Grandmama,
> How glad am I that I may join to the thanks for your last kind
> letter the warmest congratulations for the birth of another
> great-grandson! The Lord's blessing is upon your house, and
> may it for ever continue to be so! I hope that May and her
> boy will prosper, and that he may add a new ray of sun-
> shine in the pretty lodge to the sunny little circle in a happy
> home . . .[3]

Despite the animosity of the Prince and Princess of Wales
towards the German Emperor, May and George liked him and
remained on good terms. There was no hiding the fact that
William admired May. He paid her particular attention, and she
liked it. To her, accustomed as she was to travelling round the
minor courts of Germany, there was a mystique about the 'All
Highest' from Berlin. The friendship continued until
the outbreak of the First World War, and it was noticeable that
George V and Queen Mary never said a harsh word about him
after it was over, feeling sympathy for the lonely exile at Doorn.

May was now the mother of four children and, if she had
had her way, that would have been the sum total, for there was
little of the mother about her: one of her contemporaries said
that 'she was no mother at all'.[4] Her nature was such that she
'found it impossible to express her feelings by hugging or kissing
them'.[5] Nevertheless circumstances had been against her. Ever
since her marriage, family and state affairs had occupied her
time and taken her away from Sandringham. Her mother-in-law
spoiled the children outrageously and treated them as if they
were her own, while Queen Victoria intimidated them. The
second boy, Bertie, would shrink away and burst into tears at
the sight of her. May was not the real mistress of her household.

She had got away to a bad start by engaging an entirely
unsuitable nurse. In those days it was the custom for children
to be imprisoned in the nursery all day except between the hours
of five and six in the evening when they were dressed up and

---

* Afterwards Duke of Gloucester.

brought downstairs for the edification of their parents. This first nanny was a problem. She developed a great affection for the eldest boy, David, but took an aversion to the second, Bertie. On the way to the evening interview, Nanny would pinch David's arm to make him cry: Bertie, who was a weak child and on the wrong diet for a gastric stomach, would follow suit. Now all George wanted to see was smiling little faces and laughs when he tried to be funny. He regarded his children in much the same way as he did puppies in the kennels. Two infants bawling their heads off was altogether too much for him, and he would signal Nanny to take them away. This was what she wanted. Fortunately May was apprised of the character of the nurse and she was replaced by 'Lalla', a woman who brought some sunshine into the lives of the York children.

When George was away, the evening interludes were more pleasant and informal. May would play tunes such as 'Clementine' on the piano, organize games and teach her children to do tapestry. She would allow them into her room as she prepared for dinner and, as her hair was being done, Bertie, the one who loved her best, would lisp how beautiful she was.

The real influence in the lives of the York children was their father. As they grew up from babyhood, he became stern with them: he once said that just as he had been afraid of his father, he was determined that his sons should be afraid of him. And they were. This did not apply to the girl, Mary – she was always spoiled and petted. The schoolroom was the one sphere in which George reigned supreme. He held his grandmother, Queen Victoria, in the greatest respect but he did not completely trust her and would warn May, when summoned to the presence, to be careful what she said. He got on well with his father for the very good reason that he always agreed with him, which was just what Bertie wanted. His mother had a strange hold on him which she kept until she died.

George had to be the 'big chief' somewhere in his life and he made his headquarters in the dark study at York Cottage. The desk was covered with stamps and shooting magazines. The walls were hung with the same red cloth as was used for making the trousers of French private soldiers. No human pressure would make him change it, but at length moths made their home in it and he had no alternative. The red cloth was decorated with printed mottoes urging the importance of not crying over spilt milk or for the moon, and other so-called great truths of the day. It was to the HQ that his sons were summoned if the tutor's report for the day was not satisfactory. Then George would snap questions as to why the culprit had failed in his task, and immediately provide the answer before the boy could reply. He held to the belief that, as a boy, he had himself been a paragon, though in fact he had been both troublesome and rude. Ordered under the dinner table by Queen Victoria for misbehaviour, he emerged stark naked when told that he might return to his chair. Yet, on his second son's fifth birthday, he sent young Bertie the following note: 'Now that you are five years old, I hope that you will always try and be obedient and do at once what you are told, as you will find it will come much easier to you the sooner you begin. I always tried to do this when I was your age and found it made me much happier.'

The boys naturally feared him and, to a certain extent, they rebelled. No boyhood pranks were permitted. When David and Bertie were given bicycles, they were reprimanded for showering gravel from the Sandringham paths on to the lawns. On the medical side the treatment of the boys amounted to little short of cruelty. Both Bertie and Harry were forced to wear splints to correct knock-knees. Bertie, who was naturally left-handed, was made to use his right, a practice which led to the stammer which haunted his later life.

As a husband, George was more successful. In the first place he was faithful, probably the first prince – excepting Prince Albert the Consort – to be so since the arrival of George I. But the truth was that he simply did not possess the panache to court a Daisy Brooke or a Lily Langtry. Secondly, he was in love. He had found the mother-mistress figure that his eldest son was to find in Mrs Wallis Simpson, different though the two women certainly were. Thirdly, he was intensely loyal to his wife, always paying tribute to the job she did. But their minds were a mile apart. As John Gore, biographer of George V, said, 'In the most ideal marriages, if hearts may become as one, minds never can, and the nature of one individual is never wholly fusible with another's.'[6] Intellectually, May was in a very different class, and always seeking to learn more. Her husband was quite content with the little that he knew, and studying the writings of William Bagehot, as was necessary in his preparation for kingship, was a real effort. May was full of energy and curiosity: she needed encouragement and co-operation and the fact that she did not get it showed. She hid herself away in corners filled with antiques, tapestry and history. Mabell, Countess of Airlie, wrote of her, 'As a girl she had been shy and reserved, but now her shyness so crystallized that only in moments of intimacy could she be herself. The hard crust of inhibition which gradually closed over her, hiding the warmth and tenderness of her own personality, was already starting to form.'[7] Sir Henry Ponsonby, the Queen's Private Secretary, found her decidedly dull: the Empress Frederick said that each time she met her she had to start getting to know her all over again. Discerning people saw that if May could break down her stiffness, she could be of great help in society. What she needed was a husband who would lead her out, encourage her self-confidence and make her sparkle, and George could not do that.

Perhaps her greatest handicap was her in-laws. They were a mutual admiration society, a clique lording it over the Sandringham estate and the countryside around. Albert Edward* and Alexandra had rebuilt the 'Big House' and put their names above the door; it was their temple. As a family, the Wales were not intelligent and had no wish to be so. They defended themselves with chaff and poked fun at cleverness. The Prince of Wales saw Sandringham as his private kingdom and the way of life there was of his making and had to be rigidly observed: for example, all guests arriving at the 'Big House' had to be weighed. The Princess of Wales was intensely possessive: she tolerated her husband's aberrations but knew full well she was the most important woman in his life. This was in fact true. He

---

* Albert Edward, Prince of Wales, was known throughout the royal family as 'Bertie'.

was dependent upon her in his public life and he was fully aware of his debt to her. She backed him in the scandals in which he was involved and their affection for one another was very deep. Their children sheltered under the parental umbrella and the girls were often condescending and sarcastic. May discovered that she could not alter the decoration or arrangement of her own rooms without first getting approbation from above: returning once from a visit she found that the furniture of York Cottage had been moved around. She could not even alter the planting of her little garden without first getting permission. She was a poor relation caught up in the cogwheels of a big machine.

The question arises, did she, during the difficult days when she was Duchess of York, seek comfort of a spiritual nature? Was she in fact the woman who was referred to as 'The Lady of the Roses' in the history of a Catholic Church in the West End of London, where a veiled lady would arrive in solitude and pray for a while? The Sacristan of the church was direct. He said, 'Her Majesty would come into the church and give £5 with which to buy roses for the altar.' Hence the pseudonym.

There is no reason to doubt that it was she. It is known that the interest was there. She discussed the Catholic faith in detail with the Queen while on holiday with her in the south of France. The Queen was 'very wise'[8] on the subject, but emphatically against confession, which, looking back at some of her actions and friendships, can be readily understood. Can it be that the tradition and discipline of Rome appealed strongly to the restrained woman who hid her emotions so well? Was the Catholic faith a secret safety valve for the troubles which dogged her early life? The last time she, then Queen Mary, left the shores of Britain, she had audience of the Pope.

On May's paternal side the Catholic influence was strong. An ancestor of the Duke of Teck had founded the monastery of St Martin, the largest in Hungary. It became an arch-abbey, under the direct control of the Holy See. Among the foundations abroad was the Church of St Stephen at Mount Coelis in Rome and a college for priests on Vatican Hill.[9] And it must be recalled that May had spent her most impressionable years in Florence. She revelled in spectacle and was a witness of Passion Week —

the dove, the holy candle, the fireworks, the echoing 'Gloria in excelsis'.

May's swing towards Catholicism was in keeping with the feelings of her example and mentor, Queen Victoria. During her married years the Queen had been strongly against the influence of Rome, for the simple reason that her husband was. Prince Albert had brought with him from Germany a horror of Catholicism and spoke of the Reformation as the time when 'our ancestors shook off the yoke of a domineering priesthood'. Having attended a Roman Catholic wedding he informed his heir that the rites followed were 'perfectly ludicrous' and that when one got among the believers 'all the nonsense becomes apparent'.[10]

It was the Empress Eugenie of France who brought about the change. The illness and death of Napoleon III, the services at the church at Chislehurst, Princess Beatrice's strong liking for the Prince Imperial, his tragic death in Africa and his mother's lonely vigil by the Ityatosi river brought the two women together. It was through the influence of the Empress Eugenie that Queen Victoria became the first woman of Protestant faith to be conducted over the monastery of La Grande Chartreuse, the mother-house of the order of Carthusian monks. The Pope gave his consent.

May needed faith during that dark winter of 1899–1900. In the autumn, Mafeking, Kimberley and Ladysmith were besieged. In December, three British generals were defeated in turn. 'Black Week' for Britain came with the defeat of Sir Redvers Buller at Colenso. Then it was that Queen Victoria made her famous remark to Mr Balfour at Windsor, 'Please understand that there is no one depressed in this house. We are not interested in the possibilities of defeat. They do not exist.'[11] But it was a gloomy Christmas at Sandringham and all festivities were cancelled. Each week the magazines carried full pages of pictures of officers who had been killed. There was always the worry for May that she would see the likeness of one of her brothers there. Then, seven months pregnant, she had to deal with the tragic death of her father – there was no one else to do it. Next her baby arrived. But, with the month of May, began the first glittering summer of the twentieth century, glittering in both weather and actions. On the nineteenth, Mafeking was relieved and Britain went mad with delight. Five days later, the Queen celebrated her eighty-first birthday and six extra men had to be rushed to Balmoral to cope with the flood of congratulatory telegrams from all over the world.

On 11 July came May's last important public appearance with Queen Victoria. It was the day of the Garden Party at Buckingham Palace. It was swelteringly hot. The heat inside one of the tea tents was so intense that several ladies felt faint. An officer cut a hole in the fabric with his sword to let in air. The sword pierced the backside of a waitress who was standing without.

The Queen drove round in a victoria drawn by two beautiful small white horses. May, voluptuous and upright, marched behind the carriage. Lady Monkswell was watching the Queen. She wrote, 'I noticed how vivacious the dear old lady was, how she wagged her head about, looked this way and that through her spectacles. I am sure nothing escaped her.'[12]

The Queen was indestructible, or so her people thought. She would soldier on into her nineties, as her old enemy, Mr Gladstone, had done. The possibility that she would soon die never entered the heads of those about her. If it had, then arrangements would not have been made for George and May to make a forty-five-thousand-mile tour of the British Dominions in the New Year, the highlight of which was to be the opening of the first Commonwealth Parliament in Australia. In the event of the Queen's death, the new King would be left without the support of his heir. He would not have tolerated that: as things turned out, he tried to stop the tour.

Queen Victoria died from three causes: overwork caused by the Boer War; grief over the deaths and troubles of relations; and eating too much ice cream and raspberries. When the doctors advised her to ease up on her diet, she cut out the raspberries but kept on with the ice cream. At Balmoral in the spring, the doctors had found her in good shape for her age. She deteriorated as the summer ended and when they saw her again in Scotland in September, they were horrified at her decline. She was put on a diet of arrowroot and milk. Still the seriousness of her condition was not realized, despite her age. It was the same right up to the end, the doctors keeping their worst fears to themselves. Perhaps the person who saw the danger clearest was Kaiser William of Germany.

On 16 January 1901, the Queen was unable to take her afternoon drive in her donkey cart in the Osborne grounds. The doctors said that she must not do any more business and the despatch boxes began to pile up. On the nineteenth, George was shooting at Grimston Carr when he received a message that his grandmother was deteriorating. He hurried to London, leaving May at York Cottage. The Duke of Connaught was summoned from Germany; the Kaiser decided to come with him, driving the train himself, to his uncle's consternation. On the twenty-first, the Prince of Wales, George and the Kaiser went to Osborne. By the next day hope had gone. May was called from Sandringham and arrived at half past five. The Queen was cradled in the arms of the Kaiser. All her family stood around the bed and she looked at them and called them by their names. She died at half past six. Soon after, May wrote to her Aunt Augusta, 'Now she lies in her coffin in the dining room which is beautifully arranged as a chapel. The coffin is covered with the coronation robes and her little diamond crown and the garter lie on a cushion above her head . . . You would howl if you could see it all . . .'[13]

On the twenty-third, George travelled to London to attend the Privy Council meeting at St James's Palace to approve the Royal Proclamation and to take the Oath of Allegiance. On his return to Osborne he felt unwell. German measles was diagnosed and he went to bed. May nursed him. On 1 February she sat at a window in Osborne House watching the royal yacht *Alberta*, carrying the coffin of the Queen, moving between lines of warships towards the Gosport shore. The minute guns rang out and the setting sun picked out the yacht in red and gold.[14]

> We took Her silent form to glide
> Where reached from shore to shore
> Her glorious Fleet. Each warship's side

Rang, mile on mile, above the tide,
The Queen's salute once more.[15]

May did not attend the funeral service at St George's Chapel, Windsor, nor the interment at the Frogmore mausoleum two days later. But her children – David, aged six; Bertie, five; and Mary, three – were at both services. They never forgot the ordeal. It was freezing cold and the waiting seemed interminable. They were lost and miserable among the sobbing women in their black crêpe veils, the kings and the princes, the premiers and the grand dukes.

It was strange indeed, and out of character, that May attended neither service. Osborne was geared for death: the best doctors and nurses were at hand and the staff accustomed to dealing with illness. She could have accomplished the journey to Windsor and back in a day. One would have expected that the experts could have coped with a case of German measles. The answer must be that George had become so dependent on his wife that he could not bear to part with her, even for a few hours; or maybe she hated the idea of death.

CHAPTER VIII

Princess of Wales

MAY ENTERED THE REIGN of King Edward VII in a temper. The reason was that she was not immediately given the title of Princess of Wales. She became Duchess of Cornwall and York, George inheriting the dukedom of Cornwall traditionally held by the heir. And that was not good enough for May, about to depart on a world tour when the title of Princess of Wales would carry weight. She did some research and came to the conclusion that this was the first time an Heir Apparent had not been created Prince of Wales. Here we see a reflection of Francis, Duke of Teck. May had always had the importance of rank drilled into her and she writhed at being robbed of what she considered to be her right. She loosed off a complaint to her Aunt Augusta, whose opinion carried considerable weight with the new King. The Grand Duchess replied, 'My *ire* was up and hot that the legitimate historical Title is not to be continued nor borne by you and George! Oh! what a terrible mistake so to upset old traditions! and *why*? because *he* will not be superseded? what can it be else? . . . What reason can the King give?'[1]

The reason that the new King gave was simple. He considered that by giving the title to George he would create misunderstandings, and in particular mistakes in the mail. In reality, he considered the title to be his alone – he had held it for sixty years. In this he was backed by his wife, who had been Princess of Wales for nearly forty. Alexandra turned out to be the stumbling block and it was nine months before she would agree to the conferment of the title. Even then she was never to write to May as Princess of Wales – always 'Her Royal Highness Victoria Mary, Princess of Wales'.

There were other rows in those first few days of the new reign. The King wanted George to take on Osborne House, where his two aunts, Louise and Beatrice, already had homes. George and May, thinking of the expense of its upkeep and ever conscious of money, would not have it under any condition. So Lord Esher's suggestion that Osborne would make an excellent site for a new naval college was accepted. Next, the King wanted George and May to move into Marlborough House when he and the Queen moved into Buckingham Palace. This led to ructions. Alexandra did not wish to move and it was some time before it was instilled into her that she must. Then May declared that she would not move into Marlborough House unless it was redecorated: 'We really cannot go into a filthy dirty old house – *not* even for him (the King).' Terming her beloved London home as 'filthy' was hardly likely to please Alexandra. But May got her way and redecoration was approved.

It was a miracle that there was not a major clash between Alexandra and May in the opening days of 1901. That there was not was due to May's superb tact. She had learned from handling her mother, and to a lesser extent her companion, Mlle Bricka, who had a fiery temper, that the best approach was the indirect one. May's suggestions were always backed by the opinion of others with influence. She did not approach the King direct. She had never been wholly at ease with her father-in-law, but now she was even more formal than before, due to her reverence for monarchy. She differed with him on points of tradition, Edward VII being inclined to ignore the creed of Queen Victoria. She believed in rigid adherence to tradition while he did not, a reaction to his mother's authority.

One factor, an element of peace, overshadowed all others in the opening weeks of 1901 – George and May's world tour, due to start in March. Neither the King nor the Queen wanted them to go: they could not bear to part with 'Georgie boy'. The King was in poor health when he succeeded. He was recovering from pleurisy and was breathless due to bronchitis and excessive smoking. He was subject to fits of depression. His wife did not understand this, though she did try to cut down his habit of overeating. He would fly into fits of uncontrollable temper, when only Alexandra could stand up to him. On being told that she was late for an appointment and that the King was angry, she replied, 'Keep him waiting. It will do him good.'[2]

Edward therefore turned for consolation to two ladies – Mrs Alice Keppel and Sister Agnes Keyser. Mrs Keppel, a voluptuous woman of half his age, provided the fun and the romance, having the King's private ear: Sister Agnes, who ran a nursing home in Grosvenor Crescent, provided the sanity, the sympathy and the peace which none other of his loves had given. The associations piqued Alexandra as they made it appear that she was unable to provide the necessary sentiments. In fact she was not easy to get on with at this time. She had never got over the death of Eddy, which had been followed by that of the Hon. Oliver Montagu, a trusted friend whom she loved deeply in a platonic way. She had lost her mother, the Queen of Denmark. She dreaded the thought of being Queen and did not fully appreciate the sacrifices and the duties which the office demanded.

Both Edward and Alexandra hated the thought of being separated from their only surviving son. To the King, George was more like a younger brother than a son: he followed the Sandringham way of life and he did not argue. To the Queen, he was part of her being and she dreaded the loneliness without him. So the King said their proposed tour was off. The Secretary of State for the Colonies, Mr Joseph Chamberlain, was equally adamant that it should go on. Mr Chamberlain won. George and May agreed, May overcoming her hatred of the sea, for she was a bad sailor.

May's days were now full indeed. It was necessary to do much reading about the countries which she was to visit, for this was the first time she had travelled outside Europe. She had to supervise her wardrobe, which it was decreed should be all in black; only on board ship and in the tropics were white and grey to be permitted. And, most important of all, she had to arrange for the care and education of her children while she was away.

On this point May had many misgivings. It was obvious that the children should move across Sandringham Park and stay with their grandparents in the 'Big House': what she feared was the effect the stay would have on them. Both Edward and Alexandra spoiled children outrageously and May feared what would happen in the fields of education and discipline. Herself a glutton for learning, she had already noted that her two elder sons did not take after her: both were backward in their lessons. So she drew up a strict curriculum indicating how the days were to be passed and put Mlle Bricka in overall charge. Surely, she thought, the indomitable Bricka would be able to cope with the King and Queen. She was sadly mistaken. Another precaution she took was to arrange that the headmaster of the local school at Sandringham should travel with her on the *Ophir*. It was to be his task to send back information to the children as to the doings of their parents, together with geographical information, and to receive from them weekly letters telling of how they spent their days. These letters would thus be criticized. May also laid down instructions as to diet. She was later to discover that she had wasted her time.

The sixteenth of March was the departure date of SS *Ophir*, a converted P&O liner of seven thousand tons, painted white and decorated to May's instructions. The royal family travelled in strength to Portsmouth with George and May and there followed scenes of extraordinary and apparently unnecessary emotion. At a farewell luncheon on the ship, the King choked back his sobs. The Queen and Princess Victoria relapsed into floods of tears, and their ladies followed suit. George was so upset by the scene that he could scarcely bring out the words in answer to the toast. The *Ophir* moved out and George sat down and wrote to his mother, 'May and I came down to our cabins and had a good cry and tried to comfort each other.'[3]

It is difficult to see what they were crying about. Anyway it is open to doubt whether May cried: it was quite out of character. In any case she was setting out on a cruise which most people would have envied and changing the English winter for tropical sunshine. At last she had her husband to herself. And, to make matters easier for her, her youngest brother, Alge, was a member of the suite on board. As for George, he was, as a sailor, well accustomed to leaving British shores and had been round the world as a boy. It was, in truth, just another example of the

closeness of the Wales family and their reliance upon one
another.

May soon had other thoughts to occupy her mind. It was
rough in the Bay of Biscay and she was seen little. Alge tried to
persuade her to come on deck and face the waves, but to no
avail: she remained prone in the swing-cot in her cabin.

The fleets at Gibraltar and Malta gave the *Ophir* a grand
reception, and trips ashore, there and at Port Said, cheered May
up. But she went through hell in the Red Sea and wrote home
from the Indian Ocean, 'I *detest* the sea ... I like seeing
the places and being on land, the rest of it is purgatory to
me.'⁴

It was when they reached Australia and New Zealand that
May came into her own. She had always known, inside herself,
that she could handle the big task, given the chance. Now she
had that chance and there is no doubt that she outshone her
husband. At first glance she had the advantage. Firstly, she was
tall, upright and well built and fulfilled the local inhabitants'
idea of what a woman should be. Secondly, she was much
prettier than photographs had led people to believe – photographs which were condemned as 'caricatures'. Thirdly, May's
wide store of knowledge impressed the authorities deeply. She
had ideas on social welfare well in advance of the age and her
work with her mother in the charitable field stood her in good
stead.

Her success gave her self-assurance and she became a different woman. She laughed more easily and approached her many
appointments with confidence: it was George who was the shy
one. For the first time in her life she was on her own, free of the
overpowering aura of her mother, the carping of the Wales girls,
her awe of Queen Victoria and the patronization of Edward and
Alexandra. She wrote to Mlle Bricka saying how wonderful it
was to be able to do things without always being told that she
had done them wrong. Lady Mary Lygon, in waiting on May,
wrote home, 'Her Royal Highness has quite got over all her
shyness abroad ... Her smile is commented on in every paper
and her charm of manner: in fact, she is having a "*succès fou*".'
And in a later letter, 'Every state has successively fallen in love

with her looks, her smile, and her great charm of manner. She
is at last coming out of her shell and will electrify them at home
as she has everyone here.'

George approached the tour in the somewhat clinical way
apparent in certain members of the royal family. He kept a
check of the miles covered by sea and on land, the number of
foundation stones laid, the number of troops reviewed, even
minutiae such as the total number of hands shaken and the tons
of coal used by the *Ophir*. But he fully appreciated the treasure
that he had beside him and wrote to his mother from Sydney,
'You will have read the accounts in the papers of our doings
here and at Brisbane . . . Darling May is of the greatest possible
help to me and works very hard, I don't think I could have done
all this without her. Everybody admires her very much, which
is very pleasing to me. I hope you are as proud of your daughter-
in-law as I am of my wife.'[5]

It was May who provided the personal touch. This was the
first royal tour of this nature and it was comparatively restrained.
It needed the starlight of David, Prince of Wales and another
Duchess of York, afterwards Queen Elizabeth and Queen
Elizabeth the Queen Mother, to convert such journeys into
the walkabout bonanzas that came in later years. Yet, for the
period, it was a triumph for May and helped to develop
the personality she would demonstrate as Queen. It proved
her potential. And it also proved her strength. After visiting
South Africa and arriving in Canada, where the long trek from
coast to coast began, George was tired out. In Quebec he was
so fatigued that May had to step into the breach and keep an
appointment for him.[6]

In the meantime, at Marlborough House, Balmoral and
Windsor, Osborne and Sandringham, a girl and two boys were
having the time of their young lives. Where the King and Queen
went, there went they. They bowled their hoops down the Long
Corridor at Windsor and explored the castle's turrets; they raced
their bicycles along the steep paths at Balmoral; they splashed
in the sea at Osborne; they went to the circus in London; and
they joined in the gay social life at Sandringham and ate with
the grown-ups. It was all in thrilling contrast with the dark

schoolroom at York Cottage and the organized walks in the afternoon.

Lessons were of secondary importance, their grandparents putting little store by them; the two of them just revelled in having young folk with them. Edward was intrigued. He let the children have races rolling butter pats down the seams of his trousers. When the appointed hour came for the afternoon educational session to begin, Mlle Bricka would appear at the dining room door and point at her watch. Edward would wave her away. He grew bored with the persistence of the Alsatian lady and on one occasion, when visiting Sandringham, he left her behind in London. This was too much for Bricka and she hurried off a letter of protest to May. Fortified by the distance apart, May sent a stiff letter to Alexandra, stressing the importance of lessons and discipline. Alexandra replied with a hotch-potch of English which made little sense, and the spoiling continued just the same.

Overall, the tour of the *Ophir* benefited all concerned. It broadened May's outlook, gave her confidence and proved to her that she could handle the big occasion. It humanized George and destroyed some of his old-fashioned concepts. It took the nervous pressure off Edward and Alexandra and having the children always about them brought them closer together. As for David, Bertie and Mary, they learned what the word happiness meant. They were never to forget those golden days with their grandparents.

The King revelled in pulling the children's legs: among the stories he told them was that, because of the hot sun in the tropics, their parents would be black-skinned on their return. David was old enough to doubt this, but Bertie and Mary became convinced that the *Ophir* would come back with a coal-black Mammy aboard. It was with much relief that they saw an unchanged Mama waving to them from the deck on 1 November. In fact May was paler than when she had left, owing to a stormy Atlantic crossing.

Any disapproving reaction to the lax treatment of the children was quickly avoided. On 9 November, the King's birthday, George and May were created Prince and Princess of Wales.

Well satisfied, George hurried back to Sandringham to indulge in his beloved shooting. May purred with pleasure at her elevation and shortly afterwards became pregnant.

Being pregnant had its disadvantages for May that coronation summer. Endless duties were allotted to the Prince and Princess of Wales, and then came the climax. Three days before the ceremony, fixed for 26 June, the King developed acute appendicitis and an immediate operation was essential. The coronation was postponed and a deep gloom enveloped London. The responsibility for all the emergency steps to be taken fell square on the shoulders of George, who turned to his wife for help. If Edward were to die – and that possibility was real owing to his age and state of health – then they would become King and Queen. May was already despondent, suffering from prenatal depression. The situation proved too much even for her. She broke down. 'Oh, do *pray* that Uncle Wales may get well,'[7] she sobbed to Bricka. 'George says he is not ready to reign yet.' Which was true, and she knew it.

Upon George and May fell the task of entertaining the royalties and heads of state gathered in London, and seeing them off on their way home. Then followed weeks of anxiety over the King's recovery, culminating in the coronation on 9 August. Tired out, May retired with her children to Abergeldie Castle on Deeside. It pelted with unceasing rain. She wrote to George, who was at Cowes, 'Really this weather is too depressing and I feel quite in the blues and wretched.'

The rain continued and depression overcame May to a degree that she had never known before and was not to know again until her son's abdication. She threatened to leave the children at Abergeldie and return to England alone. George, perturbed, offered to postpone his duties in the south and come to Scotland to comfort her. It was a measure of her low spirits that May replied that not even he could lighten her gloom: all she wanted was to be able to sit all day in the garden in the sun. She returned to York Cottage and on 20 December her fifth child – a son named George* – was safely delivered.

---

* Afterwards Duke of Kent.

1903 was a brighter year for May. It began with a wedding. On 10 February her youngest brother, Alge, married Princess Alice, only daughter of Prince Leopold, Duke of Albany,* youngest son of Queen Victoria, who had died in 1884. From the viewpoint of the Teck family the union with a granddaughter of Queen Victoria was most welcome, but the King had hoped for a grander match for Alice and made his opinion clear.[8] Despite the fact that his daughter-in-law was a Teck, he still regarded her family as poor relations. The wedding took place at St George's Chapel, Windsor, and May's daughter, seven-year-old Mary, was a bridesmaid. May was delighted. She wrote: 'I am in a great state of excitement over it . . . for I seem to have "bemothered" Alge all my life, he being seven years younger than me.' It also gave her increased status.

Her next interest was in redecorating Marlborough House, out of which Queen Alexandra had at last been prised, complaining bitterly. It was an Herculean task, but because she had inherited from her father the flair for interior decoration she revelled in it. She and her ladies worked eight hours a day, hanging pictures and arranging furniture, and in April she and George moved in. Next month she gave a house-warming party, inviting the King and Queen and a tribe of relations. May engaged Gottlieb's Vienna Orchestra, and a housemaid was surprised to hear her whistling their favourite tunes as she went along the corridor to her bedroom. This was the first gay season since Queen Victoria's death and, installed in Marlborough House, May was riding high.

She travelled widely on the Continent during her years as Princess of Wales. The main reason behind this was that the King wished his heir to familiarize himself with the courts and the leaders of Continental countries. George was a stranger to Europe – he had scarcely made any visits at all while he was in the navy and Queen Victoria was alive. In addition he was a lamentable linguist, owing to his poor education, and it was necessary to polish up his French and German. He made no secret of his dislike of Continental travel: as he was to say later

---

* Prince Leopold married Princess Helena of Waldeck-Prymont in 1882.

in his life, 'Abroad is awful. I know. I have been.' In May he found the perfect guide and companion. She had been travelling round the courts since she was a baby, spoke perfect German and had many relations in the capitals she visited. In addition she was deeply interested in their historical background.

Outstanding among her journeys was the official visit to Vienna in 1904. Here reigned seventy-three-year-old Emperor Francis Joseph, overseeing a court whose customs and etiquette had not changed for two centuries. He was a strange and impressive old man: he dined at five in the evening, went to bed at eight and rose at four in the morning. But even May was nonplussed by the reception at the railway station, where an army of archdukes and archduchesses was waiting to receive them, and each one had to be spoken to. Once again May scored a great personal success: her ease and charming manner were in contrast with those of the stiff archduchesses, none of whom could rival her for good looks. At a grand ball she danced until four in the morning.

George was somewhat lost in the archaic splendour and jumped at the chance of going out into the countryside to shoot. While he was away, May took the opportunity to explore Vienna, where her father had served the Emperor before his marriage. She examined every room in the Schönbrunn Palace and revelled in the wonders of the imperial city. She regretted that George was not with her, but the fact was that he had no interest in works of art or historic buildings: it had not been included in his upbringing. May wrote, 'Alas for my poor George all these things are a sealed book, such a pity and so deplorable in his position! And he misses so much that is interesting in one's life.'

In 1905, May had her last child. A son, John, was born on 12 July. George was beside her and followed his usual procedure during convalescence of bringing her her breakfast at nine and spending much of the day reading to her. Their children now totalled six and there were to be no more. May recovered quickly and prepared for further travels.

During the winter of 1905–6, George and May spent four months in India. They travelled in HMS *Renown*, which they

joined at Genoa. The battleship proved to be far superior to the
Ophir and May overcame her dislike of the sea. The tour was
one of the happiest of her career and she fell in love with the
subcontinent. In later days she would murmur, 'lovely India,
beautiful India', and she forecast that when she died the word
INDIA would be found written across her heart. Before leaving
she did an immense amount of research – her children called
this 'swatting up' – and it stood her in good stead. She grew up
that winter, became a fully developed woman. It showed in her
letters home. There was less restraint in her descriptions and the
detail rivalled that of Queen Victoria in her Highland Journals.
She travelled widely – Bombay to Peshawar and on to Rangoon,
Mandalay, Mysore, Benares and Chaman. Much of the time
was spent in their special train, interspersed with visits to Indian
princes and British governors. But May was not content with
seeing only the élite side of India. She insisted on walking
incognito through the side streets of the towns – 'adding to my
store of knowledge', she termed it. She was perturbed, as was
her husband, by the status of women there and the couple
commented on this to Indian leaders.

They returned home slowly, spending a week in Cairo and
then calling at Corfu and Athens, where were King Edward and
Queen Alexandra, holidaying in the royal yacht. While George
chatted with his numerous relations and sailed, May again set
off on her voyage of discovery, delighting in the Acropolis and
the Parthenon and browsing in the British School of Archae-
ology. For contrast, she watched the Olympic Games.

While he was in India – away from May at the time on a
shooting expedition – George heard from the King that Princess
Ena of Battenberg, only daughter of Princess Beatrice (Princess
Henry of Battenberg)* had become engaged to young King
Alfonso of Spain, and that George was to attend the wedding
in Madrid. There was no mention of May. Being Catholic-
minded, she badly wanted to attend and asked George to put in
a word for her. She ended her note, 'You might try and arrange
this for me, for I believe I was a help to you in Vienna, wasn't

*Prince Henry of Battenberg died in 1896.

[123]

I, and my goodness that was stiff!' George obliged, but in reality May's presence was already arranged, as the Queen-Mother of Spain, Queen Christina, had written to Edward VII asking that she should come.

The news that his cousin Ena was prepared to change to the Catholic faith surprised and perturbed George. He forecast that all hell would be let loose in London – and it was. The fact that the future British King and Queen were to be present added fuel to the flames. As soon as the news of the engagement became known, an ecclesiastical clamour broke out. The King had early warning of the trouble ahead, for in January the Archbishop of Canterbury and the Bishop of London had informed him of the obvious signs of public disapproval. Now the correspondence columns of the newspapers became filled with provocative letters on the subject, the Church Association and the Protestant Alliance called on the King to refuse his consent, and the Bishop of London made a direct appeal to Princess Beatrice not, as he said, as a daughter of Queen Victoria, but as a devout member of the Church of England.[9] King Edward made some masterly and evasive replies; George, backed by May, condemned the opposition as 'a put-up job'; and the plans for the wedding continued. Only a few weeks after their return from India, May and George set off on the tiring rail journey to Madrid. They were facing the most dramatic moments of their lives. But for a coincidence and a stroke of luck they would have been blown to pieces and there would have been no story of King George V and Queen Mary in British history.

Being among the senior guests gathered in Madrid, May and George were lodged in the Palacio Real. Here they found that the old-world atmosphere of Vienna was completely outdone. They were allotted twelve rooms and each was guarded by a halberdier armed with a pike. Each time they left their apartments an official would clap his hands and the halberdiers would present arms, crying, '*Arriba Princesa! Arriba Principe!*' This charade appealed to May strongly.

The wedding was fixed for 31 May, at the little church of San Jeronimo. Alfonso had been warned that an anarchist was on the prowl and, when the bride's procession was late in

Princess May with her parents,
the Duke and Duchess of Teck
and her three brothers, Adolphus,
Alexander and Frank

May with her mother, the Duchess
of Teck and her first child born in
1894. He was christened Edward
Albert Christian George Andrew
Patrick David, and became
Edward VIII and Duke of Windsor

The Royal Family with their children – Princes Edward, Albert, Henry, George, John, and Princess Mary at Abergeldie.

arriving, he feared that an attempt had already been made. Among the members of the press allotted seats was an American reporter who had been taken ill a few days previously. In all innocence, he handed over his pass to none other than the assassin, Matteo Morral. Fortunately the American recovered from his illness and claimed his pass back. May commented afterwards, 'Thank God that the anarchist did not get into the church in which case we must all have been blown up!'

Matteo Morral made his way to the Calle Mayor, a narrow street on the processional route back to the palace. He climbed to a high balcony of No. 88. In his hands was what appeared to be a bouquet of flowers. Hidden in the flowers was a bomb. As the wedding coach approached he dropped his 'bouquet'. It fell short of its target. George described what happened:

> Our carriage was just in front of the one in which Queen Christina and Aunt Beatrice were driving and they were just ahead of Alfonso and Ena who were at the end of the procession. Just before our carriage reached the palace, we heard a loud report and thought it was the first gun of a salute. We soon learned however that when about two hundred yards from the palace in a narrow street, the Calle Mayor, a bomb was thrown from an upper window at the King and Queen's carriage. It burst between the wheel horses and the front of the carriage, killing about twenty people and wounding about fifty or sixty, mostly officers and soldiers. Thank God! Alfonso and Ena were not touched although covered with glass from the broken windows. The Marquesa Torlosa and her niece were killed. The two wheelers were killed and another horse, the carriage went on about thirty yards. Sir M. de Bunsen, Morgan, Lowther and four officers of the 16th Lancers, who were in a house close by, rushed out, stood round the carriage and assisted Ena out of the carriage; both she and Alfonso showed great courage and presence of mind. They got into another carriage at once and drove off to the palace amid frantic cheering . . . Naturally, on their return Alfonso and Ena broke down, no wonder after such an awful experience. Eventually we had lunch about three. I proposed their healths, not easy after the emotions caused by this terrible affair.[10]

Calm as Ena had remained at the time of the explosion, reaction hit her when she reached the palace. Her dress torn and blood-stained, she kept repeating, 'I saw a man without any legs! I saw a man without any legs!'[11] Her mother, who had been in the carriage next to the wedding coach, was so shattered that she could be of little help and comfort. The task fell upon May, the bride's nearest English relation there. She was superb and remained calm, giving Ena the support that she badly needed. Princess Frederica of Hanover reported home that she was the only one to show proper feeling.

The danger was not yet over, for Matteo Morral had escaped capture and there was no doubt in most people's minds that he would try again. Alfonso was defiant. On the day after the wedding he drove out alone with Ena. He decreed that his guests must wear their uniforms and continue with their appointments, regardless of the fact that it made them conspicuous targets. This did not suit some of the guests, including George and the Ambassador, who considered it to be taking an unnecessary risk. He damned the Spanish police, describing them as the worst in the world, and was horrified at the lack of security arrangements at the Palacio Real. But May was in agreement with the Spanish King and insisted on full dress and went about her appearances as if nothing had happened. Three days later, Morral was cornered, shot a soldier and then himself.

May's bravery throughout inspired much comment, none more pointed than that of Prince Alexander of Battenberg,* Ena's eldest brother, who was playing an important part in the celebrations. He enthused. 'She was magnificent,' he said, 'as brave as a lion. She was frightened of nothing.'[12] May's reputation spread throughout the courts of Europe.

She was tireless and dauntless as well. A week after her return from her shattering experience in Spain, she sailed to Trondheim to attend the coronation of the new King and Queen** of Norway. Her varied experiences indeed fitted her to be Queen herself.

---

* Afterwards Marquess of Carisbrooke. ** Her sister-in-law, formerly Princess Maud of Wales.

CHAPTER IX

The Final Preparation

MAY WAS OUT OF TOUCH with the human side of life. For example, she had no understanding of a child's mind.[1] She tried very hard to be a good mother: she kept a diary for each of her six children in which she recorded their progress – the cutting of their teeth, their first steps. But, as the Empress Frederick said of her, 'She does not seem to have the passionate tenderness for her little ones which seems so natural to me.'[2] There was always a superior consideration – that she was Princess of Wales and future Queen. She did not romp with her children as their grandmother, Alexandra, did. She could not bring herself to hug and kiss them. She had a clinical approach to illness and minor injuries, such as cut knees. She expected her children to behave as she had behaved when she was young.

It was left to George to oversee the upbringing of their brood. As was not unusual in the age, George was somewhat of a bully. He treated his offspring as he had treated the sailors under his command in the navy, expecting them to toe the line, obey instantly and, on the lighter side, put up cheerfully with chaff.

May had no interest in games, athletic pastimes being beyond her ken. She trudged round after the men when shooting, but only because it was the thing to do. Frankly it bored her. She did not hunt. She did not even enjoy the contemporary craze for cycling. While the King's family raced round the garden – and even the rooms of the 'Big House' – on their machines, May would draw back. She was eventually brought into the fun by the provision of a heavy tricycle for her use. Her attitude to games was summed up in a letter which she wrote to her third son, Henry, when he went to school: 'Do for goodness sake

wake up and work harder and use the brains God has given you
... All you write about is your everlasting football of which I
am heartily sick.'[3]

Yet her intellectual bent was appreciated in later life by her
children. David (Duke of Windsor) wrote of the evening sessions
when she would have them brought to her boudoir and there
read and talk to them: 'Looking back upon this scene I am sure
that my cultural interests began at my mother's knee. The years
that she had lived abroad as a young girl had equipped her with
a prodigious knowledge of royal history. Her soft voice, her
cultured mind, the cosy room overflowing with personal treasures are all inseparable ingredients of the happiness associated
with the last hour of a child's day.'[4] She was noticeably more
maternal when George was away on state business or shooting
in the shires.

In due season the boys graduated from the care of their
beloved nurse, 'Lalla', and into that of a tutor, Mr Henry
Hansell. A strange, silent man, Hansell was a crack shot, sailed
well and did not argue, and therefore George considered him
ideal for the job. His interest lay in cathedrals and their precincts
and his holidays were spent tramping from Salisbury to Canterbury, Lincoln to Wells, and this appealed to May. He did not
succeed in instilling much learning into the boys' heads, but his
advice that they should be sent away to school was wise. His
advice was ignored. May's brothers had all been sent to educational establishments, but George would not hear of it. He
and his brother Eddy had been educated at home, and so should
his sons. The navy would teach them all that was necessary. So
David and Bertie were thrown into the tough training colleges
of Osborne and Dartmouth, mixing with boys who had all been
through the mill of the 'prep' school. Out of their depth, they
were teased and bullied and had their backsides kicked and
chastised with ropes. They did not do well in the classroom and
anyway there only absorbed knowledge about knots and the
points of the compass, and little that was to be of use in the role
of king. Here May was at fault, and she was so warned by her
wise old Aunt Augusta, who quoted to her the example of
William IV, the sailor king. She should have stood up to her

husband and insisted upon a more humane and wider upbringing. Clearly she was unaware of some of the goings-on at
Osborne and Dartmouth, and took it for granted that it was the
right thing to do. Yet some of the truth must have got through
to her, for Henry was spared the naval training, being privately
educated at Broadstairs and then going through normal school-
ing. Although she defended her children when she considered
that her husband was being too stern, she was too impressed
with George's position to lay down the law. She was apt to
underestimate dangers and was a mistress of understatement.
She had dismissed the laxity of the police at the wedding of
Alfonso and Ena as 'Not very wise'. As she watched her husband
submerge in a submarine for the first time, she was heard to
murmur, 'I shall be very disappointed if George doesn't come
up again.'⁵

May encouraged her children to indulge in useful pastimes.
While she was reading to them, she would provide them with
wooden rings into which were fitted brass pegs. Wool yarn had
to be looped round each peg, thus forming crochet stitches which
in the end became woollen comforters. These she sent for sale
for the benefit of one of her charities. But generally both she
and her husband worked on the principle that the operative
word in a child's upbringing was 'Don't'. Right was found by
pointing out the wrong. The result of this lack of encouragement
was to make the young people nervous and 'jumpy', often ending
in fits of tears or temper. Then came the reprimand, 'Don't
behave like a baby.' Always 'Don't', when an encouraging word
would have made all the difference.

Apparently May did not expect to receive the love that a
child, by nature, feels for its mother. She wrote to George about
David, 'I really believe he begins to like me at last, he is most
civil to me.'⁶ Both parents seemed to be surprised by the manifes-
tations of childishness in children, expecting them to have the
power of reasoning from the time that they could talk. Above
all, the children must be standard. That the boys had inherited
knock-knees from their father and grandfather could not be
tolerated. Bertie was left-handed. That would not do at all. May
summed up her wishes for her brood: 'I do so hope our children

will turn out common sense people, which is so important in this world.' A little more love in the early days might have led to more common sense in later days, for the seeds of the abdication were sown in the schoolroom at York Cottage.

It was in the reign of King Edward that May developed her passion for collecting royal memorabilia. The hobby began with the death of George, Duke of Cambridge, in 1904. The old Duke was a rich man and had an unrivalled collection of family pictures, plate, jewelled snuff boxes and Fabergé works. Much of it had been inherited by him from his father, Adolphus, Duke of Cambridge, of whom he was the eldest child and only son. The remainder had come in the form of presents over his long life and during his forty years as Commander-in-Chief. He had once promised Queen Victoria that he would leave family possessions to the royal family, but this he did not do. Nearly everything went to his three sons by Mrs FitzGeorge. After offering the royal family the chance to buy in what they wanted at valuation, they allowed most of the Duke's treasures to find their way to the auction rooms. There was no catalogue and the FitzGeorges knew little about the subjects of pictures or who had painted them, or who were the original donors of the many bibelots. There was no reason why they should, or why they should even be interested, as Queen Victoria had ignored their very existence. So it was upon May that the task fell of sorting out what should be bought and what valuation accepted, and even checking at the auction rooms to ensure that items of family interest did not go for a song. The experience taught her one great lesson – the importance of cataloguing.

May was not the connoisseur of antiques and art she has often been taken for. She never bought a good picture in her life. She was a collector of royal possessions and had a unique knowledge in her field. Her experience led her in later life to purchase – or 'scrounge' with regal pressure – items which took her fancy, but her real obsession was with the memorabilia of royalty.

Her mania for thus collecting is easy to understand: there were two main reasons for it. The first was that she had had the importance of the royal connection drummed into her since childhood. Involved with the houses of Hesse and Nassau, Strelitz and Württemberg, Cambridge and Cumberland, and with ties to the houses of Denmark and Greece, she had mixed with a multitude of royalties at the yearly gatherings at the castle of Rumpenheim. There were few European courts which she had not visited. Her socially-minded mother had known everybody and was familiar with every page of the *Almanach de Gotha*. With an innate interest in history, May had no difficulty in memorizing the inmates of the palaces.

Her second reason for concentrating on royal items was financial. Throughout her childhood, the Tecks had been haunted by poverty. Presents from rich relations, such as jewelled snuffboxes, meant security – their only way of obtaining it. The more diamonds that sparkled on the bosom of Mary Adelaide, the more credit could she obtain from the tradesmen. Thus events such as birthdays and confirmations were looked forward to. As she grew older this nightmare of poverty reappeared before Queen Mary and her possessions became more important to her.

She had no training in the field of art, was taught nothing of woods or craftsmanship. She was self-taught, by wandering round museums and galleries and by reading copiously. Her mother had only a surface knowledge and Mlle Bricka had no interest at all. Contemporary paintings did not appeal to her and she was known to have passed a masterpiece without a glance but gurgle with delight at recognizing the faded likeness of a remote archduchess. Yet, in the end, the order that she brought to royal galleries and collections and the detailed cataloguing which she organized were of immense value to the history of Britain.

As Princess of Wales, May played a part about which little was known but which was of the utmost importance to the country. Behind the scenes she was acting as secretary and adviser to the King who had a high opinion of her intelligence and tact. From 1905, Edward was a sick man. That year, he had a serious attack of bronchial catarrh. There was a repeat attack in February 1906 and his doctors advised him never to spend that month in London, owing to the danger of fogs. In

1907, his physicians were summoned urgently to Buckingham Palace.

Worry was a subsidiary reason for the King's ill health. Britain and Germany were close to war. Admiral Sir John Fisher,* First Sea Lord, was violently anti-German and had put to Edward the astounding plan that the German fleet should be scuttled at its moorings. The Admiral claimed that he could capture the Kiel Canal and Schleswig-Holstein. In November 1906, a rumour spread through Germany that Fisher was ready to attack. Kaiser William, watching the situation, wrote, 'Fisher can no doubt land 100,000 men in Schleswig-Holstein, and the British Navy has reconnoitred the coast of Denmark with this object in view.'[7] Edward refused to listen to Fisher's belligerent plan, but the strain told on him. In his bouts of depression, he would mutter, 'Willie is only waiting until I die to declare war.'[8] He needed people beside him in whom he could confide and trust. He found them in George and May.

Edward was in marked contrast with his mother in that he showed his heir the contents of all the Despatch Boxes – their desks were side by side at Windsor. And, further, he told George that May could see them. As a result she saw everything. Her experience was much wider than her husband's, whose time in the navy did little to broaden his intellect. Because of her knowledge of Germany she was called to advise on problems with that country. On the home front, her work in the charitable fields allowed her to advise on social problems. Quite naturally, George turned to her for guidance.

George was surprised when his father told him that May should be allowed to see all papers, pointing out that the Queen did not. 'No, but that's a very different thing,' was the King's reply.

Her husband's reliance on May peeved Queen Alexandra and led to outbursts of temper. On one occasion, when she was unwell and unable to attend a Drawing Room, Edward invited May to do the honours. Alexandra was furious and forbade any of her ladies to attend. The King had good grounds for keeping

* The situation was dealt with in detail by Admiral Lord Fisher in his books, *Memories* and *Records*.

information from his wife. She was biased towards Denmark, Russia and Greece, where dwelt her relations, and she was violently anti-German. She backed Fisher's wild schemes wholeheartedly and was in favour of invasion. She hated Kaiser William. On the other hand George and May got on well with him. To heal the rift between Britain and Germany, the King invited the Kaiser and his wife to visit Windsor. On the surface, the visit was a success, May and George helping with the entertaining. Although at the time their placatory attitude was of the greatest assistance to the King, in the outcome it was Alexandra's view which turned out to be much nearer to being correct.

During the last three years of King Edward's reign, May and George travelled little abroad. George considered that he had done his share and obviously did not enjoy sightseeing. After a visit to Germany, demanded by Kaiser William, to inspect his regiment of Cuirassiers, they stopped off in Paris. But he saw little of his wife as she disappeared on her voyages of discovery, swallowed up in the Louvre or Versailles. She even drove as far as Chartres to see the fine windows of the cathedral. She proved a disappointment to the *couturières*, who had reckoned on making dresses for the Princess of Wales. She avoided them and bought nothing, having a horror of the fitting room. In this she was encouraged by her husband, who not only feared for his purse strings but hated change. His view was that he had 'bought' May dressed in a certain way and that it was only fair that she should continue in the same mould. She did on one occasion experiment with a smart hat but was met with a wave of derision. Anxious to display more of her fine legs, she cut the length of her skirt. The reception was so cool that she reverted to the customary measurement.

In his middle forties George was set in his ways and each year he moved in the same pattern. On the same dates each year he moved from Marlborough House to Sandringham, Abergeldie to Frogmore. He sailed and fulfilled the demands of the season, and then concentrated on his great love – shooting. Being more at home during these years suited May, for she had a very real mother's problem on her hands. Her youngest son,

John, was subnormal and early suffered from epileptic fits. He was cared for by nurse 'Lalla'. By nature a happy child, he grew at an immense rate. His mother loved him, spent much time with him and treasured his quaint little sayings, but he was an everlasting worry to her. He was kept apart from his brothers and sisters, as was the fashion of the day, and an aura of mystery built up about him. At the age of eleven he was given his own establishment, under the care of 'Lalla' and a male nurse.

King Edward's health deteriorated. May and George never guessed that he had not long to live: as he weakened they were engrossed in plans for a tour of South Africa.[9] The doctors knew the truth, and so did Queen Alexandra, but Edward put on such a brave face that others did not guess. He was still in his sixties. He travelled abroad frequently, yearly to Marienbad, Homburg and Biarritz. In 1908, he met the Emperor of Russia at Reval and the following year paid a state visit to Germany. He was still the leader of society, still sailed at Cowes and often attended the theatre and the race course. And Mrs Alice Keppel was his lady friend and he smuggled her out to Biarritz for his spring holiday. In his excitement, he appeared a young man when he won the 1909 Derby.

He was at Biarritz in March 1910 when he suffered a severe attack of catarrh. Alice Keppel nursed him through it. Worried, Alexandra begged him to join her at Genoa and cruise to Corfu with her in the royal yacht. He refused and returned to England. He caught a cold at Sandringham and was very ill by the time he reached Buckingham Palace.

May and George were at Marlborough House. A message was sent to the Queen at Corfu and she began a dash for home. May and George met her at Victoria station on the evening of 5 May. 'We felt very much worried about Papa,'[10] May wrote in her diary. George spent the next day at the palace, anxiously watching his father fighting against death. Edward insisted on dressing in a frock coat to receive Sir Ernest Cassel and Lord Knollys. He smoked a cigar.

May was sent for at seven o'clock. She saw the King try to rise from his chair and walk. The effort proved too much for his heart and his pulse almost ceased. Alexandra herself administered the oxygen, which gave some relief. The family knelt around the bed, the Archbishop of Canterbury saying prayers.[11] At quarter to twelve, King Edward VII died. 'What a loss to the Nation and to us all. God Help us,' was May's comment. She did not cry, comforting Alexandra and her sister-in-law as best she could. Soon after midnight she returned to Marlborough House. Now she was the Queen Consort of Great Britain and Ireland and of the British Dominions beyond the Seas, Empress of India.

CHAPTER X

❧

Early Problems as Queen

It was decided to call the new Queen Mary. She had always signed herself 'Victoria Mary', but Queen Victoria was considered to be out of the question, so plain Mary was chosen. And thus henceforth she will be called.

Mary found no problems in the role of Queen itself. In fact, as she once related, the shyness which had haunted her all her life now deserted her. She knew the drill. She had been trained in court etiquette since she could walk and knew all the royalties of Europe. She had watched Queen Victoria closely. She had been trained by her mother in the fields of social welfare and charity. She had been the confidant of King Edward VII and he had leaned on her for advice. And from the historical viewpoint, her knowledge of state ceremonial was unrivalled. She was better fitted to be Queen than her husband was to be King. Yet her problems were many, appearing at times insuperable to her, and they were personal problems. In order of seriousness they were: the attitude and behaviour of her mother-in-law, Alexandra; the fear that she was drifting apart from her husband and losing his love; the animosity shown towards her by the gay social circle of King Edward's day; the libellous statements that were circulating about the King's name; the domestic upheaval of moving house – Marlborough House to Buckingham Palace, Frogmore to Windsor Castle, Abergeldie to Balmoral; and the continuing concern for her brother Francis (Frank).

This was an intensely personal worry and not one that she could share except with her other brothers. The Tecks were a close-knit family, with a difficult history. Frank had proved to be the black sheep and caused deep rancour. Retiring from the army in 1901, he had lived a life of ease in London and overspent his very small income. He drove around in an electric brougham and, as George said, was very busy doing nothing. The rift with his sister came when he gave his mother's famous Cambridge emeralds to his mistress. This was too much for Mary and for years she never spoke to him. When at last he showed signs of improvement and began working hard to raise funds for the Middlesex Hospital, May forgave him and they became very close. Soon after King Edward's death Frank underwent a nasal operation, developed pleurisy and died. At his funeral in St George's Chapel Mary broke down and cried. This was most unusual for her – perhaps unique. Overwhelmed with grief as she was, it was not only for Frank that she wept. Other problems had piled up and she was finding life intolerable. She wrote to her Aunt Augusta, 'I wish the old life were coming back. I don't like this.'[1]

She was referring in particular to the behaviour of her mother-in-law. Alexandra was being awkward, although she did not realize how difficult she was making life for Mary. It began with the funeral of King Edward. At this she insisted on taking precedence over Mary, which was against tradition. Her reason was that in Russia the widow came first at the service and Alexandra was being advised, and egged on, by her sister, the Dowager Empress Marie of Russia. Mary gave in and thus set a standard. The next prick of the thorn came over the Queen Consort's jewels. Alexandra refused to part with 'the lovely little Crown', which she had no right to retain. Mary wrote to her Aunt Augusta, 'The odd part is that the person (Alexandra) causing the delay and trouble remains supremely unconscious as to the inconvenience it is causing. Such a funny state of things and everyone seems afraid to speak.'[2]

That was the crux of the matter – people were afraid of the former Queen Consort. Although Alexandra could be a formidable opponent when in a temper, which was seldom, the heart of the problem was inherited seniority. In those times seniority was even more powerful than class distinction. Seniority was rampant through the armed forces – when young Bertie went to Osborne Naval College he was not allowed to speak to his elder brother because David was a year senior. The same advantage of length of service ran through the professions, the public schools, the royal household and the social procedure – a woman who did not receive her correct position when going into dinner was furious and felt insulted. And Alexandra was very senior. One brother was King of Denmark and another King of Greece. Her sister was Dowager Empress of Russia. She was the widow of King Edward VII and she had no intention of taking one step backward. To her, Edward remained the King, his rightful successor, Eddy, being dead. Her second son she regarded merely as a 'stand in' and she always wrote to him as 'King George', never 'The King'. May, with her Teck background, was not in the same class when it came to seniority. She had done her task, agreed to marry the wayward Eddy and on his death taken over George. She had provided him with six children and had nursed him through two lengthy tours abroad. Had she played her role? Was she now to go back to the status of a poor relation? Britain already had a Queen very close to its heart – Alexandra.

Just as Alexandra had been rebellious about moving into Buckingham Palace, now she was equally rebellious about getting out, raising all kinds of problems. But a point which riled Mary even more was that Alexandra continued to live in the 'Big House' at Sandringham, while she, the Queen, with a large family and a sovereign's household, was condemned to be squashed into sordid little York Cottage. Here May made a mistake. The Tecks had never had a home of their own, always living in grace and favour quarters, and she did not fully appreciate the strength of the ties which bound Alexandra to Sandringham. She and her husband had rebuilt it together and their names were side by side above the door. There were nearly fifty years of memories crushed into the house and every room was crammed with mementos. The 'Big House' had been left to Alexandra by Edward in his will – it was hers absolutely. The thought of moving out never entered her head.

But it entered the heads of certain members of the household, condemned to do their work in a corner of the schoolroom or even in a passage. They sowed the seeds of discontent in Mary.

'Selfish old woman,' she termed her mother-in-law. But her husband saw the matter from his mother's viewpoint and was content to remain where he was. When an adviser dared to point out the advantages of the 'Big House', George went puce with anger and told him to mind his own damned business.[3]

This was not the only occasion when George backed his mother, and Mary did not like it. Alexandra was, in truth, claiming back her 'Georgie boy'. It was a natural reaction for a lonely widow to cling to the surviving son, and now George received all the affection that once had been shared by King Edward and Eddy. She behaved more like a queen than she had when her husband was alive, for he had always been somewhat jealous of the starlight about his wife and the affection in which she was held by the British public. Now Alexandra fussed about George, forever rushing in to see him when he was laden down with state business, forever making demands for Denmark and Greece and asking favours for her relations. George adored his 'Motherdear' and was somewhat frightened of her. Tired out with the strain of picking up the reins of kingship, he was incapable of handling his personal affairs. Although he was never separated from his wife from May to October 1910, the two drifted apart. Conversation in the evenings was restricted to impersonal subjects, criticism of statesmen, the weather, the progress of the boys. After seventeen years, May and George were back in the position they had been in during their engagement – unable to show their real emotions or confide in one another. Mary had no way of telling whether she was being a helpful Queen Consort or not.

In November, George went to Sandringham to shoot, leaving Mary in London. As had happened before, the answer to her problem came in a letter. George, it showed, was well aware of the lack of communication but lacked the power to speak, as later happened in the case of his eldest son. He wrote:

> I fear, darling, my nature is not demonstrative, but I want you to understand that I am indeed grateful to you, for all you have done all these busy months for me and to thank you from the bottom of my heart for all your love and for the enormous help and comfort which you have been to me in my

new position. I can't imagine how I would have got on at all without you. I shall never forget it.[4]

May answered by return, saying what a pity it was that he could not bring himself to say what he wrote. 'It is such a blessing to know that I am a help to you.'

Now other problems brought the two together, Mary backing her husband. There was criticism of George to countermand. Kings have seldom taken up their role without encountering a wave of opposition: George IV was pilloried because of his affairs with women and his profligacy with money; William IV was said to be senile and likely to be put in a straight waistcoat; Victoria was hissed at Ascot for her treatment of Lady Flora Hastings; the press expressed the opinion that Edward VII was unfitted to be King after his many affairs and the Tranby-Croft baccarat scandal; Edward VIII got into trouble over Mrs Wallis Simpson; and George VI was to be dubbed a 'rubber-stamp' King and not up to the job. George V fared likewise. His red complexion was cited as evidence that he drank too much. It was said that he had not inherited his father's love of horse racing. And the old rumour was resurrected that he had been married in Malta in 1890.

George was a temperate man, but his hearty laugh and bluff manner led some people to imagine this was not so. More marked upon was his red and patchy complexion, in truth the aftermath of the attack of typhoid fever in 1891, coupled with the curse of chronic indigestion. So serious did the accusation become that the Austrian Ambassador wrote to Vienna, 'At pious meetings in the East End of London, prayers are said for Queen Mary and the royal children, begging the protection of Heaven on their unhappy drunkard's home.' Mary saw her task as that of protecting her husband as much as possible and she gave the lie to this rumour in no uncertain manner.

As to his lack of interest in horse racing, this was also untrue, although it did apply to Mary, who also disliked shooting. But George saw racing in a different light to his father. Edward VII was not a brilliant horseman, but was attracted to the racecourse by the lure of the social life and gambling associated with it. His first big success as an owner came in 1896, when his horse Persimmon won the Derby. When a guest at Sandringham admired the estate, he waved his stick and said, 'It is all due to Persimmon.' George liked racing as a sport. He had had bitter experience of the financial side when he had been forced to help out his wife's brother, Frank, after his disastrous £10,000 bet at Punchestown. George, like his wife, was always careful over money. He liked a small bet and would say to an equerry that he would have half a crown on a horse in the three-thirty. But if it lost, he would quietly forget the wager. The unfortunate equerries put their heads together and opened a credit account for the King. Thus in due course he received an account which he could not ignore.

There was also rumour that Mary was afraid of the King, as she always deferred to his wishes and did not smile at him in public. Apart from her undemonstrative nature, this was caused by her obsession with the importance of the monarchy. All these minor rumours died out with the years.

George and Mary's major trouble was the resurrection of the rumour that he had married the daughter of a British Admiral in Malta in 1890. In 1910, a journalist named Edward Mylius republished the story. The case was taken to court, the King cleared and Mylius sentenced to a year's imprisonment. Mary fumed with fury over the libel. She told her Aunt Augusta, 'So many people believed it that when this scoundrel Mylius was found with the incriminating papers it was thought best to prosecute.'

Mary and George had another difficulty to face: this lay in the field of their social life. It was summed up in a cartoon by Max Beerbohm which showed Lord Burnham, Sir Ernest Cassel, Alfred and Leopold de Rothschild and Arthur Sassoon walking along a corridor of Buckingham Palace, clearly on their way to meet the new King. The title was, 'Are we as welcome as ever?' [5] Frankly, they were not. It was not that George and Mary were anti-Semitic – it was simply that they were out of tune with the business tycoons who had had such a strong influence on King Edward's life for the past twenty to thirty years. They enjoyed a domestic life, did not play bridge and went early to bed –

eleven was quite late for them. There was no desire to sit up drinking and at midnight move off to the bowling alley. Corridor creeping and gambling for high stakes were out. They did smoke, George considerably, Mary on occasion. When cigarettes were handed round after a women's meeting and she was omitted, she said, 'Can you spare one for little me?'[6]

Mary was early nineteenth century by training. She had never been allowed to forget that her mother was a granddaughter of George III, while her father was steeped in the tradition of the German courts of even further away in time. Her mother's friends came from among the oldest families in the country.

The revolution which came to Britain when May was a schoolgirl passed her by. It was a financial revolution, and in part responsible for the enforced exile of the Tecks in Florence. The climax of the revolution came in 1879 – 'Black 79', it was termed. The price of corn plummeted from fifty-three shillings a quarter down towards the thirty mark, and cargoes of it came from the rich and quickly expanding fields on the plains of Canada. The disaster spread from the upper classes to the farm labourers. The gentry could no longer afford houses in London for the season and their incomes would not stand the losses on their home farms. They were forced to sell their land, and their cattle and expensive new steam equipment were jobbed off at auction sales where there were few buyers. Tradesmen looked for settlement of their bills and the curtain came down on the Tecks.

Other royalty suffered, including King Edward when Prince of Wales. He was already losing £30,000 a year on Sandringham estate alone, and the debit increased. He was so sorely pressed for money that when he went to Paris his hotel was surrounded by moneylenders. The Prime Minister, Lord Salisbury, was perturbed to such an extent that he despatched men from Scotland Yard to protect the Prince.

In the meantime, the international financiers saw their chance – attractive estates and beautiful houses going cheap – and moved in. They had made their money on railways, by speculating in silver and by cornering commodities. Most of them were frowned upon at the courts of Berlin, Vienna and St Petersburg.

Yet Britain was offering bargains in the estate market and soon these smart gentlemen, perfectly attired, were to be seen in the hunting fields of the Quorn and the Cottesmore.

Queen Victoria, still under the sway of her gillie, John Brown, and miserly with money, would not come to her son's rescue. But it was soon noticed that the Prince of Wales had no more financial difficulties. His investments flourished. He took up horse racing and won big races. The whole rhythm of social life in England altered. New faces appeared at court functions, new names appeared in the Honours List. It was considered an essential of marital life to have a lover. Actresses became idols. It was all in violent contrast with the quiet life Mary had lived with her ill father at the White Lodge. She was considered staid and a bore. But even when Duchess of York and Princess of Wales she steered clear of the fast society and George, close to his father as he was, remained unaffected, content with his shooting and his stamps. John Gore, in his biography of George V, summed up the situation:

> In the inner ring of Edwardian society, malice was not wanting. There were many in or on the fringe of the circle of King Edward who felt that his death was the death knell of the good times and marked the end of the 'great days' or the 'happy days' of society. In a narrow sense perhaps they were right. Some of them were inclined to vent their spleen on the new King and Queen. In many an Edwardian drawing room and stronghold lampoons were soon enough circulating. The new court was to be dull and decorous, lights would be turned low and colour banished from the doings of society. A drab and puritanical regime, with economy and convention as its watchwords, would succeed to the brilliance and initiative of Edwardian social life.[7]

Society had been mixing with George since he was a boy and thought that it could cope with him. But Mary was a different kettle of fish. She had never had an affair nor made a slip. She was said to be prudish and staid. People spoke of the opening of a 'sweeter, simpler reign', a throwback to the days of Victoria and Albert, and they did not relish it. Evenings were to be spent in tapestry work and singing and the high tide of hilarity which had followed the Boer War was over. There was a popular satirical poem in which the verses ended alternately with 'The King is duller than the Queen' and 'The Queen is duller than the King'. George was described as spending the evening chatting to a rural dean about district visiting; Mary was pictured sewing designs on yard after yard of calico.[8]

Mary did not smile, she did not hunt and she did not enjoy shooting. People made fun of her past, her fat mother, her morganatic father, her enforced exile in Florence, her occupation with study and reading. She was seen as a reincarnation of Queen Victoria at her dreariest. Fortunately the new Queen was helped by the advent of great regal occasions – the coronation; the investiture of David as Prince of Wales; the Delhi Durbar; and visits to Berlin and Paris.

Mary found little difficulty in the ritual of the coronation; she turned to the history books and found there the answers to queries. She discovered that Alexandra, nine years before, had played havoc with tradition. For example, her train had been carried by six pages: May learned that all previous Queen Consorts had been attended by six earls' daughters. So she selected a team of pretty girls and put history to rights. What did worry her about the coronation arrangements was her trousseau. In her methodical way she kept a list of all clothes ordered, the cost of each item and the maker's name. In all she spent little over £2000. There were no strong colours, grey-silver, gold and white predominating. She wrote to her Aunt Augusta of 'my tiresome trousseau of clothes which has meant endless trying on. The fashions are so hideous that it has been a great trouble to evolve pretty *toilettes*'.[9]

Another problem lay in the vast number of guests, most of whom had invited themselves. All George's cousins decided to attend, and they were legion. Early in June they began their journeys from Russia, Norway, Greece, Mecklenburg, Bavaria, Hanover, Denmark, Spain and Montenegro. They had to be housed with due deference to seniority and whether they got on well together. Honours and titles had to be carefully watched.

Coronation day was 22 June, the weather being dull and chilly, contrasting with the brilliant sunshine which had warmed

London for George and Mary's wedding day. It was an ordeal for both of them, mental and physical, the weight of the crown giving George a splitting headache. He later admitted that he could not have lasted another five minutes. He paid tribute to his wife, 'Darling May looked so lovely and it was indeed a comfort to have her by my side.' The Master of Elibank* was watching her closely:

> The Queen looked pale and strained. You felt she was a great lady, but *not* a Queen. She was almost shrinking as she walked up the aisle, giving the impression that she would have liked to have made her way to her seat by some back entrance: the contrast on her 'return' – crowned – was magnetic, as if she had undergone some marvellous transformation. Instead of the shy creature for whom one had felt pity, one saw her emerge from the ceremony with a bearing and dignity, and a quiet confidence, signifying that she really felt that she was Queen of this great Empire, and that she derived strength and legitimate pride from the knowledge of it.[10]

This exactly described her true feelings, for she attached the greatest importance to the ceremony, both from the spiritual and historic viewpoints.

Among the guests was Crown Prince William of Germany, eldest son of the Kaiser and soon to be known in fighting Britain as 'Little Willy'. He was an honoured guest, housed at Buckingham Palace, and on more than one occasion Mary was noted in deep and informal conversation with him. He and his wife received much applause from the crowds lining the streets and *The Sphere* labelled him 'our most popular Coronation visitor'. Tragically, shortly before his death in 1951, he reminisced, 'Once, in one of the great moments of their history, the English cheered me! *Sic transit gloria mundi*.'[11]

The Crown Prince was fond of practical jokes. To keep up his strength during the hours to be spent in Westminster Abbey, he took along with him a bottle of brandy. He was seated next to the Crown Prince of Turkey, a Mohammedan and not supposed to drink. William took a swig and, out of mischief,

---

* First Viscount Murray.

passed the bottle to his neighbour. To his delight, the Turk took a long, strong pull and thanked the donor profusely.[12]

An outstanding person was missing from the ceremony – Queen Alexandra. She spent the day quietly at Sandringham, wandering about the house and garden, repeating and repeating, '*Eddy* should be King, not *Georgie*.'[13] Mary was indeed in a strange situation, for, if Eddy had lived, she would still have been crowned that day.

Mary and George moved into the brilliant aftermath of the coronation – the seven-mile drive through London's streets, the Spithead Review, the garden party, the gala performance at His Majesty's, the thanksgiving service at St Paul's and the Guildhall luncheon. Mary shone.

A wit christened the new King and Queen 'George the Fifth and Mary the Four-Fifths'.

CHAPTER XI

Great Occasions

IN THE MIDST of the coronation activities, Mary found herself face to face with a problem which comes to most mothers – the vagaries of an adolescent child. She now had three in their teens – David, Mary and Bertie. Mary and Bertie were proving little trouble: Mary was the brightest of the brood, best at lessons, best on a horse and her father's darling; Bertie was an ordinary boy, somewhat backward in the classroom, tending to poor health and entirely concerned with the navy. David was where the problem lay.

With a brother like Frank, one would have thought that Mary would have come to understand some of the problems of young men. Yet, as has been pointed out, she did not get to know Frank until he was middle-aged. She could not understand or tolerate a rebel. And David was showing signs of becoming one. His comment after a visit to Denmark with his grandmother was, 'What rot and a waste of time, money and energy these state visits are.'[1]

George had created David Prince of Wales on 23 June 1910 and, before the coronation, had invested him with the Order of the Garter. Now, at the instigation of Mr David Lloyd George, an old custom was revived: it was planned that, at a ceremony at Caernarvon Castle, David would be presented to the people of the Principality of Wales. When David learned what he had to wear, he objected, and there followed a blazing row with his father at Windsor, a row which was calmed down by his mother. In his own words:

> When a tailor appeared to measure me for a fantastic costume designed for the occasion, consisting of white satin breeches

and a mantle and surcoat of purple velvet edged with ermine, I decided things had gone too far. I had already submitted to the Garter dress and robe, for which there existed a condoning historical precedent; but what would my navy friends say if they saw me in this preposterous rig? There was a family blow-up that night: but in the end my mother, as always, smoothed things over. 'You mustn't take a mere ceremony so seriously,' she said.[2]

So, on a swelteringly hot day in July 1911, George V invested his heir as Prince of Wales, the Home Secretary, Mr Winston Churchill, calling out his titles. David was half fainting with nervousness and the heat. After it was over, he made a discovery about himself. While he was prepared to face up to the pomp and ritual that his position demanded, he recoiled from accepting homage. When he told his mother this, she was dumbfounded. Homage was part and parcel of the royal rigmarole and she had always accepted it blindly. What had happened to her son? She had few confidants with whom she could discuss the matter, and anyway she was always loath to dig too deeply into people's minds, but at last she found one in an old friend, Lord Esher,* who had been King Edward's mentor. She cornered him at Balmoral and for two hours walked him up and down the Deeside paths, probing his mind, discussing every detail of David's character and education and the temptations open to him. Poor Lord Esher was worn out. George proved wiser than his wife, saw something of David's viewpoint and allowed him to go to sea as a midshipman, which was all the boy wanted to do and the only life that he understood. If the advice of Mr Hansell, the tutor, had been followed and David had been allowed to attend ordinary school and mix with other boys, he would not have been so handicapped, with only his naval training to rely on.

After his cruise was over, David was informed that the time had come for him to alter his life-style. He was to leave the navy – 'Too specialized,' said his father – make educational trips to

---

* Chairman of the War Office Reconstitutional Committee, 1904; permanent member of the Committee of Imperial Defence, 1905.

France and Germany to brush up his languages, and then go to Oxford. Mary once again showed how little she knew of David. For his trip to Germany she arranged that he stay with her Aunt Augusta, who was ninety, at Neu Strelitz. The Grand Duchess wrote back saying that surely David would be bored visiting an old lady for three months. Mary dismissed this: 'There would be no question as to his being bored; he is quite a contented person and never rushes about after amusements.'[3] In the event David became very bored indeed at Neu Strelitz and made every excuse to go to Berlin and indulge in the night-life there.

A great mistake made by George and Mary in the training of their heir was not to allow him to accompany them to the Delhi Durbar* in India in the winter of 1911–12. He deeply wished to go. The occasion was unique, the majesty unrivalled and the experience might well have overcome the derisory feelings which David harboured towards royal ceremonial. In fact he never forgave his parents for leaving him behind.

There were a number of opponents to Mary going on the trip. Some said that the security risk was too great; others pointed out that, for a considerable portion of the time to be spent in India, George would be away on an up-country shooting expedition – as Lord Crewe said, he had 'an unholy fascination' for killing animals – and what would Mary do then?

If there was one thing in life that Mary craved it was to attend the Durbar. She announced that she was well able to dispose of her time while her husband was away from her: she would go to Agra and have another look at the Taj Mahal. The question of security she just waved aside. Mary got her way through sheer determination. It was a pity she did not use the same enthusiasm to put the case for David.

1911 was to be the first time that a reigning sovereign had attended a Durbar. It was to prove the last, and so George and Mary occupy a unique place in history. They left on 11 November in the brand new P&O liner *Medina*: designed to carry six hundred and fifty passengers, she was now occupied

* The Durbar was a ceremonial gathering to pay homage. There had been two previous Durbars, the first in 1877 and the next in 1903, each being presided over by the Viceroy.

solely by the royal party, which numbered twenty-four. But space was no antidote to seasickness and, owing to violent storms in the Bay of Biscay, Mary did not rise from her bed until the third day. George was sick and so were many of the crew.

But after Gibraltar there came sunny peace and Mary sat on deck and wrote letters to her Aunt Augusta and her children. There was a Marine Artillery band on board which played three times a day and she enjoyed it. But this did not apply to all of the company. The repertoire of the band was limited and, when it ran out of ideas, it invariably played the King's favourite, *In the Shadows*. As the tune echoed round the decks for the umpteenth time, a reporter was heard to pour curses on that —— band.

They reached Bombay on 2 December. Mary went ashore wearing a dress of yellow flowered chiffon, slashed by the brilliant blue of the Garter ribbon. Her flat straw hat was piled high with artificial roses. 'It is marvellous being in India again,' she wrote. 'I who never thought I should ever see it again. I am so glad I came.'[4] Awaiting them was the royal train in which they had travelled six years before. At Delhi they were in for a surprise. The Durbar Camp was the largest ever pitched, consisting of forty thousand tents to house three hundred thousand people.[5] Six great tents awaited the King-Emperor and the Empress: there was a drawing room, an anteroom, an office, a boudoir, bedrooms and a dining room opening on to the main reception tents. Mary's tent was lined with *vieux-rose* silk, hung with embroideries and carpeted with Oriental rugs. On the evening of the twelfth George wrote in his diary:

> Today we held the Coronation Durbar, the most beautiful and wonderful sight I ever saw . . . The weather was all that could be wished, hot sun, hardly any wind, no clouds. May and I were photographed before we started in our robes. I wore the same clothes and robes as at the Coronation with a new Crown made for India which cost £60,000 which the Indian Government is going to pay for. We left the camp at 11.30 with escorts . . . in an open carriage with four horses, the whole way to the Amphitheatre lined with troops. The Amphitheatre contained about twelve thousand people, there were eighteen thousand troops inside and over fifty thousand on the Mound.

On our arrival we took our seats on the thrones facing the centre of the crescent. I first made a speech giving the reasons for holding the Durbar. Then the Governor General did homage to me followed by all the Ruling Chiefs, Governors, Lieutenant-Governors and members of the different Councils. We then walked in procession, I holding May's hand, our trains being held by young Maharajahs ... We returned in procession to the first thrones when I announced that the Capital will be transferred from Calcutta to Delhi, the ancient Capital and that a Governorship would be created for the Presidency of Bengal, the same as Madras and Bombay, which was received with cheers: the secret had been well kept. The whole of the people present then sang the National Anthem and the most wonderful Durbar ever held was closed . . .[6]

George left for Nepal to shoot, the royal bag consisting of thirty-one tigers, fourteen rhinos and four bears. Mary left for Agra for a second look at the Taj Mahal and then toured in Rajputana. She was perfectly content on her own, well able to fill her days with visits to historic sites and local maharajahs. But George, despite his fascination with shooting, was feeling the strain and confessed in a letter to a sense of incompleteness. 'Each year,' he wrote, 'I feel we become more and more necessary to one another.'

One of Mary's hosts fixed up a minor tiger-shoot for her. She climbed into a tree-hut and spotted a bear and some wild boars. She began knitting. Suddenly she pointed one of her needles towards the jungle and said to Lord Shaftesbury, who was in attendance, 'Look, Lord Shaftesbury, a tiger.' She said it quite softly, not loud. The tiger disappeared before anyone could get a shot at it, and Mary, probably relieved, went on knitting.

Mary and George met again for the visit to Calcutta and then began the long journey home, Portsmouth being reached on 5 February. They were different people now, both in their own eyes and in the eyes of those who looked at them. They were Emperor and Empress. Gone for ever was the image of he being the bluff second son of Edward VII and she the demure Princess May of Teck. Mary felt it in the confidence she now had in herself. They were made.

But these were sombre times, and Mary had to come to terms

with political unrest such as she had never dreamed of. Since 1907, the movement for better living conditions for the factory workers and the miners had been gathering momentum and in 1912 it reached its climax. There were strikes on the railways and in the mines. Mary fumed at the unrest and the waste of money, and blamed the Government. George stood up for the Prime Minister, Mr Asquith. Mary replied, 'Well, I do think the unrest is due to their extraordinary tactics in encouraging socialism all these years and in pandering to the Labour Party . . . I have felt the strain very much; after all there is a limit to one's endurance.'[7]

In June 1912, Mary and George went to see conditions for themselves, undertaking a lengthy tour of the Welsh mining districts. Thus, it may be said, was born the first 'walkabout'. It soon became apparent that the couple were more at home with the working class than they were with high society. They went to the pitheads, riding on the colliery trams, to meet the men as they came up from a shift. Mary insisted on seeing the inside of a miner's cottage and when she managed to gain entry to Mrs Thomas Jones' dwelling, she refused to remain in the parlour but wandered off to the kitchen where she sat down and accepted a cup of tea. As they left by train that evening two postcards were tossed into their compartment. One read, 'With love from Mabel,' the other, 'With love from Annie,' mementos from two of the local women.

Diarist A. C. Benson heard a woman say that Mary looked every inch a queen. He commented, 'Now that was *exactly* what she was not. She had no majesty of mien, or ease or stateliness. She looked a hard-worked and rather tired woman, plainly dressed, doing her best to be civil to nervous people. It made me feel a sort of affectionate admiration.'[8] She was practical. Having been taken to see a brand-new maternity ward, she expressed approval but pointed out that the lighting was much too strong for a baby's eyes. Politician Margaret Bondfield remarked that she would have made an excellent factory inspector.

The suffragettes were a further trouble to Mary. Having no time for rebels, she dismissed their antics. She was particularly annoyed at their practice of carrying hammers in their muffs and producing them to smash windows and mirrors. She described as 'very unpleasant' the occasion at court when 'a tiresome suffragette came and fell on her knees before George and held out her arms in a supplicating way, saying, "Oh! Your Majesty, stop torturing women."'[9] She was at the Derby when Miss Davidson threw herself under the King's horse at Tattenham Corner and was killed. Her diary was full of entries about the suffragettes. 'Those horrid suffragettes burnt down the little tea house close to the Pagoda in Kew Gardens yesterday morning.'[10] It was not to be expected that Mary, with her love of the orderly, could sympathize with these unruly women.

George and Mary had planned to make a number of trips to foster goodwill in Europe, but troubles at home forbade them, although Mary did manage a short visit to her Aunt Augusta at Neu Strelitz. They had hoped to make a state visit to Kaiser William, but Sir Edward Grey, the Foreign Secretary, warned them against it, as such an affirmation of friendship with Berlin might alarm France and Russia. But the chance to visit Germany came in the spring of 1913. The *raison d'être* was a wedding. The Kaiser's only daughter, Victoria Louise, was to marry Ernest Augustus, Duke of Brunswick-Lüneburg, who was a cousin. He was the grandson of the last King of Hanover and a son of Queen Alexandra's sister, Thyra. Thus came to an end the feud between the houses of Hanover and Hohenzollern which had existed since the war of 1866.

Queen Alexandra decided not to attend, having doubts not only about the wisdom of the marriage but also about visiting Germany at such a time of crisis. Mary and George decided to go, but only in the role of relatives. This was explained to the French. But there was nothing unofficial or private about the great military display which the Kaiser staged for the entry of the British King and Queen to the capital. The scene at the Brandenburg Gate was awe-inspiring and all morning the zeppelin *Hansa* circled over the city. George wore Prussian uniform and William British.

Inside the palace the pomp and ceremony was exaggerated. Outside each royal lady's door stood a magnificent majordomo in gold and scarlet, his sole duty being to empty the slops from the washbasin, the colours of which matched his uniform exactly. Next day the Emperor of Russia arrived, accompanied by a hundred secret police. The Kaiser would not allow George to join the official reception procession, so, incognito, he went round the backstreets to Berlin station.[11] After the wedding there was a magnificent dinner at which twelve hundred guests sat down at the same time. The Kaiser kept standing up to make speeches, giving toasts and swearing eternal friendship with everybody.

The high spot of the evening was the famous Torch Dance in the White Hall. This was only danced at royal weddings and only royal highnesses could take part. In former times it was Prussian ministers who carried the flaming torches and at the end of the dance escorted the bridal couple to their chamber. But on this occasion pages took the place of ministers and giant candlesticks were used instead of torches. The dance consisted of the bride taking partners by the hand and dancing round the room with them. Her groom followed, doing likewise.[12] At the end of each circuit the partners were changed, until all the royal highnesses had danced with the bride and groom. Proceedings ended with the bride's garter being cut into little pieces and distributed among the guests.

The evening proved a triumph for Mary. She stole the show. She was glittering. Her dress was of Indian cloth of gold, with gold spun into her train of Irish lace. Diamonds, pearls, pendants and orders wreathed her neck and covered her corsage, and her diamond-studded tiara flashed in the candlelight. During the Torch Dance she was the object of all eyes. Artists were sketching the scene, and in the following week pictures of her had full-page coverage in the London magazines. It was the showpiece of her life.

Entranced as she was, Mary tended to overlook the warlike schemes which monopolized Kaiser William's thoughts. She wrote of the goodbye at Berlin station, 'William and Victoria* accompanied us to the station – Took leave of them all with regret after charming visit . . . I cannot tell you how much we

* The Kaiserin.

enjoyed our visit to Berlin or how touched we were at the kindness shown by William and Victoria and indeed by everybody. It was a most interesting time and so beautifully arranged in every way: nothing could have gone off better.'[13]

One more year to go.

Next it had to be Paris – Paris in the spring of 1914. It was to be Mary's first state visit as Queen and she rather dreaded it. She knew comparatively little of France and although she spoke French well, her husband did not. The French, bearing in mind the great reception which Kaiser William had staged for them, determined not to be outdone. The programme arranged for the couple was brilliant and wide, and organized down to the smallest detail. To one point Mary took immediate exception, and that was that the ceremonial was to begin on the ship crossing the Channel. She knew her stomach well and was not going to risk coming on deck to greet people in case she felt sick.

Lunch on the train bound for Paris was at a long table in the dining car, set with thirteen places. Mary announced firmly that she would not eat with a party numbering thirteen. A way out was sought. Someone suggested that if one of the ladies present was pregnant, she could count as two. No lady could oblige. At length the royal doctor, Sir James Reid, tactfully announced that he did not wish any luncheon and departed from the scene.[14]

As the train neared Paris, George sent for his Assistant Private Secretary, Sir Frederick Ponsonby. Mary asked him to admire her toillette. She pirouetted before him, telling him that she had gone to great pains to get a gown of the latest fashion. Sir Frederick said that it was charming, although he could see clearly that it was several years out of date.[15]

Visits of British queens to Paris have always produced rapturous receptions – Victoria, Alexandra, Elizabeth, Consort of George VI, and Elizabeth II. Mary was no exception. The arrival of the King and Queen in Paris was to the French a heart-warming symbol of the *entente cordiale* and they milled round the royal carriage. The Gala Opera, the military review, the dinner given to President and Madame Poincaré at the

British Embassy were overwhelming successes. Mary drove with Madame Poincaré through the sunlit streets lined with chestnut trees in flower. She was dressed in pale blue, her hat was piled high with light blue ostrich feathers, and there were ropes of magnificent pearls round her neck. The crowds loved it; they had not seen such display since the days of the Second Empire. Mary's enthusiasm showed clearly in her diary: 'Wonderful reception during nine-mile drive ...'; 'Beautifully decorated streets ...'; 'Crowds in the streets until all hours of the night ...'; 'The Bois looking too lovely ...'

One more month to go.

King George V and Queen Mary in their Coronation robes.
The ceremony took place on 22 June 1911

King George V and Queen Mary at the Delhi Durbar in 1911.
They are attended by their pages

Queen Mary's only daughter, Princess Mary, served as a nurse in the first World War. Here she is seen in her V.A.D. uniform

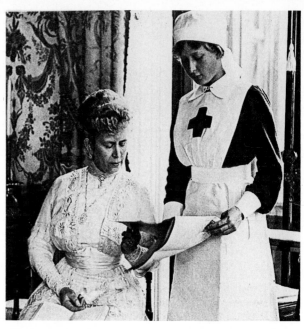

A rare photograph of the four sons of King George V and Queen Mary, taken together at the time of the King's serious illness in 1928-29. They are (left to right): Lieutenant Prince George, R.N. (afterwards Duke of Kent); Lieut.-General the Prince of Wales (afterwards Edward VIII and Duke of Windsor), as Colonel-in-Chief of the Seaforth Highlanders; Air Vice-Marshal the Duke of York (afterwards George VI); and Captain the Duke of Gloucester, of the 10th Hussars

CHAPTER XII

Years of War

On 28 June 1914, Mary was at Buckingham Palace. An urgent telegram arrived. It told of the assassination of Archduke Francis Ferdinand, heir to the throne of Austria, and his morganatic wife, the Duchess of Hohenberg. She was appalled, as the Archduke and his wife had twice been her guests at Windsor. But she saw the crime as just one more outrage by the anarchists – she had no inkling that it was the signal for the outbreak of world war.

Certainly the German royal family did not expect the assassination to lead to war. The Kaiser's brother, Prince Henry of Prussia, was yachting at Cowes; his sister Sophie, Queen of Greece, was on holiday with her children at Eastbourne. But events moved inexorably on. On 28 July, Austria declared war on Serbia. On the same day an Imperial Council in Berlin voted for war against Russia and, as a natural consequence, against France, Austria being dragged into the conflict by her determined ally, Germany. On 31 July, Emperor Nicholas ordered the mobilization of the Russian forces. On 1 August, a state of war existed between Germany and Russia and German troops penetrated French territory. By the third, France and Germany were at war and the next day German troops crossed into Belgium, the sanctity of which country was guaranteed, by treaty, by Britain.

The British public were at first strongly against war, but now their mood changed. Mary wrote in her diary on 2 August, 'After dinner a large crowd assembled in front of the palace and sang "God Save the King" and we went on the balcony . . .' On the fourth, Britain stood by her pledge and went to war. David, Prince of Wales, recalled,

> At 10.30 came the news that Germany had declared war. A Privy Council was at once summoned for Papa to sign our declaration of war and, as soon as this was known in the crowd outside, excitement became intense. Then amid an unparalleled demonstration of patriotism the parents showed themselves at 11.00 before going to bed. But the people remained singing, cheering and whistling for another three hours and I was lulled to sleep by their fearful shindy at 1.30.[1]

Mary's first problems were personal. Bertie was a midshipman on HMS *Collingwood*, patrolling in the North Sea.* It was with the fleet that the immediate danger lay. David was kicking his heels in the palace and shouting for a job – he was commissioned in the Grenadier Guards on 6 August. Queen Sophie of Greece had returned to Athens, but her children and their English nurse were still at Eastbourne. Arrangements had to be made to get them home. But right beside Mary was a problem which, small as it might appear, was of the greatest importance to her. Her daughter's personal maid, Else, was a German. Else was more than a maid, she was a confidante and friend. All the royal family adored her. Now the Queen summoned her and announced that she must either return to Germany at once or be interned. Else decided to return home and her employers wept as they said goodbye to her.[2]

Mary did not have long to wait for personal anxiety. On 23 August, Bertie, steaming off the north coast of Scotland on *Collingwood*, collapsed with violent pains in the stomach and was injected with morphia in the sickbay. Six days later he was landed at Aberdeen and rushed to hospital. He was operated on for appendicitis and thereafter sent to Sandringham to recuperate.

On 5 November, Mary attended her first memorial service for the fallen. Her husband's cousin, Prince Maurice of Battenberg, son of Princess Beatrice, was killed in action. To add to

---

* He later took part in the battle of Jutland.

the poignancy, between the death of Prince Maurice and his funeral service, Prince Louis of Battenberg,* the First Sea Lord, resigned, unable longer to bear the shafts of criticism aimed at him on account of his German ancestry. Prince Louis had been a close friend of George and Mary for many years, and they felt his passing from office deeply. George, as a sailor, knew how brilliant a man Britain was losing.

On 16 November, David left for the front line.

On a wider field, it is ironic that it took a world war to allow Mary to develop the great organizing ability within her. She saw the situation straight. While some people regarded the outbreak of hostilities as a picnic and a diversion to be over by Christmas, she was in agreement with Lord Kitchener and suspected that it would drag on for years. Her great fear was that there would be a repeat of the shambles that had taken place in the Boer War, when the volunteer ladies' organizations had tackled the problem from the wrong angle, sending out to the troops 'comforts' which were not needed and omitting those that were. On 4 August, she summoned her lady-in-waiting, Lady Bertha Dawkins, and told her:

> We must have everything ready. I do not want to have that state of things which prevailed during the Boer War, with everybody just sending what they liked, without relation to the real needs of our soldiers, without organization. It entails too much waste, and too great loss of time. Let us strive for central organizations from which to control and direct. Soon, too soon, there will be thousands of women wanting to do something to help and not knowing what to do. Let us be ready for them . . .[3]

Her first action was to get the Needlework Guild, which by this time was called Queen Mary's Needlework Guild, working on the right lines and producing the 'comforts' which would be required. On 5 August, she wrote in her diary, 'Set to work to make plans to help the existing organizations with offers of clothing and money etc.' On the eighth, 'I am to arrange my Relief Clothing Fund.' For this purpose the King put at her

* Married Princess Victoria of Hesse and by the Rhine in 1884.

disposal the state apartments at St James's Palace. On the same day she inspected the offices of the National Relief Fund and launched an appeal to help the fund which brought in a quarter of a million pounds in the first twenty-four hours. She visited the Red Cross, which was beginning to function at Devonshire House.[4] All this Mary accomplished within five days of war being declared. She had laid a firm foundation.

Under this dynamic leadership, the ladies of the voluntary organizations set to work with a will, making shirts, scarves, gloves — anything that was demanded of them. Then came a sudden shock — their efforts were misfiring. There had to be some quick thinking. What had happened was that due to a moratorium and other industrial steps inevitable with war, tens of thousands of women working in the clothing industry had been thrown out of work, and as the members of the voluntary organizations turned out more 'comforts' for the troops, more workers were sacked. 'Damn these knitting women,' exclaimed a Labour politician.

It is necessary to understand the conditions under which the women in the clothing industry were working. Their wages were often as low as three farthings an hour and they were turning out fine blouses for sixpence, blouses which later sold in the West End of London for twenty-five shillings. It took them three weeks to earn a pound and they took their children with them to work, keeping them busy making 'presentable chains' to bring in a few more pence. They had no chance to save against a rainy day and starvation stared them in the face on the day that they were sacked. There was no social security and the crisis built up quickly.

In the forefront of the fight to relieve the plight of these women was Mary Reid Macarthur, thirty-four. The daughter of a draper in Glasgow, she broke with the Conservative traditions of her family and in 1903 came to London to be a secretary of the Women's Trades Union League. In 1906, she founded a new general trade union for women — the National Federation of Women Workers. The Anti-Sweating League, which she helped to found, and her evidence before the Select Committee on Home Work, did much to convince the public of the necessity of the Trade Boards Act, passed in 1909; it was mainly due to her efforts that boards were established in various sweated industries. She was a firebrand.

Queen Mary decided that it was essential for her to meet Miss Macarthur and she instructed the Marchioness of Crewe, who was young and enthusiastic, to make contact. Fortunately Lady Crewe and the trades union leader liked one another from the start. Mary Macarthur agreed to go to the palace and whispered in Lady Crewe's ear, 'I am a Tolstoyan, you know.' Lady Crewe did not know what a 'Tolstoyan' was, but kept on smiling.

The meeting between the Queen and the draper's daughter, who was preaching what the majority of people thought was sedition, was one of the most revolutionary in the whole royal story. It was Mary Macarthur who got the shock. She was expecting to meet an imperial symbol, far removed from the problems of the working people. Instead she was led into the presence of a quiet woman showing little signs of royalty. She soon discovered that the Queen had expert knowledge of the problems involved. Decisions were made that afternoon which were quickly implemented; there was no conflict. A friendship was forged which lasted until Miss Macarthur's early death; those who worked with them knew them as 'Mary A' and Mary R'.

When Mary Macarthur returned to her trades union office, she was smiling and almost shouted, 'The point is the Queen does understand and grasp the whole situation from the trades union point of view. Here is someone who *can* help and *means* to help!' Mary Macarthur came in for some ribbing from her companions. She was asked if she had come out backwards from the Presence. 'No,' said Mary, 'not being a gymnast, I did not.'[5]

Out of that interview was born the Central Committee on Women's Employment, under the patronage of the Queen (she wanted to serve on the committee but was advised not to) and with Mary Macarthur as Hon. Secretary. The Central Committee was for administrative work only. As there had to be funds for its administration, the Queen formed a 'Collecting

Fund' to supply the Committee, and she became President of the fund. This was the first message she sent out:

> In the firm belief that prevention of distress is better than its relief, and that employment is better than charity, I have inaugurated the Queen's 'Work for Women' Fund. Its object is to provide employment for as many as possible of the women of this country who have been thrown out of work by the war.

Mary's whole outlook changed almost overnight, and she reversed the accepted role. Firstly, she accepted the fact that what was wanted was work and not charity. Charity was necessary as a means of relief and security, but firstly the unemployed women must be given an occupation and a pride in that occupation. Secondly, she realized that the royal practice of merely asking questions must stop, and be replaced by the ability to answer questions. Thirdly, she realized that a royal patron must not only be a patron, but must get down to work as well. The Bishop of London commented, 'I can tell you that there is no one who has more interest in all that makes for the welfare of the poor than our Queen: no one who will bring such common sense and influence to bear on it; and no one who will do more for the general welfare of her people.'[6] Mary Macarthur said that she prayed that there would never be a revolution in her lifetime because, if there was, she would have to go and stand by Queen Mary.

'Like mushrooms in the night, local workrooms sprang up everywhere, in London and outside. In some they made cradles from banana-crates; in others maternity outfits and appurtenances for the sick room. New clothes were made from old; fruit was preserved and, in the training centres, women were trained in market gardening, fruit and flower growing, as well as for all ramifications of domestic science.'[7] In addition the Central Committee made contact with hundreds of firms whose workers had been thrown out of employment. The Queen had a full-time job for the duration of the war.

But soon there came other calls upon Mary's time. The wounded started coming back from France and visits to hospitals

featured almost daily in her programme. Here she did not fare
as well as she did in the field of organization. She recoiled from
illness and mutilation and found it hard to express the cheering
banter that was so necessary when standing by the bedside.
Nevertheless she was a very expert visitor. Sir Clement Kinloch-
Cooke paid tribute to her:

> When Queen Mary goes to see a hospital she pays no mere
> cursory visit, but inquires about everything, making an inspec-
> tion of each department, even to the operating-room. She talks
> to the doctors about their patients, and to the nurses about
> their work, and goes into the kitchens to see how the food is
> cooked. If she notices that anything is amiss or might be
> improved, she does not hesitate to say so. Everyone knows
> that Her Majesty's knowledge of hospital equipment and
> requirements is very thorough and after an experience in
> hospital inspection extending over the greater part of the
> Empire, her criticism is of no inconsiderable value.[8]

It was the human side which came hard to her: shyness and a
rigid sense of royal decorum kept her from expressing her
compassion. 'What a relief,' she sighed to Queen Marie of
Romania* as they left a London hospital filled with war
wounded. 'I never know what to say to them.'[9]

Then came the day of a grim test. In one hospital there was
a sailor who had lost most of the front of his face, blown away
in an explosion: to tend him was an ordeal, even for the staff.
He had lost all confidence in himself and was the victim of
moods of deep depression. The matron said to Mary, 'We think
that if you could possibly sit and talk with him for a while
without betraying any consciousness of his appearance, it would
do him more good than anything else in the world.' Mary went
in and for a long time sat alone talking with the sailor in his
room. She sat near enough to touch him and looked him straight
in the face. Afterwards she said, 'It was indescribable. I thought
I could not do it. But then, of course, there is simply nothing
that one cannot do!'[10]

Mary was in contrast with her mother-in-law, Alexandra,

---

* Romania declared war on Austria-Hungary on 27 August 1916.

[163]

whose knowledge of nursing was wide. On hearing that a soldier was depressed because he would always have a stiff leg, Alexandra laughed and said, 'Well, I have a stiff leg and look what I can do!' And she swung it high over the bedside table. The same contrast showed when it came to condolence, as the daughter of a member of the Sandringham staff recalled. When news came of the death of a servant or a tenant (and Sandringham suffered heavily), Mary would arrive at a cottage door and stutter out stilted condolences. She would ask in what regiment the dead man had served. 'Oh,' she would say, brightening up, 'in the ———. A jolly good lot, what, a jolly good lot.' And then go away tapping her stick on the path. Half an hour later Alexandra – always late – would come running up to the house, burst through the door and, clasping the widow in her arms, would whisper, 'Oh, my poor dear, my poor dear.' Mary simply could not give her heart in that way.[11]

On the point of rationing Mary was a tartar. Long before the coming of the Food Controller, she stopped all luxuries and introduced a code of rationing which was practised in the royal dining room before application to the servants' hall. The cellars were locked and no alcohol served. It was rumoured that George, judging by the colour of his face, kept a bottle of whisky in his dressing-room cupboard, but he was not blamed for that. Sir Frederick Ponsonby gave an interesting account of the strict regime:

> The King and Queen decided to take the rations very seriously and at breakfast those who were late got nothing. When I say late, the ordinary meaning of the word hardly conveyed the wonderful punctuality of the King and Queen. One was late if the clock sounded when one was on the stairs, even in a small house like York Cottage. In order to make sure of getting something to eat one had to be before time. Lord Marcus Beresford, who came to stay, quickly got the hang of this and dogged the Queen's footsteps into the dining room. The point was that there was just enough and no more for everyone: but as most people helped themselves too generously, there was nothing left for the person who came last. (Sir Bryan) Godfrey-Faussett was kept on the telephone one day and came into the dining room after everyone else had sat down. He found

nothing to eat and immediately rang the bell and asked for a boiled egg. If he had ordered a dozen turkeys he could not have made a bigger stir. The King accused him of being a slave to his inside, of unpatriotic behaviour, and even went so far as to hint that we should lose the war on account of his gluttony.[12]

It was the same with heating. Going round a hospital where a new system of central heating had been installed, George commented to a patient, 'How lucky you are. We have to live in the corner of one room to keep warm.' And then added, 'And you can have baths every day! I only get a hot bath once a week. You just can't lather soap in cold water, can you?' The first Food Controller, Lord Devonport, said of the Queen, 'Of all the practical women in this world – my own wife included – there is not a more practical, a more understanding, a more helpful woman than Queen Mary.'[13]

The King made five visits to the Western Front. The tour of 1914 passed off without incident but that of October 1915 – the month Nurse Cavell was executed at Brussels – was dramatic. George was inspecting troops. Three cheers were given, so heartily that his horse took fright. It crouched on the ground, then reared straight up in the air: its hind legs slipping, it fell right on top of the King. For three minutes, he lay quite still: then he opened his eyes and asked for help to get up. Support was given and he rose to his feet. That was a mistake, for he had a double fracture of the pelvis and should have laid still until a doctor arrived.

In great pain George was driven back to the château where he was staying and his doctor was sent for. A telephone call was put through to Buckingham Palace. Mary was having tea with Alexandra at Marlborough House. They were merely told that the King had had a fall from his horse and that the Queen was not to travel to France. It was essential that the degree of injury and the length of the stay in France were kept secret, for, if German spies found out, the château would undoubtedly be bombed.

It was not until early November that a hospital train took the King to Boulogne. Mary made preparations for his reception at Buckingham Palace. She sent him a note, 'Nobody to meet you *anywhere* and I will wait in my room until *you* send for me, for I presume you would rather be settled in your bed before you see me.'[14]

An examination in London showed that George had been injured more seriously than had been supposed, but the real truth does not seem to have been appreciated even by his family. Thereafter he suffered recurring pain and this played upon his nerves and his temper. He had always been irascible and now his outbursts were more marked. He was never to be the same man again; in fact the accident aged him by years.

Mary had another problem – her Aunt Augusta was ailing. Princess Augusta Caroline, Dowager Duchess of Mecklenburg-Strelitz, was ninety-four and had been born in the reign of George IV. Ever since Mary's childhood her aunt had been her mentor, confidante and favourite person – they were even closer than Mary had been with Mlle Bricka, her companion who had died in 1914. Ever since the death of the Duchess of Teck, Augusta had taken the place of mother and weekly letters flowed between Strelitz and London. The war hastened her end. There was no staff at Neu Strelitz and the *schloss* was icy cold. It tore her heart out to see the country of her birth and that of her adoption engaged in bitter strife and she lived for the weekly letters from her niece, which reached her by diplomatic channels via Sweden. She became ill in the autumn of 1916 and died in December. Her last act was to send a message of loyalty to King George V and her last spoken word was 'May'.

Despite her aunt's great age, her death flattened Mary. She felt that she had finally crossed the bridge dividing youth from old age. Her aunt probably meant more to her than anyone in life: it was only to her that she could open her heart and confide the innermost feelings that she found so hard to express. It must be remembered that Mary was tired out through the strain of war: her hair had turned to silver. Her husband's accident exacerbated matters, for he was expected to go on doing what he had done before, and he just could not tackle it. After a taxing week when they had toured the north of England, visiting furnaces and shipyards from Liverpool to Newcastle, George went on to Scapa Flow and Mary returned to London. He wrote to her, 'Very often I feel in despair and if it wasn't for you I should break down.'[15] Trouble was brewing in the engineering and munitions works and the Government stressed again and again the importance of royal visits. The doctors advised Mary to rest, but she found it impossible. Her brain, she said, was pulp. She reached her fiftieth birthday and greeted its coming with the word 'dreadful'. In July, the King went to France again, and Mary went with him, but they undertook separate tours. She saw for herself the clearance stations and the ambulances at work, and learned much.

Mary saw the need for progress in the development of artificial limbs for the disabled and studied a method by which the muscles were used to work artificial arms. She was a frequent visitor to Roehampton hospital, to which she had lent her name, and took a great interest in the workshops there and at Brighton. Here was a practical problem which appealed to her organized mind. When she visited the limbless, it was noted that she always had plenty to say.

The ties of the royal family to the reigning houses of Europe brought many a heartache to George and Mary. George was very touchy on the point of his German background. When H. G. Wells referred to his court as 'alien and uninspiring', he roared, 'I may be uninspiring but I'll be damned if I am alien.'[16] But people recalled what his grandfather, Prince Albert the Consort, had said, 'I am German through and through and always shall remain so.' And Kaiser William was George's first cousin.

Mary, on the other hand, viewed herself as British through and through, and said so many times. No more British figures could be imagined than her mother, Mary Adelaide, or her uncle, George of Cambridge, Commander-in-Chief for forty years. Her father had been a somewhat remote princeling from southern Germany and had lived in England all his married life. The link did not antagonize the public as did that with the Hohenzollerns.

Then there was Greece, to which George was tied through his mother, Alexandra, whose brother had been King George of the Hellenes. Her nephew Constantine, known as 'Tino', now reigned there and was married to the Kaiser's sister, Sophie. Public feeling in Britain was strongly against 'Tino', who was generally believed to be in league with Germany and a spy. After the disasters of the Gallipoli landings, there was no controlling the flood of hate and recrimination. King Constantine sent two of his brothers, Princes Andrew and Nicholas,* to try and heal the breach. They were cordially welcomed by the royal family, but the newspapers howled their hatred and criticized George and Mary. Without doubt, this outburst of criticism influenced George** when the time came to rescue Emperor Nicholas and his family from Russia. George could have done more to save them, but, as Sir George Buchanan, the British Ambassador to Russia, said, the arrival of the Emperor in England might have led to strikes in the docks, munition factories and mines – even to general revolution.[17]

As the German submarine campaign intensified, the food shortage in Britain became even more acute. When at Windsor Mary spent her spare time planting potatoes. At Sandringham she and her household picked up horse chestnuts, which were needed in the munitions factories, and organized the school-children to collect jam-jars, bottles and scrap iron. This work appealed to the thrift in her and it gave her satisfaction that she was doing something to help.

On 6 July 1918, Mary and George celebrated the Silver Jubilee of their marriage. They were photographed at Buckingham Palace with their family – Mary, twenty-one, the 'pin-up' girl of the Forces; Bertie, twenty-three, in RAF uniform, having been invalided out of the navy; Henry, eighteen, at Sandhurst and in khaki; and George, sixteen, a naval cadet. Two were missing – David, twenty-four, who was at the front, and John, a tragic monster boy of thirteen, living in a separate establishment.

The tide of victory began to run for the Allies and hopes ran high as the summer turned to autumn. On 9 November, Mary wrote in her diary, 'Heard that William had abdicated and his

* The fathers of Prince Philip, Duke of Edinburgh, and Princess Marina, Duchess of Kent.
** The King was also influenced by the fact of it being necessary to divert ships for the operation, and by the influence of politicians.

son renounced his right to the Throne. What a downfall, what retribution to the man who started this awful war.' And two days later:

> The greatest day in the world's history. The armistice was signed at 5 a.m. and fighting ceased at 11. We went on to the balcony to greet the large crowd which had formed outside. At 12.30 we went out again and the massed bands of the Guards played the National Anthem and patriotic songs and the anthems of the Allies. Huge crowds and much enthusiasm. The Army Council, the Lords of the Admiralty and members of the air board came to offer congratulations. At 3.15 we drove to the city in pouring rain and had a marvellous reception . . . The Prime Minister came to see us at 7. Afterwards we went on to the balcony, the band played popular songs, and we had another wonderful scene.[18]

Thus, at the eleventh hour of the eleventh day of the eleventh month, war came to an end. London had never witnessed such a spontaneous demonstration of joy: the tops of the buses were packed with people waving flags and banners and the roofs of taxis became grandstands for the scene. In the evening, under the gas-lamps burning around Buckingham Palace, the crowds gathered by the hundred thousand, cheering, shouting, weeping as the King and Queen returned time and again to the balcony. *The Times* commented, 'In part it is a personal tribute – and none was ever more richly deserved – to the conspicuous example which the King and Queen have set to us all in public service and in private self-denial. They have done their duty well, and they have their reward today.'

CHAPTER XIII

Restless World

AT HALF PAST FIVE on the morning of 18 January 1919, Queen Mary was called to the telephone to be told that her youngest son, John, was dead. She woke George and arranged to drive to Sandringham. At Wood Farm, Wolferton, where the Prince had been cared for, she looked at the dead boy on the bed. 'Little Johnnie looked very peaceful lying there . . . He just slept quietly into his heavenly home, no pain, no struggle, just peace for the little troubled spirit. The first break in the family circle is hard to bear . . .'[1] Reticent by nature, Mary said little of her loss, but it made bitter the early months of the peace for which she had longed. And that peace was not turning out to be the paradise which people had brought themselves to think it would be. In her low spirits after the death of John, she wrote to an American friend of the great unrest which the end of the war had brought in its train. She was saddened that while during the war all classes had worked together for the common good, now they were at one another's throats, thus missing the chance to reconstruct the world on the right lines. To her, it seemed that a great opportunity had been missed.

It was a strange new world in which she found herself, and it was hard to adjust. For example, her family name of Teck had disappeared. In July 1917, the King had proclaimed that his family should in future be known as the House of Windsor. All German titles went and Mary's family name switched from Teck to Cambridge. Her elder brother, Adolphus (Dolly), Duke of Teck, who had married Lady Margaret Grosvenor, became Marquess of Cambridge, their children being the Earl of Eltham, the Ladies Mary and Helena Cambridge, and Lord Frederick

Cambridge. Her younger brother, Alexander (Alge), whose wife Alice was the daughter of Prince Leopold, Duke of Albany, was created Earl of Athlone: their children became Lady May Cambridge and Viscount Trematon.

Mary had also to make adjustments in her own family circle. During the war she had not been able to see as much of her children as she would have liked and in 1919 she found herself almost a stranger among them – except for Princess Mary. She noticed in her sons that the old order had indeed changed, yielding to the new. Pleasure was the order of the day, a natural reaction to a young generation who had survived four years of war. There was an air of restlessness about them and a tendency to wish to do away with the ceremonial of pre-war days. Her daughter was different. She had always been at home and was known as 'the permanent third'. She was her father's delight and kept the conversation going at the dinner table.

In 1919, only Princess Mary was at home with her parents. David was setting up his own establishment at York House, St James. Bertie was serving with the RAF. Henry, in the army, and George, in the navy, only appeared at time of leave. To the younger boys visits to Windsor and Buckingham Palace were tantamount to staying at the headmaster's house. To them, their father, at fifty-five, was of a very different generation, a relic of the past and a force to be reckoned with. He did not speak to them much, but at times would blast them with fits of accusation and temper. Although he did not ask them what they were doing, he seemed very well informed: in fact his staff was a 'secret service'. One evening at Buckingham Palace, Henry secreted dance pumps in his pocket and after dinner slipped out to a night club. He was spotted by an equerry and reported. Next morning he committed the crime of being late for breakfast. He took one look at his father's face, heard the opening blast of reprimand and then fainted on the floor.

Bertie was the staid one. He always agreed with his father and heard more of the confidences of his mother than the others. Handicapped by poor health and a stammer, he found visits to the palace a strain and they upset his nervous system. It was always Mary, the 'Peacemaker' as she had been known as a girl in the Teck family, who smoothed over the rows and quietened down the King. She would remonstrate with him in secret, but not in front of the children.

David was the joy of Mary's secret life – it was almost a love affair. He was handsome beyond words and he reminded her of the royals of long ago, in particular of her own father. Mary saw David as the epitome of everything that she herself had wished to be and had not been. She had sat shy and silent at dinner parties; now she saw David smiling and taking the conversational lead. His laughing photographs adorned the walls of factories and shops, dormitories and nurseries. He was extrovert and spoke well. Time and time again as she plodded round hospital wards she had listened to tributes to her 'very darling David' from the wounded. As little more than a boy, he had done so much and been so brave. He was her dream come true. She was never intimate with him, wishing to keep him the cavalier of her dreams and not daring to break the china image. She was content to know that her eldest son was probably the most popular figure that the world had ever known. She did not realize, or wish to, that David was of the flesh and blood of herself and George and in truth was subject to the same weaknesses and drawbacks, and inside was a very different person to the image which he showed to the world. The star quality came from his grandparents, Edward and Alexandra, but both of them had their latent weaknesses.

Despite general appearances, the throne was not so strongly entrenched in 1919 as it had been in 1914. The tumbling of the crowns of Europe at the war's end, coupled with changes in industry inevitable with war and the ensuing political unrest had whittled away the power of the British monarchy. Although George and Mary had done a sterling job in the war years, they were ageing now and lacked panache. Someone was needed to put back the magic. Wise counsellors such as Lord Esher and Lord Cromer saw this and their advice was to use the Prince of Wales more widely. His name was legend among the fighting men of the Empire and now he should be sent to the far corners of the world to show the flag and add glamour to the royal role. The Government backed this view, and so began the six years

Queen Mary in high spirits walks with her husband and her mother-in-law, Queen Alexandra, to watch the Victory Parade held at the end of the First World War

Queen Mary, with King George and Queen Marie of Romania, attending the opening of the British Empire Exhibition held at Wembley in 1924

Queen Mary and King George with Princess Mary and Lord Lascelles after their wedding in 1922

Albert (Bertie), the second son of Queen Mary and King George V, who was created Duke of York. He married Lady Elizabeth Bowes-Lyon in 1923

Lady Elizabeth Bowes-Lyon, who married Queen Mary's second son, the Duke of York, in 1923. In 1936 she became Queen Elizabeth, and, on her husband's death in 1952, Queen Elizabeth the Queen Mother.

Prince Henry, Duke of Gloucester,
Queen Mary's third son, born in 1900

Prince George, Duke of Kent,
photographed with his fiancée,
Princess Marina of Greece.

Lady Alice Montagu-Douglas-Scott,
daughter of the Duke of Buccleuch,
who married Prince Henry, Duke of
Gloucester in 1935

'David', Prince of Wales, with the
happy smile which endeared him to
the British public and the peoples of
the many countries which he visited

After the First World War King George V and Queen Mary gave a garden party at Buckingham Palace for the hundred winners of the Victoria Cross. Here they are seen chatting to Private Samuel Harvey.

After the King's serious illness in 1928 Queen Mary took him to Bognor Regis to convalesce

of overseas tours which were to enrich the Empire and better relations with foreign lands and, in the process, tire David out. It was a task which in the end was to gain him little thanks.

David went off to America and Canada. New York went mad, the crowds roared their approval and the newspapers carried such headlines as, 'What does David wear in bed?' He became the most eligible bachelor in the world, open to a temptation which defies description. Mary was thrilled. She wrote to George, 'What a splendid reception David got in New York: he really is a marvel in spite of his "fads" and I confess I feel very proud of him, don't you?' But George did not altogether see it that way nor entirely approve. Firstly, the 'road show' staged for his son was too personal for his liking: he never approved of the American way of life. Secondly, he felt that he was being moved down a place. All his life he had played second fiddle – to his brother, the Duke of Clarence, to his parents and, since his accession, to Queen Alexandra, who ordered him about and was the darling of the public. He considered that now he should play the leading part. There was to be rivalry between George and David right up to the end.

Who was to be David's bride? Thoughts of matrimony for her brood dominated Mary's thoughts during the postwar years. Frankly, she was ill equipped to cope with it. Both of her engagements had been engineered and she had never known romance. The old practice of turning to the *Almanach de Gotha* and thumbing through it until a suitable candidate was found was over. Germany, the long-time primary source of brides and bridegrooms, was out, and few foreign countries were welcome. The alternative – to find a home-bred product – was unusual: so far the only such unions in recent times had been those of Princess Louise, fourth daughter of Queen Victoria, and the Marquess of Lorne, heir to the Duke of Argyll; and another Louise, eldest daughter of Edward VII, and the Duke of Fife.* Yet it was this course that was followed for the first marriage of the children of the King and Queen. In November 1921,

---

* The Earl of Fife was created Duke on marriage. Queen Victoria had no wish to do this, but yielded to the pleas of the Prince of Wales.

Princess Mary, twenty-four, became engaged to Henry, Viscount Lascelles, eldest son of the Earl of Harewood. Lord Lascelles was approaching forty and had been a friend of George for some years. It was a strange romance, for he was gaunt and unattractive, certainly not a ladies' man and disapproved of 'modern girls'.[2] But he had his advantages: he was immensely rich and he would not take his bride away to a foreign country. He was addicted to country sports, which appealed to George; and he was a collector of art treasures, which appealed to Mary.

The wedding took place on 28 February 1922, at Westminster Abbey. It was the first big state pageant since the war and was treated as a day of national rejoicing. But the mother and father had to pay a price. Mary wrote to David, who was in India, 'The wonderful day has come and gone and Mary is married and has flown from her home, leaving a terrible blank behind her . . .'[3]

A 'terrible blank' indeed there was, more so in the case of George than his wife, who was able to fill her days with interest and once remarked that she was never bored. The family of Edward VII and Alexandra were all noted for their tendency to rely on others, and George had relied on his daughter almost as much as on his wife. Now he went right back into his shell. He did not like being entertained and could only be persuaded to dine out four or five times in the London season. Day in, day out, George and Mary faced one another across the dining-room table – very much alone together. The position was exacerbated by the effect that the dreariness had on the boys. They shrank from being present at evenings which ended at ten o'clock and began to manufacture excuses for their absence from Buckingham Palace. Worried, Bertie wrote to David, 'Things will be very different here now that Mary has left and Papa and Mama will miss her too terribly . . . I feel that they can't possibly stay in and dine together every night of their lives . . .'[4] But what was the alternative?

The royal days were prescribed. Mary was called at a quarter past seven and at nine o'clock precisely she breakfasted with George. His parrot, Charlotte, ruled the table. Sometimes affable, more often bad tempered, she would roam among the plates, picking at a boiled egg or helping herself to marmalade. When she messed, George would slide the mustard pot over it so that his wife should not see.[5] The meal over, George would stroll out on to the balcony, light a cigarette and tap the barometer, the weather being of great interest in his life. At half past nine, Mary would retire to her room and work on her correspondence until lunch time. This was another lone session with George and Charlotte. In the afternoons, if she had no charitable engagement, she would set forth to explore art galleries or antique shops, often in the company of her brother Dolly, who had the same interest. Then back for tea. There followed a rest, when she would work on her embroidery while her lady-in-waiting read aloud to her. Dinner was the crisis time, for by this hour George was tired after working on his 'red boxes'. Tiredness meant irascibility: when a footman, serving spinach, touched the royal chair with his foot, the King let out, 'That's right. Pour it all over me. ' Conversation was difficult. If Mary recited her afternoon's activities, she was met with, 'There you go again, Mary: furniture, furniture, furniture!'[6] They had in truth very few common interests. George would have liked to discourse about shooting, but the subject was anathema to his wife. It bored her stiff, so much so that, after a shooting party she once said, 'I would have turned cartwheels for sixpence.'[7] And so, shortly after ten, to bed.

Mary did little to alter the situation. If she did, it only met with reprimand. She was discovered by George learning some new dance steps from Sir Frederick Ponsonby, and was laced down properly. She was apt to accept things, particularly when they centred on the monarch. She did not see herself as a pioneer – more as a wife whose duty it was to provide a peaceful and comfortable life for her husband. If small things were difficult, like conversation, she put up with it. She always had her 'one great hobby', as she called it, to fall back on. And her 'one great hobby' was the care and collection of royal treasures.

The work done by Queen Mary on the royal collection was both invaluable and incalculable. The war had interfered with her task but now she spent endless hours cataloguing, matching up and reorganizing. She started to fill notebooks with details of the contents of the palace rooms and deposited them in Windsor Library. Although Windsor was the main scene of her activities, she carefully checked the contents of Buckingham Palace, Balmoral and Holyrood House, finding sets of chairs which had been broken up and bringing them together, matching up pictures and dining services. And as she worked, she learned. When she began, it was only the royal connection which intrigued her. Now she began to appreciate beauty and line and this led to her collecting on her own account, consulting museum directors and antique dealers. One example of her diligence came with a Greek and Etruscan dinner-set, the figures chocolate on a red background. All details of its origin had been lost. One day Mary announced to her lady, 'I have been reading Fanny Burney and find that she mentions a dinner-set given to George III.' A search began, ending among remote archives in the British Museum. It transpired that George III had presented King Ferdinand of the Two Sicilies with two cannon for his yacht. So delighted was the Sicilian King that he ordered a dinner-set to be made in the royal potteries and in 1787 he gave this to his British counterpart. There was a great thrill for Mary in that piece of detective work.

She became the Perfect Guide to Windsor and whenever a guest raised a query, George would say, 'Ask May. She will know all about that.' There was not an object with which she was not familiar. After a tour of the castle, an expert commented about Mary's knowledge:

> As one walks along the magnificent Grand Corridor, on to which most of the private suites open, and looks up and down, round and about at the innumerable pictures and treasures ranging from General Gordon's Bible, presented to Queen Victoria by Miss Gordon, to that breathlessly beautiful carved ebony cabinet of Flemish workmanship presented to Charles II by Louis XIV of France, with its drawers consummately inlaid and signed by the various masters who carved them – at the paintings of Zoffany, Reynolds, Gainsborough; the innumerable miniatures, panellings, tapestries, statuary – it is almost overwhelming to realize how much of caring, study, observation and reading has gone to make the Perfect Guide.[8]

How did other women view the British Queen? Here is a vignette of her by one who, many years before, had been selected to be the wife of George – Queen Marie of Romania:

> She looks dull in the eternal photos we see of her in the many papers. Always the same hat, the same cloak, the same parasol, the same smile, the same shoes. But she has a nice sense of humour. Only there is this, she told it to me herself: she does not like uncomfortable things. She likes prosperity, collecting, putting things in order. She likes wealth and position, jewels and dresses. She has little imagination, but she likes reading; history interests her, family trees. She likes to be amused, but decorously, though occasionally a risqué little story can make her blush with the pleasure of having understood it. She has watchful but kindly eyes. She is always very smartly dressed, even in the early morning. Her clothes fit as though built for her. Her collars go right up under her ears. She wears what is politely called a 'transformation' so that there is never a hair out of place . . . She has endless diadems which she wears often as it is neither difficult nor painful to attach them to the 'transformation'. She passes smoothly through life – honoured, guarded, appreciated, recognized.[9]

She liked 'prosperity, wealth and position . . .' That sounds somewhat strange for a woman who would sit down for an afternoon committee meeting with Mary Macarthur or spend hours sorting out parcels for the Needlework Guild. But it was true, and the other side of her. She had inherited her two faces from her mother and her father. Mary Adelaide had always over-staffed herself and insisted on royal recognition and privilege; always poor, the love of prosperity was increased. Francis revelled in the regal, always adhering to etiquette and seeking royal advantages.

Mary, on the rare occasions when she travelled alone, travelled in state. When on a visit to Holker, a home of the Cavendish family, she sent a list of requests ahead of her. She wished a chair to be placed outside her bedroom door on which the page or footman could sit all night; barley water was to be brought to her room every two hours; ice was to be provided at half past eleven at night; and six clean towels were required every day. Pillowcases and sheets, she added, she brought herself. The staff travelling with her totalled nine: two dressers, one footman, one page, two chauffeurs, one lady-in-waiting, one maid to the lady-in-waiting, and a detective.[10] This was reminiscent of Queen Victoria, upon whom Mary modelled her life. When the old Queen travelled abroad, she took with her an entourage of over one hundred, and refused to trim the number.

It was on a visit to a country house that Mary came to the conclusion that she had found the bride for one of her sons. She was shown around and instructed by a young woman who proved to be in the same category as herself – the Perfect Guide. The place was Glamis Castle, Scotland – the girl was Lady Elizabeth Bowes-Lyon, youngest daughter of the Earl and Countess of Strathmore. Mary knew Elizabeth as she was a friend of her daughter and often came to Buckingham Palace. The two shared a common interest in the Guide movement and, when the Princess became engaged, Elizabeth was invited to be a bridesmaid. Bertie first met her at the RAF ball at the Ritz in the summer of 1920. She was dancing with his equerry, James Stuart,* and he cut in. Thereafter there was only one girl in the life of Bertie, by this time Duke of York.

Bertie was a slow but dogged suitor. He was always talking about Elizabeth and his mother pricked up her ears. When the Prime Minister made it clear that foreign marriages for the Princes would be unpopular in Britain, Mary commented to Lady Airlie, her Lady of the Bedchamber, 'I don't think Bertie will be sorry to hear that. I have discovered that he is very much attracted to Lady Elizabeth Bowes-Lyon.'[11] Lady Airlie knew Elizabeth well and Mary asked her to find out how the land lay. She added, 'I shall say nothing to either of them. Mothers should never meddle in their children's love affairs.'[12] But, intrigued, Mary could not resist finding out more for herself and when at Balmoral she motored over to Glamis. Lady Strathmore was unwell and it was left to Elizabeth to do the honours. The manner in which she handled this somewhat awesome task, and her detailed knowledge of the historic castle, filled Mary with admiration. Here, indeed, she thought, is the ideal daughter-in-

---

* Afterwards Viscount Stuart of Findhorne.

law. But her first reaction was that she should be David's bride, not Bertie's. This was understandable: her generation reckoned that the eldest went first and the romantic angle took second place. But she was not dealing with an heir who accepted set ways of thinking and it is a pointer to how little Mary knew David that she should have considered such a course. Or, for that matter, how much she knew of Elizabeth, for she and David would have been on a collision course within weeks.

Since 1918, David had been in love with Mrs Freda Dudley Ward and he was in contact with her daily: he had the same penchant for married women as had his grandfather, Edward VII. But his attachment did not restrict him from flirtations on his travels. His was a new kind of love, breaking the Edwardian tradition of one mistress at a time. George and Mary simply did not begin to understand, could not accept it. They kept tabs on the affair, even going so far as to open a file. The friendship was frowned upon because Freda was married and because her father had commercial interests: George called her 'the lacemaker's daughter'. But it was beyond Mary's horizon that such an affair could be a deterrent to finding a future Queen of Great Britain and Empress of India.

The sexual side was difficult for Mary to understand, for, like her husband, she was imbued with Prince Albert the Consort's belief in faithfulness: he once said that the very idea of extra-marital sex made him feel sick. This way of life was shattered by the behaviour of George's heir, who slept around with abandon. It was impossible to reconcile the views, or understand the values. There was an obvious desire in Mary to be *au fait* with the seamier side of life – as already noted, she blushed with pleasure when she picked up the point of a risqué story. With that same blush, and seemingly out of character, Mary would recount the story of an adventure of Edward VII in Paris. Attracted to a young woman at a house party, he arranged with her that she should leave a rose outside her bedroom door to denote where she slept. In the early hours, Edward tiptoed along the corridor, tapped and heard '*Entrez*'. Sitting up in bed was a startled kitchen-maid: his chosen partner had played a joke on him.[13] Mary thought that this was most

amusing. Yet she had been far from amused when her brother
Frank had taken a mistress, and even ceased to speak to him.
She never faced up to David's aberrations, always believing that
in due course he would turn to the question of providing an heir
to the throne. She could not bring herself to think otherwise.
But, as regards Elizabeth Bowes-Lyon, having listened to Lady
Airlie and appreciating Bertie's adoration of her, Mary changed
her mind and decided that her second son was the right man.

Now she turned to a task far more to her taste and ability –
the planning of the engagement. With George's assistance, the
fulfilment was engineered with naval efficiency. In January 1923,
Bertie was asked to spend the weekend at the Hertfordshire home
of the Earl and Countess of Strathmore, St Paul's Waldenbury.
Having arranged a telegraphic code-word system, Mary and
George went to Sandringham and waited. Bertie took Elizabeth
into the garden of her childhood home and braced himself to
ask the question. The answer was 'Yes'. Elizabeth later said that
she was surprised: if she was, she was the only person in the
network of the two families to be so. Mary and George were
having tea at York Cottage when a telegram arrived. It read,
'All right, Bertie.'[14] It might well have read, 'Mission accomplished.' So, on a showery day in April 1923, Mary watched
the wedding of Bertie and Elizabeth in Westminster Abbey. 'I
have not lost a son,' she said. 'I have gained a daughter.'

CHAPTER XIV

Over the Bridge

QUEEN MARY went abroad three times between 1922 and 1925 – and thereafter never left the shores of Britain. It was not that she did not want to go: it was simply that George hated foreign travel. 'Amsterdam, Rotterdam, and all the other dams! Damned if I'll go,'[1] was his view. In 1913, Mary had planned a whole series of state visits, beginning with Vienna. Then the war had shattered her dreams and now the thrones had toppled. She was the ideal visiting Queen, regal and impressive. The greater the occasion, the faster did her blood chase and the more she sparkled. And she had an absorbing interest in the historic side of foreign cities. She had been travelling Europe since she was a child and she sorely missed the palaces and the galleries.

Among the thrones still standing was that of Belgium. In May 1922, Mary and George went to Brussels – the first state visit by a British sovereign for seventy years. One of the duties in their programme was to lay a wreath on the tomb of Nurse Cavell. They stayed at the palace of Laeken, full of memories of Queen Victoria's 'Uncle Leopold', who was King of the Belgians. Laeken is a quarter of a mile in length and laced with corridors and staircases. George was given a room, nearly as large as Paddington station, at one end, while his wife and essential staff were at the other. Communication was difficult. On one occasion a lost party was found in the labyrinth. In it were Admiral Lord Beatty and Field-Marshal Sir Douglas Haig; each was trying to take command and abusing the other. Other members of the party were amused at the thought of going astray while under the command of the Admiral of the Fleet and the man who had led the biggest British army ever to take the field.

The coming of night brought loneliness to George in his isolation and, bravely, he set off on the quarter-mile trek through dim-lit corridors to find his wife. It was like the old days. Once again, as she read, Mary spotted her bedroom door opening, and then she saw, as she described it, 'his dear, sad little face'.[2] This shows clearly the bond that existed between the two. He simply could not bear to be alone, while she had the air of a mother about her – his 'dear, sad little face' being reminiscent of a lonely child who, during the dark hours, seeks the comfort of its mother's bed.

In May of 1923, a state visit was paid to Italy. This was a great thrill for Mary, for she had never been to Rome. 'How wonderful Rome is,' she wrote, 'with all its treasures and we had such perfect weather, real summer, and everything looked so beautiful.'[3] She had not been to Italy since 1885, but once again it had her in its spell. The highlight of the visit was an audience of the Pope. With her secret liking of the Roman Catholic faith, this meant much to Mary. It was for her a day of rejoicing and she refused to wear the customary black. Instead she arrived all in white, a white veil over her head; she was sparkling with ropes of pearls and round her throat was a pearl choker. The sightseers who thronged to see her in the Piazza of St Peter's were never to forget the sight.

It was in this year of 1923 that a signal tribute was paid to Mary – a tribute to her devoted service as Queen and the work that she had done for the Royal Collection, and also a token of respect and the love held for her by the leaders of the art world. The idea was conceived by Princess Marie Louise,* after she had learned that Mary was interested in dolls' houses. The Princess planned to show how a King and Queen lived in the twentieth century and what authors, artists and craftsmen were doing at the time, for the benefit of future generations. She approached the famous architect, Sir Edwin Lutyens, and obtained his cooperation. He was busy building the city of New Delhi at the time, but was enthusiastic. The doll's house was

---

* Daughter of Prince Christian and his wife, who was Princess Helena, third daughter of Queen Victoria.

eventually to be displayed at the British Empire Exhibition, held at Wembley in 1924 and 1925.

Lutyens's design showed a house on four floors, with mezzanine and basement, standing in a painted tin and velvet garden. It was designed to accommodate a family of people six inches tall. A pipe-major and five guardsmen stood sentry and a small white dog waited in the garden. Mary saw the original plan, was intrigued and thereafter cooperated to the full. All the leading figures in the art world were invited to make their contributions, and all did save one: George Bernard Shaw refused and sent a rude reply.[4] Gradually the house took shape, the dining room laid for eighteen guests, each dining off gold plate. Princess Marie Louise wrote:

> In the King's library, dominated by portraits of the Tudor sovereigns, bookshelves held two hundred volumes the size of postage stamps each written by a contemporary author in his own hand, while minute portfolios bulged with seven hundred watercolours and drawings of the same size. The Queen's saloon was lined in rose-coloured silk and furnished in the style of the later eighteenth century. The bedrooms of the King and Queen faced healthily south and west, and the bedlinen had taken a 'Franco-Irish lady' fifteen hundred hours to weave. The bathrooms were particularly luxurious, with walls of ivory and shagreen, and the floors of African marble and mother-of-pearl. Real water spurted from the taps; waste from the baths and from the lavatories ran into real tanks beneath the house. The cupboards were filled with china and glassware, the larder was full of food, and the wine-cellar was stocked with miniature bottles of wine. The kitchen stove was perfect in all its details, and the gramophone in the children's nursery played *God Save the King*. In the garage beneath the dolls' house stood a series of extremely costly reproductions of the royal Daimlers.[5]

Mary herself undertook the arrangement of some of the rooms and she went to Wembley before the exhibition opened to add the finishing touches. This fabulous tribute to her drew vast crowds and, after the exhibition was over, went to Windsor.

In 1925, Mary suffered a blow which was to influence the rest of her life. The first bell tolled for George: his health broke down severely and the doctors insisted that he take a

Mediterranean cruise. The same thing had happened to his father at much the same age. The trouble was the same – bronchial catarrh. Edward VII had in the main followed the doctors' orders to be out of England at the end of the winter: he liked the sunshine and he liked going to Biarritz with Mrs Keppel. When he took a risk and exposed himself to the cold blasts of Norfolk in the spring, it killed him. Although George did not smoke or eat as much as his father, he was a difficult patient owing to his objection to going abroad.

The news from the doctors could not have come at a worse time for Mary. It meant that she crossed the bridge which led from an active past into an uncertain and sedentary future. It came at a time of other crises, for the country was in a whirl of industrial unrest which led to the General Strike, and an active leader was needed. It also came at a time when Queen Alexandra was fading away.

Alexandra had been a problem to Mary ever since she became Queen. She had never fully accepted that George was the rightful King – she looked back at the ghosts of Eddy and her husband. She was assuredly, in the public view, the symbol of royalty, dearly loved, and only the very old could remember the days before the Princess of Denmark came to reign at Sandringham. Mary had never been able to climb above the status of poor relation. Thus, before George could take his allotted role as Number One, the warning had come that he was not destined to have a long life and that his activities would have to be curtailed. It was a bitter blow to take, although the bulletins on George did not come fully home to Mary. To her, his was an irritating illness which would fade away in the Mediterranean sunshine. She could not bring herself to believe that the days of royal tours were over and that in future she was to be restricted to the shores of Britain. George was only sixty, and Queen Victoria had been running the country and travelling when she was over eighty.

Mary set about preparing the details for the Mediterranean cruise. She had never been abroad with George without having a fixed programme and she thought that it would be rather fun. In the event it was not fun. She wanted to go to Naples – he said no, as the harbour was full of dead dogs. Malta he ruled out – a bloody place, he said,[6] doubtless still bitter over the rumour that he had been married there. The problem was, how was George to fill his days? It was unlikely that he would be content wandering around with Mary on sightseeing tours and inspections of galleries. George solved the problem for himself by inviting his sister, Princess Victoria, to accompany them.

Mary's heart sank. Victoria was the bane of her life and had been since she was a girl. She was a spinster. She in no way blamed herself for this, recounting suitors who ranged from the widowed Lord Rosebery to an equerry. No, she had sacrificed her happiness to care for her selfish and eccentric Mama. She was a hypochondriac and her health had been a source of worry since girlhood – in fact Lord Dawson of Penn, the royal doctor, had once said that he could write a book about it. In truth she was not a suitable candidate to climb into the connubial bed. She made up for her deficiencies with an inflated degree of egoism. This stemmed from the days when the children of the Prince and Princess of Wales ranged wild at Sandringham, ruled the roost and considered themselves to be the cat's whiskers. They became a mutual admiration society. Victoria had never ceased to poke fun at Mary's morganatic background, had classified her as a bore and apologized to those who were placed next to her at dinner.

When George became King, Victoria strengthened her hold on him. Every morning she would telephone him, opening with 'Good morning, you old fool'; one day she said it before she was connected, which flattened the operator. Into the instrument she would pour conspiratorial mischief, often to the detriment of Mary: she and George were acting like children again. And she would make trouble by claiming back items of furniture and jewellery that she said were rightly hers. She knew that this would upset Mary, and it did. Now this bitter, fifty-five-year-old spinster was to be planted on the deck next to Mary the day through.

The worst happened. As the royal yacht passed along the Italian shores in March and April 1925, the weather broke and everyone caught colds. 'I loathe the sea,' repeated Mary once again. Victoria, who joined the yacht at Genoa, was consistently troublesome and brought out the worst in George. The two refused to join sightseeing tours at the ports at which they stopped and, if bullied into it, spoiled Mary's day by a sustained fusillade of criticism and chaff-making about ancient monuments, pictures and scenes of beauty. 'I am *so* glad to be back,'[7] was Mary's comment when she saw the shoreline of England.

They returned to find a crisis at Sandringham. Alexandra wrote to George, 'I feel completely collapsed. I soon shall go.'[8] She lasted through the green and scented days of a Norfolk summer but suffered a heart attack in November. Mary was at York Cottage and seldom left her bedside. November had always been so gay at Sandringham in the old days, the scene of Edward VII's mammoth birthday shoot and Alexandra's birthday ball. Sixty years of Norfolk memories were fading out, and with them a large slice of Mary's adult life. Queen Alexandra died on 20 November, recognizing her son and daughter-in-law to the end. She was buried in the Memorial Chapel at Windsor. 'Now darling Mama lies near dear Eddy,' was Mary's comment. The ghost of Eddy haunted her still. The shadows lengthened: two years later her eldest brother, Dolly, Marquess of Cambridge, died of peritonitis. Always Mary's favourite, his loss hit her hard. He was only fifty-nine.

Yet there was sunshine. Bertie hurried over to the palace with the news that Elizabeth was going to have a child. It had seemed a long wait – three years – but now it was a much-needed tonic to offset the gloom that preceded the General Strike. The baby, who was to become Queen Elizabeth II, was born at twenty minutes to three on the morning of 21 April 1926. A few minutes later, taps came at the bedroom doors of Mary and George at Windsor: they had given instructions that they were to be awakened no matter what time the event took place. Soon after breakfast they set off for London to carry out a personal inspection. Mary reported that the baby was 'a little darling with lovely complexion and pretty fair hair'.[9] Then Bertie, in a rare moment, opened his heart to his mother, or as much of it as was considered fit and proper in the royal family. He admitted that all he and Elizabeth had wanted to make their happiness complete was a child – and that his wife had wanted a girl.[10] Now all was perfect. The christening was at Buckingham Palace and Mary and George were godparents: the christening robe had been used at like ceremonies by all Mary's children. The baby cried, increasing the sobs when she was passed to her grandmother. It was only when she was restored to the nurse that peace reigned. It was reckoned that the secret lay in the contents of a bottle.

The events of 1925 and 1926 were a turning point in the reign of George and Mary. Firstly, they moved into the 'Big House' at Sandringham, and a dream came true. George paced the gravel and was captain of all he surveyed. Mary revelled in the space as she toured the 365 rooms she had coveted since 1910. For a third of a century she had been cooped up in gloomy and cramped York Cottage, bringing up six children under difficult conditions. Little May of Teck had indeed come into her own. Sandringham had always seemed the last step on the long climb up from penurious exile in Florence.

Secondly, the birth of the York baby – named Elizabeth but known in the family as 'Lilibet' – sent Mary and George rocketing up the popularity scale. With no Alexandra to cope with, and the star of David, Prince of Wales, turning to the wane, the moment had arrived for the King and Queen to take their rightful place. The propelling force which sent up their rating was provided by baby Lilibet. First in line of succession in the second generation, there was already talk of the future seeing another Good Queen Bess. There had been excitement at the births of two sons* to Princess Mary, but it was nothing to the explosion which greeted the new baby. Picture postcards poured off the presses by the hundred thousand. There were Lilibet hats and rompers, Lilibet cakes and dolls. Her every movement was religiously followed. Her pram excursions became royal processions. And once she could talk, the sayings attributed to her were legion. A glimpse of the pram of the Princess who lived in Piccadilly was the high spot for sightseers in London.

The popularity of Lilibet brushed off on to Mary more than

* George, born 1923; Gerald, born 1924.

anyone else in the family. Lilibet's mother was still rather a stranger and had spent much of her time abroad since her marriage. Now Mary was photographed every time she went to a children's home or a hospital, and always with a baby. She was photographed playing with her grandchildren in the palace gardens and postcards of her holding Lilibet were best sellers. There was far more excitement and interest in the new baby than there had ever been over her own children. Now she looked so happy. In fact she did not really enjoy babies until she became a grandmother – all of the fun and none of the worry.

There was another reason for her happiness, for Lilibet brought a new kind of life to George. She filled the gap left by Princess Mary. Whenever he was bored or irascible, Mary sent for Lilibet and the two would play together. And, fortunately for her, Lilibet was always handy in 1927. In January, Bertie and Elizabeth went on a world tour, among their engagements being the opening of the new Parliament House in Canberra, and were away for six months. During this time, Lilibet stayed in the care of her grandparents at Buckingham Palace.

It was on 21 November 1928 that George became ill and retired to bed. 'Too tiresome,' commented Mary, as she did of all illnesses. Next day she deputized for him at his engagements. The crisis built up. On 2 December she wrote, 'George was very ill in the evening as the heart began to give out. Terribly anxious.' [11] The doctors diagnosed septicaemia but could not locate the source of the poison.

Londoners thronged to see the bulletins, seeming to sense that the King was near to death. The country came near to a stop. The serious illness or death of a senior member of the royal family has always deeply affected the British public, as in the case of the Prince of Wales in 1871, the Duke of Clarence in 1891 and Edward VII in 1902, when illness caused the postponement of the coronation. Now George and Mary were treated to bigger, bolder headlines than they had been given since their accession. They monopolized conversation, even in places where royalty was seldom mentioned. Fuel was added when it was learned that the Prince of Wales had been recalled from East Africa. He made a sensational dash to reach his

Queen Mary with her eldest
grandchild, George Hubert Lascelles,
son of Princess Mary, born 1923

Queen Mary, King George and Princess
Elizabeth driving back to Balmoral Castle
from Crathie church

King George and Queen Mary on the balcony at Buckingham Palace on the occasion of their Silver
Jubilee. With them are Viscount Lascelles, Hubert Lascelles and the Princesses Elizabeth and Margaret

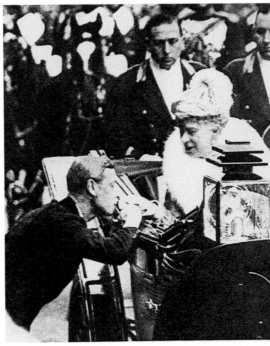

King Edward VIII saluting Queen Mary at Windsor

King George V's funeral. The coffin
nears St George's Chapel, Windsor

The Royal family in their coronation robes after the
crowning of George VI and Queen Elizabeth in 1937

father's bedside: on his arrival George opened one eye and grunted, 'Damn you, what the devil are you doing here?'[12]

The patient was X-rayed. The radiologist, Dr Graham Hodgson, brought his equipment into the palace garden and fed the cable in through a window. It was the first time a case had been so treated outside the big hospitals. Still the truth did not emerge. Lord Dawson made one more attempt to find the seat of the poison. This time his syringe brought out sixteen ounces of noxious matter. George was operated upon for the removal of a rib and drainage, and his life was saved. 'Anxious work,' wrote Mary. But he was far from over his troubles and it was not until 6 January that real hope came. He sent for his wife that evening and she reported, 'He was perfectly clear and we had a talk for twenty minutes which cheered me up much after not having spoken to me for practically six weeks. George signed his name just to show me he could do so.'[13] Mary's outward calm was a worry to her family. It was quite obvious how she felt, but she kept those feelings strictly to herself, not even unburdening herself to her children. She could have shared her emotional strain with the Yorks or with Princess Mary, who had come up from her Yorkshire home of Goldsborough. But she kept herself bottled up and the fear grew that if the King remained long in his crucial state, or if he died, she would have a complete breakdown. David said to Bertie, 'Through all the anxiety she has never once revealed her feelings to any of us. She is really far too reserved: she keeps too much locked up inside herself.'[14]

In February, George went to Craigweil House, Bognor, to recuperate. It was then that Elizabeth was able to make a really useful contribution towards his recovery: she sent Lilibet to stay with him. The two took little walks together, she guiding him by the hand and prattling away. One afternoon they made sand castles in the garden. The Archbishop of Canterbury saw them and was of the opinion that they were some of the most epic sand pies ever turned out and that they should be preserved. Mary was kept busy deputizing for her husband. The only engagements that she dreaded were the courts and standing alone before that glittering throng. But that she felt she must do because the dress trade relied so strongly on the making of the dresses.

In May, she and George returned to Windsor to a rapturous reception all along the way. The National Thanksgiving Service for George's total recovery was scheduled for 7 July: then another abscess developed. He made it to St Paul's, but Mary found it strange to hold a thanksgiving service for a man who had an open wound in his back.

CHAPTER XV

The Great Divide

THE LAST FIVE YEARS of George's life were one long struggle to stave off illness. He grew up as a monarch, but he paid the price. He laboured under four other handicaps, all great worries to him. Firstly, politics demanded much of his time. Secondly, he was worried, far more than people guessed, by the Prince of Wales: if David had married and had children, he could have viewed the future with more equanimity. Thirdly, Hitler and Mussolini were rattling their sabres in Europe and George dreaded the thought of war: he declared that if it came, he would join a mob in Trafalgar Square and shout for peace![1] Fourthly, he loathed the 1930s. He disapproved of the spread of democracy through the Empire and the disappearance of old-time cere-monial and was riled by the sartorial slackness of the politicians who came to court. He was appalled by women's fashions: one Easter Monday he looked out of his open window at Windsor, watching the visitors moving about the grounds. 'Good God,' he shouted '*look* at those short skirts, *look* at that bobbed hair!' His voice was loud and carried far. Mary abruptly told him to shut up.[2]

All these worries rebounded on Mary. She would not open her heart to anyone and she became inhibited, hiding the warmth and the tenderness which lay within her.[3]

A very welcome event was the birth of a second child to Bertie and Elizabeth on 21 August 1930. Reaction to the King's illness contributed to the outstanding public interest. In addition it was a girl. This represented quite a change in the royal family as among the children, grandchildren and great-grandchildren of Queen Victoria and Prince Albert there had been one hundred and ten boys to only sixty girls. Mary was at Balmoral at the time and motored over to Glamis Castle to see her new granddaughter. But she brought disturbing news. Elizabeth wanted to use the name Anne, but the King did not approve. So Margaret was substituted, though Elizabeth insisted on using her selected second name – Rose.

In the troubles which followed the great financial depression of the thirties politicians were apt to forget the degree of George's illness. The depression hit America in 1929, causing businessmen to leap from high windows, but did not reach Britain to the full until the summer of 1931. Mary and George had just arrived at Balmoral in August when a telegram came urging the King's return. Tired out, he had at once to make the return journey to London where he urged, successfully, that the Labour Government should give place to a National Government. Left alone on Deeside, Mary fumed at the lack of feeling and foresight of politicians. If her husband was long delayed, she declared she would join him. She then made her classic remark, 'I will not be left sitting on a mountain.'[4]

The crisis continued until the autumn, ending with a general election. George was exhausted. Sometimes he would dine alone, unable to face even his wife. This was a clear indication of the lowness of his spirits. Mary's company was an essential: he never returned to the palace after an engagement without shouting up the stairs, 'May, May, it is I.' In the early hours of the morning, Sister Black, who had remained with him after his illness of 1928–9, would often administer oxygen to relieve his restlessness.

In 1932, George and Mary made an important decision. After many misgivings and much exhortation from politicians, George agreed to make a Christmas broadcast from Sandringham. It proved a success beyond all expectation, and became a ritual, though George was so nervous that a thick cloth had to be put on the table to stop the sound of paper rustling in his shaking hands. The words had been written by Rudyard Kipling and at once passed into legend: 'I speak now from my home and my heart to you all: to men and women so cut off by the snows, the desert or the sea that only voices out of the air can reach them.' All over the Empire, that message was regarded not only as a Christmas greeting from the King, but from Queen Mary also. It had a strong effect in Canada, Africa, Australia and New Zealand and the King's advisers decided that it must be continued year by year, as indeed it was – and is.

Life for Mary and George now became a mixture of simplicity and traditional ceremony. As George weakened, meals became more and more plain. To the despair of the chef, Mary would cross out his suggestions for some ambitious gateaux and substitute stewed plums and semolina: this was a favourite dish of hers. But the running of the household was kept as it had been for generations past. George's nurse, Sister Catherine Black, thus described life at Windsor:

> Everything had to be carried on according to precedent. Old forms and ceremonies that had been in use for centuries were scrupulously observed. The rules and conditions of service laid down for the household in the reign of George III were still referred to when any doubt arose and 'It has always been done that way' was considered the last word in any argument.[5]

Ascot Week was a good example. All ladies invited were required to have four new outfits for attending the races, two new morning dresses and five evening gowns. Before dinner the Lady of the Bedchamber paraded them in a quarter circle in the Green Drawing Room, the Master-of-the Household doing the same to the men on the other side of the room. There was a check that decorations were being worn correctly. As the clock struck half past eight, the King and Queen appeared, the Master of the Household bowing and backing away from the presence. The women curtseyed and Mary shook them by the hand. The man chosen to sit at her right bowed to her, took her stiffly by the arm and led her into dinner, a hidden band playing 'God Save the King'. Inside the hour Mary would catch her husband's eye and give the signal that she was about to withdraw. As she left the table, the ladies with her curtseyed. Back in the Green Drawing Room she took up her crochet and the Lady of the Bedchamber brought up the first of the women with whom she had previously indicated she wished to talk. George spent exactly twenty minutes over his port and then led the male guests to join the ladies. Conversation and games of cards followed. As eleven struck, the guests rose and took station in quarter circles, as they had done before dinner. Mary and George wished them good night and the day was over.

The same guests were invited every year, so they came to know the drill perfectly. The exact repetition suited Mary well, for she had been trained at Strelitz and Württemburg, where the court etiquette was equally rigid. For her, it obviated the necessity of making light conversation to strangers. She adored order and detail and the evenings passed without disruption of any kind. It did not suit her sons, who on one occasion rolled back the carpet after their parents had gone to bed and began dancing. They did not try it a second time.[6]

Nineteen thirty-four brought two never-to-be-forgotten days to Mary. In September, she motored from Balmoral to Glasgow to launch the giant Cunard liner which bore her name. In October, her youngest surviving son, George, who had been created Duke of Kent, married at Westminster Abbey. His bride was Princess Marina,* a granddaughter of Queen Alexandra's brother, King George II of Greece. 'She has not a cent,' commented the King, but he was so enraptured by Marina's charm and beauty that he forgave her even that. Mary considered her 'a charming addition to the family', but thought it incumbent upon her to administer a slight reprimand when the bride reached Buckingham Palace. Marina had been photographed while smoking a cigarette on the Channel steamer.

The Kent marriage highlighted the position of the Prince of Wales. David was forty now and showed no signs of contemplating marriage and having children. Nor did he appear to be preparing himself for kingship. He seldom saw his father: George commented, 'I hardly ever see him and don't know what he is doing.'[7] In fact matters had reached a state when communication between them no longer existed. Mary was little better placed. She had always been too withdrawn to gain the confidence of her sons and it was too late to start now. She

---

* She was the daughter of Prince Nicholas of Greece and Denmark, who married Helen, Grand Duchess of Russia.

concentrated her efforts on keeping the peace and confined her talks with them to trivialities.

Keeping the peace was not easy, for George easily exploded with anger when David's name was mentioned. He told Count Mensdorff, the former Austrian Ambassador, 'He has not a single friend who is a gentleman. He does not see any decent society.'[8] The rare occasions when they met usually ended in ructions. One day George roared at David, 'You dress like a cad. You act like a cad. Get out!'[9] Reprimanding David was difficult. George tried it once, unable to contain himself when his heir made complimentary remarks about Germany in public. David would not accept the reprimand and afterwards told the German Ambassador that he considered he, David, was right. When people pointed out to the King the obvious attractive qualities in his heir, he replied, 'Yes, certainly. That is the pity. If he were a fool, we would not mind.' He told Stanley Baldwin, the Prime Minister, 'After I am dead, the boy will ruin himself in twelve months'[10] – a prophetic forecast indeed. The abrasive atmosphere further increased George's irascibility, and this rubbed off on Mary. So difficult did George become that on one occasion, when she was returning by car with him from Sandringham, she threatened to get out at Royston to finish the journey by train.

On the other side of the coin, David certainly had grounds for complaint about palace life. He unburdened himself to Lady Diana Cooper* one night at dinner, beginning with a description of his miserable childhood. 'He described the gloom of Buckingham Palace; how he himself and all of them "froze up" whenever they got inside it; how bad tempered his father was; how the Duchess of York was the one bright spot there.'[11]

David met Mrs Wallis Simpson in 1930. He was still on intimate terms with Mrs Dudley Ward but also had an interest in Lady Thelma Furness. Until 1934, he saw Wallis and her husband, Mr Ernest Simpson, at regular intervals. In 1932, they were guests at David's new home of Fort Belvedere near Windsor, Lady Thelma Furness acting as hostess. In 1933, David

* Wife of Duff Cooper, later first Lord Norwich.

gave a birthday party for Wallis at Quaglino's. The following January, Lady Furness went to America and left David in Wallis's care: by this time Wallis's marriage was breaking up. When Thelma Furness came back, she discovered that she had lost David – she knew from the look in Wallis's eyes. And the cold truth came also to Mrs Freda Dudley Ward. David washed both women out of his life without even a goodbye wave.

David's love for Wallis Simpson was an extraordinary trance. His father was to say, 'This is no ordinary love'; Winston Churchill said the same. Since 1914, the royal family had been searching for a bride for David. In that year, on turning down a candidate brought forward by Queen Alexandra, David affirmed that he would only marry a woman for love.[12] Thereafter he had companions, confidantes and flirtations, but he never came near to his ideal. In truth he required a mother-mistress – he wanted attention and he always wanted to please. This was revealed by Freda Dudley Ward in her old age. Women found this somewhat trying: when David joined Freda by the rail at a race meeting, she was overheard to say, somewhat petulantly, 'Oh, go away, David.'[13]

Mary and George were ill-equipped to deal with a position such as this. George had never experienced a case of all-de-vouring love. His brother Eddy's amours had been slight. His father's affairs had been numerous but not very serious; perhaps Edward's early passionate attachment to Lady Warwick came nearest to David's plight now. George simply did not understand a love which counted higher than the throne. Mary was even less fitted to cope. She had never passed through a stage of high exultation – the feeling was foreign to her. In addition she was still somewhat awed by, and frightened of, George. When David took his problems to Lord Louis Mountbatten, Mountbatten urged him to lay the facts before his mother. 'She'll make him see your side,' he said. 'No,' David replied, 'it wouldn't do any good. She's as frightened of Papa as we are.'[14]

Lacking a shoulder on which to lay his head, David turned to bravado and flaunted Wallis before his parents. He invited her to Buckingham Palace. George complained that she had been smuggled into his home without his knowledge or permission. 'That woman in my house,'[15] he roared. David even dared to dance with Wallis right under the eyes of his mother and father at a ball at Windsor. She felt George's eyes boring into her.[16]

This was the time that Mary should have grasped the nettle firmly. The worries of the sick King were already immense and she should have handled the matter herself, pointing out the obvious impossibility of a divorced American woman, in her second marriage, occupying the position of British Queen. She should have brought home clearly the state of George's health and urged David to prepare himself for the succession. Inwardly, David was very attached to his mother and at least would not have lost his temper and would have put his case. His views could then have been assimilated and passed on to senior royal advisers. Coming from her, note would have had to be taken. But she could not bring herself to do it. Instead she tried to evade the problem and complained only to her ladies and members of her committees whom she knew well, but this had little effect. They listened and then kept their mouths shut. So precious months passed, and there were few months to go.

At the end of April 1935, Mary and George came from Windsor to Buckingham Palace to prepare for their Silver Jubilee. On 6 May, they had been twenty-five years on the throne and that day had been chosen for their celebration drive to St Paul's for the thanksgiving service. For them it was to be a wonderful experience. They realized that at last they stood where Victoria and Edward and Alexandra had stood before them, high in the estimation of the people. Perhaps it meant more to Mary than it did to her husband. Little May of Teck, the poor relation, the morganatic Princess, had made it to the top.

Mary's diary became hectic. There were last-minute appointments with dressmakers, drives out to see the decorations going up, visitors arriving from all over the world, and the mail piled up to gigantic proportions. On the evening of the fifth, the crowds began to take up their chosen stations in the Mall. They were mostly family parties with children, preparing to camp out for the night. Mary and George were happy in their domesticity and in sharp contrast with the European dictators. The vast coming together was in part a reaction to the threat of war from across the Channel, in part a tribute to the King and Queen who had seen them through four years of war and the troubled twenties.

Next evening Mary wrote in her diary:

> We left at five to eleven in the big open carriage with six grey horses – We had a marvellous reception from the crowds of people all the way to St Paul's and back – The Thanksgiving Service at eleven thirty was beautiful – Back before one and we all went on to the Balcony where the crowds cheered us – After luncheon we had to go on to the Balcony again – At eight . . . listened to G's wonderful message to his People which was broadcasted – most moving. After dinner we had to go out on the Balcony again – A wonderful day.

George contributed one of the most feeling passages that he ever wrote: 'The greatest number of people in the streets I have ever seen. The enthusiasm was indeed most touching. I'd no idea they felt like that about me. I am beginning to think they must really like me for myself.'[17]

In the welter of post-Jubilee festivities, two events stood out – the reception of the Dominion and Empire prime ministers and the homage paid by the two Houses of Parliament in Westminster Hall. George's speech at the latter was recorded for a gramophone record. Those who listened to it noted that at the end, his voice almost broke with emotion. He was talking about Mary. He had guessed that this would happen and had told his secretary, 'Put that paragraph at the very end. I can't trust myself to speak of the Queen when I think of all I owe her.'[18] That was Mary's accolade.

It is the lot of monarchs to be tested beyond the bounds of personal endurance. It was the lot of George V. Happy as he was at the celebrations, his strength was not up to it. Mary's was. The Naval Review at Spithead was followed by the RAF display. There was a dinner at the Jockey Club in Newmarket and a reception for the delegates to the Empire Parliamentary Conference. Long drives were made through the streets of London's suburbs and visits made to children's feasts in the mean streets. Night after night George and Mary were called out on to the balcony of Buckingham Palace. By the time he reached Balmoral in August he was played out. Mary, on the other hand, was still on top of her form. She wrote of the Gillies Ball*: 'Great fun. I danced twelve dances running from nine thirty till eleven thirty.'[19] She was sixty-eight and George was seventy.

Good news came with the announcement of the engagement of their third son, Henry, Duke of Gloucester, to Lady Alice Montagu-Douglas-Scott, third daughter of the seventh Duke of Buccleuch, an old friend of George's. Sadly, the Duke died in October and the wedding was celebrated quietly in November in the Chapel of Buckingham Palace. George commented, 'Now all the children are married but David.'[20]

During the autumn evenings, the conversation of George and Mary centred on the affair of David and Wallis Simpson. He made her promise that when he was dead, she would not receive the American woman at the palace. He said, 'I pray that nothing comes between Lilibet and the throne.' When old friends urged him to speak with his heir, he answered, 'There's nothing I can do with the fellow.'[21] Mary still stood on the touchline. Her last chance slipped away.

She could not face up to the truth that George was dying. She had always shied away from the idea of death, though brave as a lion when it came. She had been the same in the cases of her mother, Queen Victoria and Edward VII. Her grandmother had lived until ninety, her Uncle George to eighty-five and her Aunt Augusta to ninety-four: she thought that everyone should do likewise. She boasted that she came from a long-lived family. She behaved in the same manner in the case of Princess Victoria. Her sister-in-law was failing fast, and this was obvious. Mary went to see her at her home, Coppins, Iver, Buckinghamshire, and reported that although she had been unwell, she was getting better now. Victoria was not getting better and died on 3 December.

This was the death knell for George. Throughout the autumn he had been saddened by the passing of old friends – the Duke of Buccleuch, Lord Jellicoe and Lord Sysonby (Sir Frederick

---

* The annual dance for the servants at Balmoral.

Ponsonby), his Keeper of the Privy Purse for twenty-one years. Now his beloved 'Toria' was gone and his world ended. It was the breaking of his links with the past, the Sandringham of his youth. Of the then Wales family only Maud was left, and she was Queen of distant Norway. The ghosts of Edward and Alexandra, of Eddy, Louise and Victoria were in every room when he arrived at Sandringham for Christmas. The dining room was gay with the great ones of the close of the nineteenth century. On the park drives he could hear the clip-clop of the ponies' hooves as his mother drove out to visit tenants in the villages. The shouts of his sisters came from the schoolroom and Eddy lay still on his bed in the little room which had been kept sacred to his memory. He was like unto a man who had done his life's work and was now prepared to leave his task in the hands of God. He craved sleep.

Mary did her best to make it a jovial Christmas. The family turned up in strength. David was there, seemingly distant and somewhat lost; Henry and his beautiful bride, whom George adored; George of Kent and Marina with their baby son, Edward; and Lilibet and Margaret. Elizabeth was in bed with pneumonia at the Royal Lodge, Windsor, and Bertie stayed with her. Knowing what joy the presence of their daughters would bring to the King, they despatched them to Norfolk.

It began to snow and ice capped the lake where Edward and Alexandra had staged their skating parties in a fairyland of magic lanterns. Lilibet and Margaret built a snowman and pelted the guests with snowballs. Then the party was over, the girls went back to their parents and Sandringham was quiet. Mary walking by his side, George rode round the gardens on his white pony, Jock. On 14 January he did so for the last time – it was the anniversary of Eddy's death and a day which was stamped for ever on Mary's memory. He sat by the fire in his room, she reading to him as he watched the flames from the wood fire.

Still Mary underestimated the situation. 'Poor George,' she wrote, 'who had not been feeling well for some days, felt worse and had to go to bed before dinner.' On the seventeenth, she sent for Lord Dawson of Penn and summoned David from Windsor. David had guessed the truth and flew up in his

aeroplane. George died peacefully at five minutes before midnight on 20 January, his wife and children about him. Mary
stooped and kissed the hand of King Edward VIII. Then she
went to her room and wrote in her diary, 'The sunset of his
death tinged the whole world's sky.'

CHAPTER XVI

The Short Reign

MARY'S CALM DEMEANOUR in the days following her husband's death was commented upon by all who were near her. She appeared less shocked than her children, who were completely overcome by their father's death. In truth they had not realized that he was dying until the last two days. And death was a stranger to them, while Mary had been at many deathbeds. Dr Lang, Archbishop of Canterbury, wrote, 'The sons were painfully upset – I suppose they had seldom if ever seen death – and it was the Queen, still marvellously self-controlled, who supported and strengthened them.'

The shock was lessened for her because, in her own mind, the two were still working together. George was an integral part of her daily programme. It was still 'he and I'. She was with him when the lid of the coffin was screwed down and carried by men of the Grenadier Guards out into the garden where a bier awaited. Twilight was passing into night as the coffin was trundled along the paths of the garden which George had loved best on earth. The wind bent the dark shrubs and flurries of rain chased across the lawns. Mary headed the party of twelve close mourners which followed the bier. Only one wavering electric torch lit the way. As they came from behind the shrubbery which screens the Church of St Mary Magdalene, they saw that the lych gate was brilliantly lit, the Rector standing alone beneath it. Thus, in moments of absolute simplicity, George's coffin was laid near the pew in which he had worshipped for nigh on seventy years. 'The Church full of our kind people,'[1] Mary wrote. She left him in their care to keep the night watch.

There was the same feeling of togetherness when, after the

funeral train reached London, Mary drove ahead to await the coffin's arrival at Westminster Hall for the lying in state. He was coming – she had her part to play. For four days the coffin lay on the great catafalque in the historic Hall and a million people filed past the remains of King George V, throughout the day and far into the night. An endless queue moved step by step along the south bank of the Thames, over the bridge and back to Westminster, light rain falling on the silent line.

'We fetched him from Westminster,' Mary wrote, and she took him to Windsor. In St George's Chapel she stood alone behind his coffin, wearing the peaked coif and thick crêpe veil of German mourning. In the House of Commons, the Prime Minister, Mr Baldwin, said, 'Do I need to say a word in this House of how his power and influence were enhanced in a million ways by that rich companionship he shared with the Queen?'

Mary went back to the loneliness of Buckingham Palace. Her days were full of residual duties, answering letters, dealing with George's will and his possessions, preparing to move back into Marlborough House where she had lived when Princess of Wales. She was determined on one thing above all – not to be a nuisance to the new King as Alexandra had been to George when Edward VII died. The King was dead but a new King reigned. She took it for granted that he would behave in the correct manner: her faith in the monarchy was sublime. She referred every point of doubt and procedure to David. If she did not see him for a few days, she wrote to him, as she had done to George when he was away from her. Would it be all right for George and Marina to have some surplus silver, as they were short for their dinner service? There was doubt as to which sword Kaiser William had given to George in 1905: would it be all right if she went to Windsor to identify it? Would it be in order to make a certain structural alteration to Marlborough House? Could a pension be granted to an old servant of George's who was retiring?

Mary cast thoughts of Mrs Wallis Simpson from her mind. George had made her promise that she would not receive her and this she adhered to. But in the dark shadow of her sorrow she lived in days past, her work of clearing up her husband's estate taking her back to the time of Queen Victoria. She was in her seventieth year. For six months, until full summer came, she worked on George's affairs and on planning her move to Marlborough House. Then at the end of July she went back to Sandringham, and that was when the full force of her loss hit her. Now the tears came to her eyes and she was near to breaking down. David was always kind and thoughtful and he came to see her off. She wrote to him from Sandringham:

> I fear I was very quiet today when you came to see me but I feel sure you realized that I felt very very sad at leaving those lovely comfortable rooms which have been my happy Home for twenty-five years, and that I was terribly afraid of breaking down – It was dear of you to come and see me off and I thank you with all my heart . . . It is very nice here and peaceful and I am sure I shall like it, but I miss dearest Papa quite dreadfully, even more than in London, and his rooms look so empty and deserted without him: I forced myself to go in and look round but felt very sad.[2]

Everywhere she walked in the gardens and park, George was with her. Every flower and shrub brought back memories of the past. The staff and tenants greeted her with affection, as if she were the squire's wife, for they were out of tune with Edward VIII and feared what changes he would bring to the Norfolk estate.

As Mary's grief increased, her children recovered from the shock of losing their father. David decided that he needed a holiday in the sunshine, and a rest from monarchy, and he chartered the yacht *Nahlin* to cruise off the Adriatic coast. Among the guests whom he invited to join him was Mrs Wallis Simpson. Mary accepted the decision without query. She wrote to him, 'I am glad you have chartered a yacht and hope that you will find sunshine and good weather.' Resting at Sandringham, the clamour of the foreign press which greeted the *Nahlin* cruise – the scanty bathing dresses, the expeditions ashore – passed her by.

Mary returned to London. Then the letters came in – letters from all over the Empire and the United States. In them was expressed concern at the manner in which Edward VIII was behaving at a time of world crisis: concern at his liaison with Mrs Wallis Simpson. Mary was urged to take action before it was too late. She read the letters, as she did the cuttings from the foreign press, and put them aside without comment. She filled her diary with records of the weather and her daily perambulations between the palace and Marlborough House. She saw Mrs Simpson's name in the Court Circular, but still she held her tongue. She told her closest friends that she did not believe in interfering in the personal matters of her children.[3] But there was another reason. She knew that, of those children, the eldest was the most obstinate and difficult to sway. In fact she feared that interference might drive him further in the other direction. And also, so deep was her respect for the throne that she hesitated to query the action of a King.

In David's mind there was but one person superior to himself – Queen Mary. He had brushed aside Cosmo Lang, the Archbishop of Canterbury, and he reckoned that he could cope with the Prime Minister, Mr Stanley Baldwin. He thought that he could 'get away with anything'. This attitude was encouraged by Wallis Simpson. But it was with some trepidation that he reported to Buckingham Palace on his return from the Adriatic in mid-September. He knew that he had broken the code of kings and had done things that called for a rebuke. He had never forgotten the cold feeling that had come to his stomach when, as a boy, he had been summoned before his parents to explain a lack of discipline or poor progress in the schoolroom, or a bad report from Osborne Naval College. He was to be pleasantly surprised. In his own words:

> My mother asked whether I had enjoyed the cruise. I assured her that I had had a wonderful time. 'Didn't you find it terribly warm in the Adriatic?' she asked. Her curiosity about the simple details of the voyage reminded me of how she used to talk to us when we returned from school. She had read in *The Times* of my meeting with King George of Greece at Corfu, and wondered how he was getting on. I told her that he had lost weight, and that he was homesick for his friends in London. 'Poor George,' said my mother. 'I don't envy the rulers of those Balkan countries.'[4]

David left the palace rejoicing. If he could get away with the *Nahlin* cruise, he reckoned that he could get away with anything – even marrying Wallis Simpson. He went off to Balmoral, and she went with him.

Then there came an event – small in itself – which triggered off a major reaction. The Duke and Duchess of York, with their children, were also on Deeside, taking their summer holiday at Birkhall. There was no contact between Balmoral and Birkhall but there came, through members of the household and the staff, news of what was going on at the castle. Wallis Simpson was acting as hostess and sleeping in Queen Mary's old room. The evenings were a round of gaiety and even David later commented that he could feel the disapproval of his austere great-grand-father, Prince Albert, when the cocktails were carried into the drawing room before dinner.[5] Then other news reached Birkhall. This concerned changes which were being made both in staff and management. Bertie, unconsulted, felt 'neglected, ignored, unwanted'.[6] He was deeply upset, for the way of life at the castle was sacrosanct and had been since the 1850s. Somewhat at a loss as to what to do, and avoiding the difficult step of going to Balmoral and having it out with his brother, he unburdened himself to his mother.

Now this letter was very different to the many that she had already received. Here was the next in line of succession to the throne appealing to her for help, her self-effacing, quiet second son. If the ways of Balmoral were interfered with, lasting damage would be done to the royal way of life as she knew it. She felt impelled to act. She consulted, and complained to, a few 'extraneous persons',[7] but without result. At last she passed the ball into the hands of Mr Stanley Baldwin and his Cabinet.

This development came at a bad time for Mary, for she was fully occupied with her move from Buckingham Palace to Marlborough House, a move which took place on 1 October 1936. The transfer of her many treasures and the organization of her staff of sixty-five was a major task for an ageing lady. Her diary told the story: 'To Marl. H. at ten twenty-five and stayed there till after one – supervising various things and arranging furniture – Went there again at three and stayed till seven thirty!!! I took my tea there and had it with Mrs Moore our housekeeper, picnic-fashion in one of the rooms – Felt dead tired on my return.' On the last day of September she wrote, 'Sad to think that this is my last day in the old Home of twenty-five years – *Toute passe, tout casse, tout lasse!*'* Next day David drove with her when she went to her new home. No mention was made of affairs at Balmoral.

In October, Mrs Wallis Simpson moved into a rented house at Felixstowe: her petition for divorce was due to be heard at Ipswich on the twenty-sixth. On the twentieth, Mr Baldwin saw the King and begged him to persuade Mrs Simpson to have the divorce proceedings withdrawn. David replied that it was not his right to interfere in other people's private affairs. Wallis duly received a decree *nisi*. The American press heated up the headlines, but British publications refrained from comment; it was obvious that they would not long continue to do so. On 13 November, the King's Private Secretary, Major Hardinge,** warned that the silence was about to be broken and that there was danger that the Government would resign. He wrote, 'If Your Majesty will permit me to say so, there is only one step which holds out any prospect of avoiding this dangerous situation and that is for Mrs Simpson to go abroad *without delay*.'[8] Furious, David did not reply, but in the days ahead he had no more dealings with Major Hardinge, Walter Monckton acting as his liaison with Downing Street. Sir Walter Monckton (afterwards first Viscount Monckton of Brenchley), was a distinguished barrister and had made friends with the King when they were at Oxford together. On the sixteenth, the King again saw Mr Baldwin and declared his intention to marry Mrs Simpson: if necessary he would renounce the throne. That evening, David dined with his mother and sister Mary at Marlborough House. In the Queen's boudoir after dinner he broached the question of Wallis. At first his audience was sympathetic, but when he revealed that he was prepared to abdicate, both women were astounded. Mary, misery lining her face, implored him to do no such thing, for the sake both of the family and the country. But

* All passes, all cracks, all tires. ** Afterwards 2nd Baron of Penshurst.

she noted that David would accept no view but his own – his happiness came first. He was told that he had no alternative but to make a personal sacrifice, but he simply would not listen. He said over and over again that if only his mother would meet Wallis, she would realize what a wonderful woman, what a paragon of virtue, she was. At last he snapped out the vital question, 'Why will you not receive her?' Mary answered coldly, 'Because she is an adventuress.'[9]

Next day, David informed his brothers. Bertie hurried over to Marlborough House and told his mother that he did not want to succeed to the throne. If the job was thrust upon him, he would do his best, but he feared that the whole fabric of royalty might collapse. Mary was understanding and sympathetic, showing deeper maternal feeling than she had ever done in her life. She later revealed, 'He sobbed on my shoulder for a whole hour – on a sofa.'[10]

There was temper in her now – it had always been there, stemming from her Teck forebears. As a girl she had determined to keep it in control. But now it showed and 'bright spots of crimson'[11] burned in her cheeks when the possibility of abdication was mentioned. Yet next day, she was able to write sympathetically to David, 'As your mother, I must send you a line of true sympathy in the difficult position in which you are placed – I have been thinking of you all day, hoping that you are making a wise decision for your future . . .'[12]

Then Mr Baldwin arrived to see her. He described to his niece what happened:

Queen Mary is one of the shyest women I have ever met in my life. This shyness puts a barrier between her and you which it is well nigh impossible to get across. I had suffered from this, though she was always very nice to me. But I was always expected to keep the conversation going, and it sometimes flagged. She had a way, too, of standing at the end of the room when one was shown in at Buckingham Palace; and she would remain there like a statue while you made your bow and walked over a sometimes very slippery floor to kiss her hand. But all that was one day changed quite suddenly and I will tell you how . . . The first time I was sent for to see her at the beginning of this Simpson story, I had a tremendous shock.

For, instead of standing immobile in the middle distance, silent and majestic, she came trotting across the room *exactly like a puppy dog*: and before I had time to bow, she took hold of my hand in both of hers and held it tight. 'Well, Prime Minister,' she said, 'here's a pretty kettle of fish!'[13]

Mary decided that an air of calm must now be induced, to scotch any rumours which might be flying around. To this end she appeared in public as much as possible, visiting exhibitions and the London Museum, and going to the big stores to buy Christmas presents. The people of south London saw her when the Crystal Palace on Sydenham Hill burned down on 30 November: she drove out to see the smouldering ruins. For her it was a symbolic tragedy, for here was buried the outstanding memory of Prince Albert the Consort, wiped out at the moment when the foundations of the British throne were shaking.

The British press broke its silence on 3 December. The large, blatant headlines shook three women to the core of their being. Mary, breakfasting at precisely nine o'clock at Marlborough House, exclaimed, 'Really! This might be Romania!'[14] Wallis Simpson, in her bed at Fort Belvedere, rioted. She decided that she must leave England at once: that night she was on the boat from Newhaven to Dieppe, en route for Cannes. Elizabeth, Duchess of York, back at 145 Piccadilly after a trip to Edinburgh, was developing influenza.

Mary hurried off a note to David: 'Darling David, This news in the papers is very upsetting, especially as I have not seen you for ten days – I would much like to see you, won't you look in some time today? Ever your loving Mama, Mary.'[15] David dined at Marlborough House that night. The Yorks were there. He explained to his mother the reasons for his apparent aloofness. 'I have no desire to bring you and the family into all this. This is something I must handle alone.'[16] He repeated that he could not bring himself to live alone as King and must marry Wallis. Before he left he asked Bertie to come and see him at Fort Belvedere in the morning.

But David did not see his younger brother for three days, making excuses each time he was asked to do so. A pall of secrecy hangs over this strange interlude. Something happened to David after he left Marlborough House, causing him to cancel his appointment with Bertie, who was left in agony of suspense. Time has made it clear that those three days were spent in final settlement of who should be the next King. There was a strong lobby, composed of politicians and senior members of the press, which was of the opinion that Bertie was not up to the task of kingship: George, Duke of Kent, was preferred. Both Mary and the Archbishop of Canterbury were strongly in favour of Bertie. The matter was decided in his favour by the evening of the seventh and David sent for him. He made no explanation for his lack of contact, merely repeating once again his decision to abdicate. But it emerges clearly that if Bertie had become aware of the doubts about him, he might have refused to tackle the task.

On Wednesday, 9 December, Mary drove to the Royal Lodge, Windsor, the country home of Bertie and Elizabeth. Twilight was gathering and fog enfolded the garden as she listened to David's final decision that he would abdicate. He wrote:

> She was already waiting in the drawing room when I arrived. I gave her a full account of all that had passed between Mr Baldwin and myself during the six days since our last meeting . . . She still disapproved of and was bewildered by my action, but now that it was all over her heart went out to her hard-pressed son, prompting her to say with tenderness, 'And to me, the worst thing is that you won't be able to see her for so long.'[17]

Mary drove back to London and George and Marina joined her for dinner. Here was another problem for her. It was unlikely that no inkling of what had been going on had reached the ears of the Duke of Kent. Thus explanations were necessary, and the task fell on his mother. George had, in his youth, been a wild young man and it had been necessary to remove a number of young ladies from his orbit. After such affairs depression set in and on one occasion he took to drugs and suffered a nervous breakdown. David had taken him away to Fort Belvedere and carried out a programme of rehabilitation, showing deep sympathy and understanding.[18] George was devoted to his eldest brother.

Marriage to Marina had brought him great happiness. They already had a son, Edward, and Marina was at this time eight months pregnant, her new baby being expected at Christmas. This was no time for shocks for the Kents. There was the danger of pre-natal depression for Marina. For George, there was the risk that the whole turmoil of the abdication would bring on a return of his former nervous troubles, and even upset his marriage. In the event, that is what was to occur, though fortunately only on a temporary basis. Thus Mary had a hard task to keep the conversation flowing.

To complete her marathon day, Bertie arrived after dinner, bringing with him the Instrument of Abdication.* Mary read it with revulsion and incredulity. Then Bertie broke down and, in his own words, 'sobbed like a child'.[19] That Wednesday was one of the worst days in Mary's life.

On the tenth, David signed the Instrument of Abdication: Bertie became King George VI and Elizabeth, Queen Consort and Empress of India. She was lying in bed with influenza at 145 Piccadilly. Mary went to see her and Elizabeth handed her an anti-germ impregnated handkerchief.[20] Lilibet's governess noted the strain: 'Queen Mary, who was always so upright, so alert, looked suddenly old and tired.'[21] Lilibet and Margaret were confused as to what the excitement was about. They had watched Mr Baldwin come to No. 145, grim and smoking his pipe, and wondered why. A servant heard Margaret ask, 'What's happening?' Lilibet replied, 'I don't know really, but I believe Uncle David wishes to get married. I *think* he wants to marry Mrs Baldwin – and Mr Baldwin doesn't like it!'[22]

David planned to leave England after his farewell broadcast from Windsor Castle late on the evening of the eleventh. He asked his family to meet him for dinner at the Royal Lodge before the broadcast. Mary did not wish him to speak on the radio and sent him a note: 'Don't you think that as the Prime

* Monckton and Sir John Simon, the Home Secretary, drafted the King's message to Parliament.

Minister has said everything that could be said, it will now not be necessary for *you* to broadcast this evening, you are very tired after all the strain you have been and are going through, and surely you might spare yourself this extra strain and emotion – Do please take my advice.'[23] But David was determined to have his say.

Thus the last scene was set. Mary decided that it should pass off with dignity and as calmly and cheerfully as the circumstances would permit. She went to her wardrobe and chose a bright, coloured frock – this was to be the first time she had been out of mourning since her husband died. She drove to Windsor with the Princess Royal, her constant support. Waiting for them at the Royal Lodge were her brother, Alge, and his wife Alice – the Earl and Countess of Athlone – and David, Bertie, Henry and George. Before dinner was over, a car came to take David to the castle and his family sat down to listen to his words. Mary considered that his broadcast was good and dignified: she heard him pay tribute to the comfort that he had received from his mother 'during these hard days'.

David came back a new man. He was smiling and obviously relieved and the tension in the family was eased. Mary went to the window and looked out over the gardens. The fog was thickening. She gave the signal to her daughter that it was time to go. 'And then,' she wrote, 'came the dreadful goodbye . . . The whole thing was too pathetic for words.'

One point, as a mother, she had omitted to enquire into: that was, what was David going to do when he reached France? She was so accustomed to kings having all arrangements made for them that she took it for granted that the details had been settled in advance. But they had not, and David had not given them a thought. He had taken it for granted that the members of his staff would attend to it, but now, as he was later to say, they seemed to evaporate – even his valet refused to go with him. It was left to Wallis to fix where he should go. She rang just before the broadcast to say that she had arranged for him to stay with the Rothschilds at their home of Enzesfeld near Vienna. Sir Piers Legh, his equerry since 1919, volunteered to go to Austria with him.

Mary need not have worried about the fog, for her way home was well policed. She was the most important person in the country now – as long as Queen Mary was there, all would be well. There was much for her to remember as she sat upright in her Daimler. She had seen four reigns come to an end – she saw again Victoria breathing weakly as she lay, cradled in the arms of Kaiser William, in her bed at Osborne; Edward VII insisting on dressing up in a frock coat on the day that he died at Buckingham Palace; George V's life moving peacefully to its close at Sandringham; and now David, her dream King, once the idol of the world, relinquishing his great responsibility for the love of a divorced woman whom she termed an adventuress.

She came to London, passing the statue of Albert high on his stand in Kensington Gardens. She saw the dark outline of Buckingham Palace, sentries before the gates and a gathering of inquisitive sightseers. She came home to Marlborough House, to the warmth and the quiet ministrations of her staff. She said, as she was to say so often in the days to come, 'All *this* thrown away for *that*.'[24]

CHAPTER XVII

Three Vital Years

THE ROYAL FAMILY spent Christmas at Sandringham. A crowd watched Mary leave with her son and daughter-in-law and her grandchildren and the sight of her upright figure gave a feeling of stability to the very unstable situation caused by the abdication. For Mary the holiday was an unnerving experience, a wild, sad dream that had nothing in it of reality.

Only a year before, she had made the same journey, and George had been with her. He was failing, but no one had dreamed that he would die so soon. He had made his Christmas broadcast; she had rejoiced at the happy year of their Silver Jubilee. Since then she had gone through the agony of his death and the ordeal of the lying-in-state and the funeral; she had changed houses; and then stood up to the daily strain of watching a reign collapse. Now the reaction came and she was shattered.

She was in a strange position, for she was in fact in charge. It was her staff which was running Sandringham. It was she who said what should be done, for she alone knew. Bertie was tired out and thoroughly upset, not feeling capable of making the traditional broadcast; Elizabeth was recovering from influenza.

Drained by the grief of her memories and the strain of the abdication, Mary retired to her room. She did not go to bed, just sat before the fire dreaming, going over and over again in her mind the events of the past year. It was not until New Year's Eve that she was able to go down to dinner. 'Thank God this sad year is over,' she said. But there had been one bright spark of comfort. On Christmas Day a daughter had been born to George and Marina of Kent and she was named Alexandra.

Back in London, Mary recovered and set about one of the

most difficult tasks of her life – the re-establishing of the stability of the monarchy. After the abdication Mr Maxton, Independent Labour Party Member for Glasgow, had said that royalty, like Humpty Dumpty, had had a great fall, and that all the King's horses and all the King's men could not put royalty together again. Mary was determined that it should be put back together.

She saw as one of her priorities that she should be seen as much as possible in the streets: this gave a feeling of continuity. Behind the scenes she had daily to help Bertie in the ways of Kingship. The new King was entirely untrained. He said to Lord Louis Mountbatten, 'Dickie, this is absolutely terrible. I never wanted this burden; I am quite unprepared for it. David has been trained for this all his life. I've never even seen a state paper.'[1] Mary had learned much about a King's duties, beginning in the days when Edward VII had called upon her for advice, and now she was always at hand to point the way. She was even better equipped to help Elizabeth, and time has shown how she put her stamp firmly upon her. There was much speculation as to how the former Duchess of York would cope with her new responsibilities and the press even employed lip-readers to pick up any asides which she might make. But she made no mistakes. Mary made a point of always being near.

As Queen Mother, without in any way embarrassing the new Queen, Mary became one of those great figures that stand out in fine relief from a whole generation. She helped Elizabeth in a great many ways. One of the most important of her assets was her unique knowledge of the royal families of Europe. Elizabeth's knowledge of them was scanty and when visitors arrived at Windsor and Buckingham Palace it was to her mother-in-law that she turned for their backgrounds. Mary's memory of people and places was inexhaustible, as had been Queen Victoria's. So whenever Bertie and Elizabeth went on tour around the country, they consulted Mary and learned who to meet and what to see. George V had always left the entertainment side of court life to his wife and thus she was able to advise his successor as to who to invite to occasions such as Ascot.

Mary passed on to Elizabeth the tricks of the role of Queen.

She taught her never to allow a family bereavement to isolate her from public life. She taught her the kind of hats to wear, so that crowds who had waited long hours to see her had a full view of her face. She taught her the kind of colours that she should wear – colours which would stand out in a crowd and be seen from afar. She taught her the art of being photographed: she herself would never face a camera when laughing as she said that she came out looking like a horse. No new Queen has ever had such an instructress.

Mary enjoyed a much better relationship with her grandchildren than she had had with her own children. And she had quite a tribe of them – Lilibet and Margaret, the Harewoods, the Kents and the Gloucesters. Lilibet was her favourite and she was openly delighted that one day she would be Queen. Throughout her childhood and adolescence Lilibet was able to look to her grandmother for encouragement, understanding and example. Mary became one of her strongest influences. Lilibet inherited her grandmother's shyness. She also inherited her well-ordered mind, her strong will, her reserved public manner, her high moral code and her sound common sense. Mary said of Lilibet, 'She always knows her own mind. There is something very steadfast and determined in her – like her father.'2 But the old Queen would stand no nonsense. Lilibet called at Marlborough House one morning and a member of the household greeted her with, 'Good morning, little lady.' 'I'm not a little lady, I'm Princess Elizabeth,' the child answered. Mary overheard the remark and called Lilibet over to her. She said, 'This is *Princess* Elizabeth who hopes one day to be a *lady*.'3

Mary noted Lilibet's unselfishness and the way she gave way on the small problems which arise in every household. Margaret she found a contrast – her impish expression, her high spirits and gift for mimicry. She described Margaret as '*espiègle*', which means frolicsome and waggish. Sometimes she had occasion to rebuke her, but on one occasion added, 'All the same she is so outrageously amusing that one can't help encouraging her.'4

Mary was not a strait-laced old granny. There was one point on which she varied widely from the accepted view of her – her partialness to extremely risqué stories. Her main source of supply of these was General Sir Arthur Slogett, a former Director-General of the Royal Medical Corps, who became her consulting physician. He was known as 'Naughty Arthur' and that distinguished author and journalist, Sir Philip Gibbs, commented that most of his stories 'made my hair curl'. When Prince Philip joined the royal family, Mary found a further source.[5]

Another duty that Mary saw as important was the training of Lilibet and Margaret, their parents' time being so fully occupied. Daily she received the curriculum for the girls' lessons and every Monday afternoon she reserved for an outing with them. Prompt at two o'clock Mary would arrive at Buckingham Palace and take the girls and their governess to see some place of historic interest. They went to the Tower of London, the South Kensington museums, the Mint, Greenwich and Westminster Abbey, Mary, as usual, a well-informed guide.[6]

As a mother, life was not easy for Mary. David was proving difficult, not apparently realizing that he was not still the King. He plagued Bertie with telephone calls, advising one course or another, and asking favours. This was just one more strain for Bertie, who was already finding his task more than he could bear. It was left to Sir Walter Monckton to tell David that the calls must cease. There were endless discussions about David's title. Although Bertie had announced at his Accession Council his intention of creating his brother the Duke of Windsor, it was not until May that the title was given legal form. The honour of Royal Highness was for him alone, and not for Wallis if he married her. There came the rub, for it was the one honour David wished for. In theory his wife had the right to take her husband's title, but the legal form contained the words 'be entitled to hold and enjoy for himself only the title style or attribute of Royal Highness so however that his wife and descendants if any shall not hold the said title style or attribute'.[7] The possibility had always to be considered that the marriage might break up.

Mary wrote often to David in Austria, but restricted her letters to trivialities and family news. She was still very angry with him and, what was worse, felt that she had been humiliated.

But her chief trouble lay with Bertie, who needed all the

support that she could give him. Detrimental rumours spread across the country, some just idle gossip but others clearly having a malignant origin. Edward VIII's fans were many and his way of thinking was theirs. The chief target was Bertie's health and the fact that he had been invalided out of the navy. His stammer was held against him as an insuperable handicap. His lack of experience in the ways of kingship was considered a disadvantage – a point with which the King himself agreed. But, in the main, it was the panache of his elder brother that was missing. There were strong doubts as to Bertie's ability to discharge his functions as a sovereign. It was said that he was only a rubber-stamp King, at the beck and call of the politicians. His health record was traced back to childhood days. There was criticism that he was not to hold a Delhi Durbar in India, although the pressure of work and the unsettled conditions on the Continent made a long absence from Britain inadvisable. There were rumours that he was not strong enough to go through the full coronation ceremony – even that the coronation would be postponed. These rumours reached Bertie's ears and upset him deeply. When he went round to see his mother at Marlborough House he showed signs of the Teck temper inherited from his grandfather. He needed placating. Mary had always been the peacemaker in the family and now proved a tower of support.

The malignant rumours led her to make a most important decision. She decided that she would attend the coronation. She discussed this with Bertie and he was delighted with the idea. By tradition, as far back as Plantagenet days, no Queen Dowager had attended the coronation of her husband's successor. Queen Adelaide, widow of William IV, had stayed away from the coronation of Queen Victoria; Queen Alexandra had shut herself away at Sandringham when George V was crowned. Stickler for tradition that she was, Mary broke with it. Her knowledge of history was well known and fears about the conduct of the ceremony faded away. Her wealth of memories and her past experience were of the greatest assistance and on 24 January, she noted that she had 'a long confabulation' with the principals concerned.

Thereafter her days were filled with the coronation. She went to Westminster Abbey to see how the Royal Box, the Annexe and other essentials were being prepared. She went to the jewellers to inspect the work of resetting the crowns for Bertie and Elizabeth. She held rehearsals at Marlborough House for the four pages who were to carry her train, and her advice was eagerly sought at the main rehearsals taking place at Westminster Abbey. In early May, she made drives around London to watch the decorations going up.

Mary really came into her own when the foreign visitors began to arrive. Her knowledge of the royal houses of Europe was unique and proved of the greatest help to Bertie and Elizabeth. It was noticed now how Mary's face lightened, wiping away the sorrow of bereavement and the strain of the abdication. She looked as happy as she had done at the Silver Jubilee. She revelled in the 'family lunch' given two days before the coronation.

> We gave our gift of a gold tea set which had belonged to the Duke of Cumbd.* to Bertie and E. I also gave E. a tortoiseshell and diamond fan with ostrich feathers which had belonged to Mama Alix, and to Bertie a dark blue enamel snuff box with *our* miniatures. Bertie then gave us his family order, his miniature on a pink ribbon, lovely, he also gave me the Victorian Chain, and to others various orders . . . Maud and I dined at the Palace, State Banquet to 450 people in the Ball Room and Supper Room, Bertie in Ball Room, E. in Supper Room. I sat opposite Bertie with Gustaf of Sweden** and Rico of Denmark*** as neighbours . . .

The morning of Coronation Day, 12 May, broke dull and rainy. Regardless of the weather, the crowds were enormous. The barriers to Whitehall were closed at five o'clock; there were fifty thousand people in the Mall alone. At ten minutes past ten Mary left Marlborough House, riding in a glass coach and escorted by a troop of Horse Guards. A crown of diamonds sparkled on her grey hair and she was robed in purple and ermine. She wore her finest jewellery. She came to Marble Arch. 'The cheering re-doubled, took on a deeper note, and after the splendid figure of the Blues came a glass coach bearing Queen

* Cumberland. ** King of Sweden. *** Crown Prince Frederick.

Mary who never looked happier or more regal. Obviously deeply touched by the warm affection of the crowd's greeting, she smiled and waved her acknowledgements again and again.'[8] From Piccadilly rose a wave of cheering and thousands of voices came as one, 'Queen Mary! Queen Mary!'

She entered Westminster Abbey with her last surviving sister-in-law, Queen Maud of Norway: *

> Maud and I processed up the Abbey to the Royal Box. I sat between Maud and Lilibet, and Margaret came next, they looked too sweet in their lace dresses and robes, especially when they put on their coronets. Bertie and E. looked so well when they came in and did it all too beautifully. The service was wonderful and impressive – we were all much moved . . .[9]

That evening Mary, wearing her own crown as Queen Mother, stood between the King and Queen on the balcony of Buckingham Palace. At first Lilibet and Margaret stole the limelight and the huge crowd roared their names. 'And then came a shout, "Queen Mary". At once it spread like a wind through a corn field, until all were hailing the woman who had been their Queen for over twenty-five years, and now, in-vested with new dignity, seemed a nobler figure than ever.'[10] She stretched out her hands towards her son and daughter-in-law.

For Mary followed days which strictly concerned herself. A fortnight later she celebrated her seventieth birthday with a luncheon party at Marlborough House. The third of June was sad. Not only was it the birthday of her husband, but on that morning, at the Château de Candé in France, David married Wallis. She merely commented, 'Alas! the wedding day of David and Mrs Warfield.'

The frequent appearances of Mary during that glorious coronation summer did much to make the days the success that they were. She went to the Derby, to the Aldershot Tattoo and to Wimbledon to see the tennis finals. She took part in the Garter Service at Windsor and laid the foundation stone of the new

* Died 1938.

Queen Mary delighted in a good cup of tea. Here she is seen enjoying herself at the centenary celebrations at University College, London

Mary, as Queen, showed a particular interest in institutions devoted to the care of children. Here she is seen at the Rachel McMillan College, Deptford

Queen Mary spent her seventy-fifth birthday sawing wood for the log fires of Badminton House, ably assisted by men of her bodyguard

Queen Mary at the christening of Princess Anne in 1950. Prince Charles steals the limelight

A family group taken at Sandringham at Christmas 1951, only a few weeks before the King died. Standing, from the left: the Duke of Kent, Princess Margaret, Princess Alexandra of Kent, the Duchess of Kent, the Duke of Gloucester, Princess Elizabeth, the Duke of Edinburgh, the Duchess of Gloucester. Seated: Queen Mary, George VI holding Princess Anne, Queen Elizabeth holding Prince Charles. Front row, Prince Richard of Gloucester, Prince Michael of Kent, Prince William of Gloucester

Bodleian Library Annexe at Oxford. In August, she went to Sandringham, taking part in local festivities there, and then set off on visits to four country houses, all belonging to close friends of her husband and herself. It brought back many memories of similar excursions which she had made with her mother long before.

Mary's interest now turned to the monuments to be raised to her husband's memory. One of the first to be unveiled was that at the bottom of Castle Hill, Windsor, designed by Lutyens and presented by the townspeople. Other statues included that destined to stand at Westminster and one of George V in the robes which he had worn at the Delhi Durbar in 1911, destined for Calcutta. A memorial which attracted Mary's special attention was the plaque of George's profile for Sandringham Church. She played an active part in getting his effigy placed in St George's Chapel – it was paid for jointly by herself and David. The designer was Sir William Reid Dick and she was a frequent visitor to his studios. She also gave him sittings to enable him to make an effigy of herself to be placed beside her husband on her death. She joked that she came from a long-lived family and it would be some years before it would be required.

Mary was most insistent that a correct image of George should be passed down to posterity. A picture of him was to be presented to the town of Ipswich – seated on his white pony, Jock, at Sandringham. The artist was Sir Alfred Munnings. Jock was duly paraded, George being impersonated by his valet, French, wearing one of the late King's homespun tweed shooting suits, 'spats and all'. French referred to his late master as 'the old toff'. On its completion a printing firm wanted to make copies of the picture and a representative, Mr Wade, and Munnings attended Marlborough House so that Mary might inspect it and give her permission. Waiting in a small downstairs room at Marlborough House, Munnings remarked to Wade in a low voice, 'I have a feeling that someone is looking at us.' Wade shared his suspicion. 'I had precisely the same feeling.' He then noticed a small aperture in the ceiling.

In the upstairs drawing room Mary inspected the work with a critical eye. She pronounced, 'You have shown the King looking too much the squire and not enough the King. He also has bent shoulders. I do not wish my people to remember him like that.' So there were no prints.[11]

Mary found great contentment in flowers. The interest had been born in her when she helped her father as a child at the White Lodge. It was colour that she liked, having an abhorrence of privet and ivy. George V had only a mild interest in gardens, but he liked banks of colour. When Mary was at York Cottage, Sandringham, horticultural matters were the province of her parents-in-law: permission had to be obtained before alterations were made. But Mary had her own little private garden at the cottage, and she lightened the background of a dark shrub with brightness and colour. On Queen Alexandra's death she showed her hand at the 'Big House' and today's gardens are largely of her planning. Balmoral has its 'Queen Mary's Garden', situated beyond the main lawn on the south side of the castle: it was made in 1923. The garden was simple in design, with a low semi-circular wall of rocks planted with alpines leading to a fountain, around which were planted small flowerbeds. It was largely due to the interest and encouragement of Queen Mary that the Savill Gardens were created at Windsor. Sir Eric Savill, who became Deputy Surveyor of Windsor Parks and Woods in 1931, conceived the idea of making a garden within the park, away from the royal home. The King and Queen backed him and the result is the masterpiece which exists today.

As a widow her interest in flowers increased. Marion Crawford wrote in 1951:

> London owes a great deal to Queen Mary's love of flowers, for many of the flowerbeds in the public parks were inspired or suggested by her. The blazing bed of dahlias at Lancaster Gate, Hyde Park, is one of her creations. It is a regular thing, season by season, for her to say, 'Let us go to Dulwich Park' – or St James's, or Battersea – 'and see how the flowerbeds are coming on.' That makes, for her, an excursion as interesting as a visit to a museum or an historic building. And of course there is Kew, so near to the scenes of her own childhood, and the more romantic because it was in those beautiful gardens that her father proposed marriage to her mother. 'Queen Mary's Rose Garden' in Regent's Park is one of the sweetest

sights of London. It is easy there for anyone to forget that this is almost in the heart of the great city, for it is like a fairyland, with bank after bank of roses reflected in the still waters of the lake. It was a happy day for Queen Mary when the rose growers of Britain sent her 2500 new roses for the Regent's Park garden. Chelsea Flower Show is still one of the greatest events of the year for her.[12]

It has often been said that the great figures of Britain have had their reputations made abroad. This was true in the case of George and Elizabeth. It was their state visit to Paris in 1938 and their tour of Canada and America in 1939 which consolidated the love and admiration for them in the hearts of the British people. George and Elizabeth were in agreement with this: they both said, 'It made us.'[13]

But leaving the country when war was imminent was a worry to the King and it was a great relief to him to have his mother as a figurehead at home. He said, 'We are not a family, we are a firm.'[14] And he left Queen Mary behind as the managing director. Mary was thrilled about the French visit, recalling the wild enthusiasm which she had received there in 1914. And the reports confirmed a repeat performance. Crowds waited up all night in the boulevards to see Elizabeth come home from a ball, her evening dress made of hundreds of yards of Valenciennes lace sparkling with silver. The charm of the couple lightened the hearts of the politicians and generals and for a time, in the splendour of the Elysée Palace and the lighted gardens of the Quai d'Orsay, they forgot the threat of Adolf Hitler.

The transatlantic tour was a much more serious venture and the happenings in Europe made it appear likely that it would have to be cancelled. It was a long-standing invitation. The Canadian Prime Minister, Mr Mackenzie King, had suggested the visit when he was in Britain at the time of the coronation. When, a year later, the outline arrangements had been agreed upon, President Roosevelt had suggested that the tour should be extended to include America. In September 1938, the Czechoslovakian crisis began. Hitler spat out his vilification of President Benes and there was hand-to-hand fighting in the troubled Sudetenland, which the German leader was determined to occupy before a plebiscite was held. The King and Queen returned to London from Balmoral; Mary came from Badminton, where she had been staying with her niece, the Duchess of Beaufort. She saw the trenches being dug in Hyde Park; on the twenty-fifth she was fitted with a gas-mask. Three days later she went to the Ladies' Gallery at the House of Commons to hear the Prime Minister, Mr Chamberlain, make a statement on the crisis. She wrote in her diary:

> The PM's speech was clear and explained everything. As he was finishing Sir John Simon touched his arm and gave him a paper which he read and then he made the astonishing announcement that Hitler would see him again at Munich tomorrow and that Daladier and Mussolini would also join them in order to find a way out of this dreadful *impasse* – It was a most dramatic and wonderful ending to the speech and the relief felt all round the House was remarkable and all the members of the Conservative and National Government cheered wildly – I was myself so much moved that I could not speak to any of the ladies in the Gallery . . .[15]

Then an unexpected letter arrived at Marlborough House. It was from ex-Kaiser William of Germany, living in exile at Doorn:

> May I with a grateful heart relieved from a sickening anxiety by the intercession of Heaven unite my warmest sincerest thanks to the Lord with yours and those of the German and British people that He saved us from a most fearful catastrophe by helping the responsible statesmen to preserve Peace! I have not the slightest doubt that Mr N. Chamberlain was inspired by Heaven and guided by God who took pity on his children on Earth by crowning his mission with such relieving success. God bless him. I kiss your hand in respectful devotion as ever.
> [16]

The floodgates of memory opened for Mary and back before her eyes came pictures of her visit to Berlin in 1913, when she attended the wedding of William's daughter. Both she and her husband had got on well with William prior to 1914, and it was noticed that they never criticized him for his part in the outbreak of the First World War. Mary sent the letter to Bertie, saying, 'Poor William, he must have been horrified at the thought of another war between our two countries.' Then the message was filed away in the Windsor archives.

An uneasy calm lasted until March while, behind the scenes, Hitler continued to plan for the smashing of Czechoslovakia. In that month the autonomist Sudeten leaders fled to Germany and begged Hitler to authorize their independence. On the fourteenth, President Benes was summoned to Berlin and agreed, under enormous pressure, to place his country under the protection of Germany. Next evening, Hitler entered Prague and Czechoslovakia ceased to exist. The King was in doubt of the wisdom of crossing the Atlantic, but he was persuaded to do so by his ministers, who were convinced that the final crisis would not come until the autumn and that the visit would do immense good. So Bertie agreed. He wrote to his mother, 'I feel that we must start for Canada on Saturday . . . I hate leaving here with the situation as it is, but one must carry on with one's plans as they are all settled, and Canada will be so disappointed.'[17]

On 3 May, Mary headed the strong royal contingent, including Lilibet and Margaret, which travelled to Portsmouth to see the King and Queen embark on the liner *Empress of Australia*. She inspected the cabins in great detail, thoughts crowding her mind of similar departures which she had made with George. She wrote, 'The ship left punctually at three – it was a fine sight from the jetty – and we waved handkerchiefs. Margaret said, "I have my handkerchief" and Lilibet answered, "To wave, not to cry" – which I thought charming.'[18]

By this time, a very firm link of understanding and friendship had been forged between Mary and Elizabeth. The awe with which the younger woman had, quite naturally, regarded Queen Mary had evaporated and in its place had come a genuine feeling of partnership and confidence. Elizabeth wrote regularly to her when she was away. Here is a letter which she sent from the *Empress of Australia* as the liner made what proved to be a most adventurous crossing of the Atlantic:

> For three and a half days we only moved a few miles. The fog was so thick that it was like a white cloud round the ship, and the foghorn blew incessantly. Its melancholy blasts were echoed back by the icebergs like the twang of a piece of wire.

Incredibly eerie, and really very alarming, knowing that we were surrounded by ice and unable to see a foot either way. We very nearly hit a berg the day before yesterday, and the poor Captain was nearly demented because some kind, cheerful people kept on reminding him that it was just about here that *Titanic* was struck, and *just* about the same date![19]

While the journey was in progress, Mary was involved in a car accident which might well have proved fatal. She was out for an afternoon drive, accompanied by Lord Claud Hamilton, her Comptroller, and Lady Constance Milnes Gaskell, her Lady of the Bedchamber. The car was in Wimbledon Park Road. Mary had just pointed out to Lord Claud that there was a caterpillar climbing up his trouser leg, when there came an almighty crash and the Daimler limousine turned turtle. Above it loomed a heavy lorry laden with steel tubing. Mary, Lord Claud and Lady Constance lay in a heap against the broken windows. Two workmen carrying stepladders rushed to the scene. One ladder was put into the smashed car, and the other on the road. Mary described the scene: 'We were in a heap at the bottom of the car and we got out by the help of two ladders.' An onlooker said, 'She climbed up and down those ladders as if she might have been walking down the steps at the coronation. She had not her hat or one curl out of place. The only outward sign of disorder was a broken hatpin and her umbrella broken in half.' As she climbed down the second ladder she joked with the workmen who held it. She announced, 'I shall be all right after I have rested a few minutes. I am going to have a cup of tea and that is all I want.'[20] As she rested in Dr Revell's house in Wimbledon Park Road, her doctor was telephoned for and a relief Daimler left Marlborough House. Lord Claud and Lady Constance also had miraculous escapes, suffering only a bruised shoulder and a black eye. When the doctors examined Mary on her return to Marlborough House, it was found that she was black and blue from head to foot.[21]

She rested a few days in bed, enlivened by visits from Lilibet and Margaret and happy with the news reaching her from Canada. The tour was proving a triumphant success. The hysteria increased when the couple reached the United States, where they were entertained in Washington and at Hyde Park, the ancestral home of the Roosevelts, by the President and his wife. Rarely has New York witnessed such rapturous scenes. Bertie and Elizabeth became close friends with Mr and Mrs Roosevelt, a friendship which was to pay a big dividend in the troubled years ahead. Elizabeth kept her mother-in-law in touch with all their doings and wrote from Hyde Park after she had attended morning service in the little parish church of St James, 'The service is exactly the same as ours down to every word, and they even had the prayers for the King and the Royal Family. I could not help thinking how curious it sounded, and yet how natural.'

When Bertie and Elizabeth came home, it was immediately apparent that a change had taken place in the hearts and minds of the British public. The reporters at Southampton described their reception as 'fantastic' and 'unbelievable'. For the drive from Waterloo to Buckingham Palace the streets were as crowded as they had been for the coronation. In the evening hundreds of thousands packed the space before the palace, singing popular songs and calling for the royal family. When the King and Queen came out with Mary, it was noticed that there was a broad smile on her face and that she looked as happy as she had on Silver Jubilee night. What had happened was that the acclamation of the Canadian and American press and radio had caused the British to wonder whose King and Queen Bertie and Elizabeth were. That evening they put matters to rights. This was the fulfilment of Mary's dream. In 1936, so many of her hopes and beliefs had been shattered and, if she doubted if the sun would ever shine so brightly again, she cannot be blamed. But it was shining, just as brightly as it had done in the summer of 1935. She was a very proud mother.

On 3 September, Mary was at Sandringham. She attended morning service at the church of St Mary Magdalene. The rector had installed his wireless set in the nave and the congregation listened to Mr Neville Chamberlain's solemn statement that war had been declared.

At half past eleven the air-raid siren sounded.

CHAPTER XVIII

The Last Scene

IN JANUARY 1915 and September 1916, German Zeppelins had dropped bombs on the Sandringham area and the *National Review* reported that this was done on the express orders of Kaiser William. On both occasions Queen Alexandra had been in residence. The memory was fresh in Bertie's mind. His fears were exaggerated by the knowledge that Hitler was an expert at snatching up important figures – it had even been rumoured that he might try and seize the King and Queen as they sailed to Canada. If German troops made a surprise landing in Norfolk, bundled Mary into a plane and spirited her away to Germany, Hitler would have a strong card in his hand when it came to bargaining. So Bertie quickly decided that the sooner his mother was packed away to some safer place, the better. The place chosen was Badminton in Gloucestershire, the home of her niece, the Duchess of Beaufort. Mary was reluctant to go, declaring that it was 'not at all the thing to do' to leave London at such a time. But she bowed to her son's wishes.

Shortly before ten o'clock on the morning of 4 September, Mary's caravan left Sandringham; she was not to see her beloved estate again for six years. And it was indeed a caravan, for she took with her her staff of sixty-three from Marlborough House and their luggage and the line of cars made an impressive departure from Sandringham, through the gathering of staff and tenants who had come to wish her *bon voyage*. They headed south-west through Peterborough and Oundle, halting for lunch at Althorp where they were greeted by Lord and Lady Spencer.*

---

* Seventh Earl. Married Lady Cynthia Elinor Beatrix Hamilton.

How fascinated would Mary have been if she could have known that it was from this household that would come the next Princess of Wales. After an eight-and-a-half-hour drive, Mary came to her new home. On the steps of Badminton House, her niece waited to greet her: she was alone, as her husband had joined his regiment. It was with considerable apprehension that the Duchess watched the long caravan of cars making its majestic way along the drive.

To begin with Mary was ill at ease at Badminton. She was a woman who liked to live in familiar surroundings, with her own treasures about her. She had been doing just that ever since she was married. Bertie heard of her unrest and arranged that Foreign Office summaries be sent to her in a red despatch box, of which she held the key. But she missed her family and felt out of the swim of war affairs: she compared her lot to that of the refugee children at Badminton village. To counteract this, she made weekly journeys to London, a long day for an old lady of seventy-two. She would call in at Marlborough House, visit her dentist or oculist, perhaps see an exhibition and lunch at Buckingham Palace. And this she continued to do until the bombing made the journey inadvisable and uncertain.

She was well guarded, a company of the Gloucestershire Regiment, the Rifle Brigade and the Royal Berkshire Regiment being quartered there. There were also four dispatch riders, whose duty it was to lead Mary to a secret hiding place in the event of a German airborne landing. These troops she soon put to a useful task, not always to their liking. She had always had a hatred of ivy and she organized squads to clear the Badminton estate of the 'enemy'. In all during the war years she supervised the clearing of a hundred and twenty acres and a sixteen-acre wood of firs remains as a memento of her stay.[1] Salvage also took her attention and she organized the refugee children into parties to collect old bottles and metal. On her drives she was always on the look-out for old iron and returned with odd items which she had picked up on the way. Sometimes these turned out to be farmers' equipment and were rescued from her 'dump' and returned to their owners. She was completely ignorant of agricultural matters, but she joined the local Pig Club, raised her own pig and dutifully handed in her bacon coupons. She drove round the estate in a farm wagon drawn by two horses, and seated in a basket chair. 'Aunt May,' remarked the Duchess, 'you look as if you were in a tumbrel!' Her aunt grinned and answered, 'Well, it may come to that yet.'[2]

Her royal duties increased as the months passed and service units were visited over a wide area. She inspected the ATS at Salisbury, the WRNS at Bristol and the WAAF at all the aerodromes in the area. She was in the streets of Bristol the day after the city was bombed. She always gave lifts to those in uniform. Some of them found it hard to believe that they had been helped on their way by none other than Queen Mary, so she had small metal medallions, bearing her crown and cypher, made and these she handed out at the journey's end, as proof of the experience. She would cross-examine her passengers about their lives and was surprised one day when a private told her that he worked in a maternity home. She chuckled over this all evening, saying, 'Now, I wonder what he does there!'

When the Americans arrived, twenty-two-year-old Private Foster from Michigan got a shock. He sat beside Mary wondering who the charming old lady was, when he heard her addressed as 'Your Majesty'. His face was a picture of surprise and Mary asked him if he knew who she was. 'You have me beat there!' he replied.[3] He was speechless when he found out and took firm hold of the medallion which she handed to him. After that Mary saw much of the Americans and watched her first baseball match when two US Army teams met at Clifton.

Mary was never idle. She had brought with her boxes of old family papers and, when confined to the house by weather conditions and in the evenings, she would sort them out into portfolios and make up photograph albums. The memories of her childhood fascinated her and she went through and annotated her diaries, which took her back sixty years. As relaxation, she worked on her ten-stitch embroidery. She gradually became part of Badminton life and when she was told that, if she chose, she could move to Windsor, she declined, saying that it would be like living in a fortress.

But she did pay visits to Windsor – three in all. In March

1942, she motored there to watch Lilibet being confirmed by the Archbishop of Canterbury. In July she went again, this time for the christening of the third child of George and Marina of Kent, who was named Michael. Since the abdication she had become very close to the Kents and rejoiced in their happiness.

Seven weeks later, tragedy struck. 25 August was a day of continuous rain and Mary passed the afternoon sorting and labelling photographs, while her lady-in-waiting read to her. After dinner a telephone call came from Balmoral where the King and Queen were staying. It told that George of Kent, who was serving in the RAF, had been killed in an air crash. There was only one survivor of that giant Sunderland which had taken off for Iceland in bad weather. Mary was so stunned that she could not bring herself to believe the news. Her first thought was for the widow, and early next morning she set off for Coppins to comfort Marina. Four days later she was at the funeral in St George's Chapel, Windsor, an occasion which Bertie described as the most moving ceremony that he had ever witnessed.

As in the First World War, Mary was a stickler for abiding by the rationing. Badminton, with its long corridors and the state rooms closed for the duration, was cold, but Mary insisted on adhering to her ration of coal. The food coupon allowance was strictly followed. Mary was always particular about her diet and cooking, but there was a house rule that plates must be cleared and she bravely attempted to do so.

The Duchess gave a luncheon party, the dining table, as usual, surrounded by dogs eager to supplement their meagre ration. Mary was seated next to a bishop who was rather deaf. She was served with some meat which was on the tough side and included a piece of gristle which it was beyond her capability to consume. She spotted a dog sitting up and begging and said to the bishop, 'Give this to the little chap,' and handed over the gristle. The bishop could not hear the instruction and, guessing that it was a royal command, popped the meat into his own mouth. Chewing valiantly, and with huge gulps, he managed to swallow it. The guests, who had heard Mary's message, were convulsed. A substitute morsel was found for the thwarted dog.[4]

The war in Europe drew towards its close. On 'VE Day' –
8 May 1945 – she listened to the radio and heard the vast crowds
cheering the King and Queen outside Buckingham Palace. In the
evening, she went to the local 'pub' and joined with the celebrat-
ing villagers in a singsong. On 11 June, she returned to Marlborough House.

She had been very happy at Badminton: never since her
youth at the White Lodge had she experienced such freedom.
She said goodbye individually to all the senior staff on the estate
and, with tears coursing down her cheeks, handed to each one
of them a carefully chosen present. She said to one of them, 'Oh,
I *have* been happy here. Here I've been anybody and everybody,
and back in London I shall have to begin being Queen Mary all
over again.'[5]

Marlborough House was in a sorry state. There was little glass
left in the windows and bomb blasts had brought ceilings down
and blown doors off their hinges. For a time refugees had been
quartered there and there were mementoes of their stay. The
house had been emptied of its treasures in 1939, these being
stored away in secret hiding places. Mary had been making trips
up from Badminton since April, deciding on the immediate
priorities, and by the time she arrived in June, her suite on the
first floor was, as she said, 'beginning to look quite nice again'.
But glass and building material were so hard to obtain that
many rooms had to remain unfurnished. As one by one they
were made habitable, she called back the relevant furniture from
its storage place. Now nearing eighty, Mary was called upon to
undertake a refurbishment even more strenuous than that she
had tackled when she moved there in 1936. In addition she had
a packed programme of victory celebrations to attend and a
great many famous people to receive, among the first, to her
great delight, being General Eisenhower.

In October came a very special visitor: David flew over from
Paris to visit her and she was thrilled to see him again. She
ordered his favourite dinner – grouse. She wrote, 'At four *David*
arrived by plane from Paris on a visit to me – I had not seen
him for nearly nine years! It was a great joy meeting him

again, he looked very well.'[6] But she remained firm in her determination, and her promise to her husband, not to receive the Duchess of Windsor. This was a thorn in David's side but, in his mother's case, he overlooked it and paid a number of visits to her in her last years.

Mary still spent her Christmases at Sandringham, giving a party and handing round presents to the staff of Marlborough House before she left. She was in fine form in 1945. She was joined in Norfolk by Mabell, Countess of Airlie, her lifelong friend and lady-in-waiting for fifty years. The Countess found Sandringham much changed from the days of George V. Baize-covered tables bearing jigsaw puzzles stood about the hall and the radio blared incessantly. The house was full of young people, including several Guardsmen invited to entertain Lilibet and Margaret – Mary called them 'The Bodyguard'.

> Only in Queen Mary's room – the one which she had always occupied, with its lovely collection of small treasures – was it possible to recapture the past. I felt as I sat reading to her that King George might come in at any moment with some letter about which he wanted to consult her . . . At about 11.30 that evening dancing began. We all danced, Queen Mary and myself included. We were foolishly pleased to discover that in the old country dances such as 'Hickey Hoo' and 'Stripping the Willow', she, at nearly seventy-nine and I, at nearly eighty, outshone the two young Princesses and their guests. At the end of an hour I stopped after a strenuous 'Sir Roger de Coverley', but Queen Mary kept on until we went up to bed at nearly 1 a.m.[7]

The overpowering interest in Mary's life now became the romance between Lilibet and Prince Philip of Greece. She had first seen him when he was a small boy at school in Paris. His parents, Prince Andrew and Princess Alice,* had brought him over to London to stay with his grandmother, the Dowager Lady Milford Haven, and he was taken to tea at Buckingham Palace. Later, when he was at school at Gordonstoun, he spent his holidays with the Duke and Duchess of Kent, the latter being

---

* Prince Andrew of Greece and Denmark married Princess Alice of Battenberg in 1903.

his aunt, and Mary saw him often. She thought him handsome and with plenty of common sense. During the war she followed his naval career with interest and knitted scarves and pullovers for him. She spoke to Lady Airlie about him in January 1946:

> They have been in love for the last eighteen months. In fact longer, I think. I believe she fell in love with him the first time he went down to Windsor, but the King and Queen feel that she is too young to be engaged yet. They want her to see more of the world before committing herself, and to meet more men. After all she's only nineteen, and one is very impressionable at that age.[8]

A problem which had first to be settled was that of Philip's nationality, the Greek and German connection being unpopular in Britain. It was not until March 1947 that he became naturalized and plain Lieutenant Philip Mountbatten, RN. At this time the King and Queen, with Lilibet and Margaret, were on a tour of South Africa. Both Bertie and Elizabeth thought that it was better for Lilibet to be away from Philip for a time so that she could make up her mind with certainty. Mary agreed: she was kept in touch with every detail of the romance. Lilibet and Philip became engaged on 10 July, and Mary was with them at the Royal Garden Party which was their first public appearance. That night there was a party at Buckingham Palace. Mary was radiant and when Mr Winston Churchill went to greet her, she held out both her hands, a gesture that she had never been known to make before. She gave Lilibet the jewellery which had comprised her chief wedding present on her own marriage fifty-four years ago. When she went to see the wedding presents on display at St James's Palace, she spotted the loincloth knitted by Gandhi, the Indian leader. She was deeply shocked, labelled it 'indelicate' and commented, 'What a horrible thing!' She made another inspection of the display the next day. As she neared the loincloth, Margaret sensed danger. She pounced on the offending garment and hid it. At the wedding of Lilibet and Philip in November, Mary looked magnificent: in her was captured all the majesty of the centuries. She was fifteen hours on her feet that day, and she was eighty.

A year later came another happy event – Prince Charles was born. Mary announced that she was delighted at being a great-grandmother. She was at the christening in the Music Room at Buckingham Palace. She gave the baby a silver gilt cup which George III had presented to his godson at a similar ceremony in 1780: 'So I gave a present from my great-grandfather to my great-grandson 168 years later.'[9] From this time on, Mary began to take life more easily and restricted her public appearances. People came to see her, rather than she going to see them. She still went to the occasional theatre and exhibition and kept fully alive her interest in royal records and antique collecting, being a frequent caller on her favourite dealers. In the winter of 1949–50, she was plagued by sciatica and was obliged to use a wheelchair, but in the spring the pain faded and she was back on her feet once more. It was in January 1950 that this astonishing old lady startled the world by producing the carpet upon which she had been working since 1942. As her contribution to the economic crisis she presented it to the nation to be sold for dollars. It was seen by 400,000 people in North America in twelve weeks, and fetched $100,000. The sum of £35,354 from its sale and exhibition was then passed to the Exchequer.[10] In March 1950, she became the oldest Queen Consort that Britain had ever known.

The routine of life at Marlborough House was very precious to her, for she revelled in procedure and exactness. Every moment of her day was filled with interest – correspondence, visitors, afternoon drives. All her life she had been an early riser and by the time her breakfast tray came up at nine o'clock, she was fully dressed and ready to tackle the day. Her taste was simple – coffee, toast, butter, marmalade and fresh fruit. On the tray were the menus for the day on which she would pencil suggested amendments. If visitors were coming to lunch or dinner, she always remembered, or discovered, their favourite dishes. Her guests were amazed to find their particular fancies.

Tea was her favourite meal, her grandchildren frequently arriving to join her. Prince Richard of Gloucester had a special fancy for chocolate cake and it was always on the table. The actual brewing of the tea was a rite which she reserved for herself.

> It was served in the antique silver tea service which had belonged to Queen Victoria, and following the cakes would come another trolley on which was a spirit kettle at the boil. From this Queen Mary made the tea herself, carrying out all the steps necessary with precision and care. They included measuring the Indian tea she liked best from the jade Chinese tea-caddy kept in the cabinet in her sitting room, pouring water into the pot, and finally snuffing out the flame under the kettle. It was allowed to brew exactly three minutes, and then the footman was given the signal to pour.[11]

The rule 'one spoonful for each person and one for the pot' was strictly followed.

A problem for Marlborough House in the postwar years was the finding of suitable staff. The old order of royal servants, who considered such service to be an honour and passed on the baton to their sons and daughters, was passing. Now young people were looking for something more exciting and rewarding than domestic service and advertisements for kitchen-maids frequently appeared in the newspapers. A handicap in finding recruits was the small wage offered. Then came a revolutionary step: in the last years of the reign of George VI, every royal servant at Buckingham Palace joined the Civil Service Trade Union and union meetings were held in the servants' quarters.

At the end of 1947, Mary was fortunate in obtaining as her chef M. Gabriel Tschumi, who had served Queen Victoria, Edward VII and George V. He had begun work at Windsor in the 1890s on a yearly salary of £15, and considered himself lucky to get it. Tschumi not only knew Queen Mary's tastes, but had a long memory. She had only to say that she would like a pudding which had been served to the sovereigns visiting Windsor in 1907, and Tschumi knew what she meant. He considered that Mary knew more about cooking and diet than any other royal personage whom he had served. Sometimes the two would clash over the ingredients for complicated Continental dishes, but Tschumi was invariably right, which made her chuckle. He put a continuity and comradeship into her last years which brought her much contentment.

From the time of Lilibet's wedding a shadow hung over Mary's life: Bertie's health. At first she put this down to mere tiredness and strain caused by the war. She remembered well his illnesses between 1914 and 1918 and how on several occasions he had stayed with her while he recuperated from them. She urged more rest and a plain diet. But after the birth of Prince Charles it was obvious that the King's trouble was more serious. He developed thrombosis in the leg, the Christmas visit to Sandringham had to be cancelled and early in 1949, he underwent an operation. He recovered well but looked an old man now. There were silver streaks in his greying hair and the lines were deep in his face. But he still held firm to his determination to visit Australia and New Zealand in 1952. It was a continuous worry for Mary, herself becoming frail at eighty-three, but happiness came to her in August 1950, when Princess Anne was born.

1951 was Festival of Britain Year and one entailing much work for Bertie. Mary, in a wheelchair, was with him at the service in St Paul's when he initiated the festival. She wrote, 'My mother was present at the Opening of the 1851* – when she was seventeen and now I her daughter was present at this opening at the age of eighty-four – Lovely service – most impressive . . .'[12] She was not so impressed with the exhibition itself on the South Bank, judging it to be 'really extraordinary and very ugly'.

The British public had now seen Queen Mary and King George VI together for the last time. Bertie developed influenza and rested at Buckingham Palace and Windsor during June and July; he then went to Balmoral. There he developed a heavy chest cold and returned to London for examination. A bronchoscopy showed that he had cancer of the left lung. He was not told, and nor was his mother, but his wife knew. Mary did however know of the risk that coronary thrombosis might occur, bringing about his death, and also that there was a chance of Bertie never being able to speak above a whisper again.

On the day of the necessary operation Mary spent 'a dreadful

---

* The Great Exhibition in Hyde Park.

morning' at Marlborough House, sitting by the telephone waiting for reports. The result was termed to be 'fairly satisfactory',
but it was several days before she was allowed to see her son.
To her great relief she found him sitting in a chair and looking
better than she had dared to hope. He kept her in close touch
with his progress:

> At last I am feeling a bit better after all I have been through
> in the last three weeks. I do seem to go through the most
> serious operations anybody can do, but thank goodness there
> were no complications and everything has gone according to
> plan. I have been most beautifully looked after from the
> surgeon to the nurses and doctors . . . I have been sitting up
> in a chair for the last week and have had my meals up as well.
> So I am getting strong and can walk to the bathroom.[13]

On 30 November, he was able to leave the sickroom and spend
a few days at Royal Lodge, Windsor. On 21 December, the royal
family left for Sandringham.

It was a gay Christmas. Bertie had made a marvellous recovery and was looking forward to shooting. He told those who
enquired after his health that he was not ill: he had merely had
an operation from which he was recovering. Mary thrived in
the family gathering: Lilibet and Philip were there with Charles
and Anne, the Gloucesters with William and Richard and Marina
of Kent with Edward, Alexandra and Michael. Mary helped
with the arranging of the presents in the ballroom and dined
downstairs each evening. But then the weather became cold,
and she developed rheumatism and on 15 January returned to
London, full of hope about her son's condition. She picked up
the threads of her usual way of life, receiving important visitors
to London, sorting the records at Frogmore, visiting art galleries
and the Royal School of Needlework and driving to Richmond
to revive memories of the days which she had spent at the White
Lodge.

On 30 January, Lilibet and Philip called at Marlborough
House to see Mary before they left for Africa at the start of their
tour of Ceylon, Australia and New Zealand. Next day, she
listened on the radio to the scenes at London Airport as their
plane took off. The King, hatless, was there to wave them

goodbye. That afternoon, she had tea with Bertie and Elizabeth at Buckingham Palace. She said farewell to her second son.

By half past nine on the morning of 6 February, Mary had finished breakfast and was already at work in her sitting room. There came a tap at the door and her Lady of the Bedchamber, Lady Colville, entered. She stood stock still and her face told the story.

'Is it the King?' asked Mary. She was told that Bertie had been found dead in his bed at Sandringham. Mary never recovered from the shock of that fearful moment. It drained from her the wish to go on living. She said, 'I suppose one must force oneself to go on to the end.'[14] The Countess of Arlie, who was in Scotland, raced south to help her.

At four in the afternoon of the next day, Queen Elizabeth II arrived back from Africa. Mary drove out of the gates of Marlborough House to see her arrive home. Mary said, 'Her old Grannie and subject must be the first to kiss her hand.' The new Queen received her at Clarence House immediately. Thus did Mary greet the sixth sovereign under whom she had lived.

King George VI rested in Sandringham Church and then was brought to London and his coffin taken to lie in state to Westminster Hall, just as had that of his father. The rain pelted down. Heavily veiled, Mary, with the new Queen and the rest of the royal family, followed the coffin and watched it placed on the catafalque in the centre of the Hall. Her courage was the subject of universal admiration. She knew that it was her duty to help the new Queen and her mother and somehow summoned up the strength to do so. As the distinguished mourners arrived in London for the funeral, she received twelve royal personages and a President in two days.

On 15 February, the King's coffin was taken in procession from Westminster to Paddington station en route for Windsor. Mary sat at a first-floor window of Marlborough House, below a half-drawn blind. Her eyes were dry. As the procession came in sight, she whispered, 'Here *he* is' and held Lady Airlie's hand. From their coach the Queen and the Queen Mother bowed to her. The royal dukes saluted. The eyes of David, his face white and strained, lingered on the figure of his mother. She rose and went inside. She watched on her television set the procession reach Paddington and, later, the burial in the vault at Windsor.

It was a necessity for Mary to have her time fully occupied and she spent the remaining winter months recasting her will. It was the third time that she had made it: the first was when her husband died, the second when Edward VIII abdicated. Now it all had to be done again, in favour of Elizabeth II. But in April she fell ill with a form of influenza and was in bed for the whole of the month. May sunshine revived her and she turned her attention to the coronation of the new Queen, fixed for the following spring. She visited Kensington Palace to study the robes which Queen Victoria had worn in 1837. The twenty-sixth of May was her birthday. She wrote in her diary:

> Nice fine day, not so hot – my eighty-fifth birthday! Spent a hectic morning with endless presents arriving and lots of flowers – Mary* kindly came at 12 and helped me, we had lunch and tea together – Between 2.30 and 4.30 a number of my family came to see me, very nice of them – Hundreds of letters, cards etc. arrived – we tried to deal with them – I felt very much spoilt and had a nice day in spite of my great age.[15]

At the end of July, she went on her usual holiday to Sandringham. The Norfolk air and the familiar surroundings gave her new strength. At Sandringham Church fête she served for an hour and a half behind a fancy goods stall. She chatted gaily with the customers who milled around her. When she left, the stall was empty and she had taken £55.

Winter set in earlier and colder than ever before that year. In October Mary caught a bad cold and her doctors advised her to stay indoors. Very few visitors were allowed, but among the few was Lady Airlie:

> It was a dull grey November day when I entered the familiar door at Marlborough House. I was taken straight to her bedroom and having been warned not to make her talk on account of the cough which was troubling her, I chatted away about trivial things. All the while I was conscious of the perfection of everything around her: the exquisitely soft lawn nightgown – the same as those worn in her youth – the nails

* The Princess Royal.

delicately shaped and polished a pale pink; the immaculately arranged grey hair. Her face had still a gentle beauty of expression; no trace of hardness as so many faces have in old age, only resignation. As I kissed her hand before leaving I noticed the extreme softness of her skin. I went back to Airlie happier for having seen her, not knowing it was for the last time.[16]

She recovered sufficiently to spend Christmas at Sandringham and returned to London a few days before the anniversary of Bertie's death. She enjoyed one more burst of activity, driving out in the afternoons and receiving acclamation wherever her Daimler went. 'Go it, old girl,' a newspaper-seller shouted. She saw the preparations being made for the coronation stands; she instructed that, should she die before the ceremony, the arrangements were to continue unaltered.

It was as if she had a premonition of death. Early in March began her last illness and the doctors had little hope. The Duke of Windsor and the Princess Royal returned from America on the liner *Queen Elizabeth*.

Twilight in the Mall – Tuesday, 24 March 1953. The outline of the stands being erected for the coronation showed through the thin fog. A crowd of some four hundred had gathered round the gate of Marlborough House, pressing forward to read the bulletin posted there. Queen Mary was dying. The Duke of Windsor drove in. Soon afterwards Queen Elizabeth the Queen Mother, dressed in black, arrived. The Princess Royal hurried over from St James's Palace. A few minutes before five o'clock, the Queen came with the Duke of Edinburgh and Princess Margaret.

At seven o'clock another bulletin was posted. The watchers came and went. At twenty minutes past ten a blind was drawn: others followed until every window was shrouded. Then the flag over Marlborough House came fluttering down.

Through the night, the presses of the newspapers rolled out her praise. 'Queen Mary was loved as no Queen before her had been loved.'[17] It was said that the last of the great Victorians had gone. The tributes to her knew no bounds.

The public admired and loved her but never came to know her as they had known Queen Alexandra and were to come to know Queen Elizabeth the Queen Mother – this woman who never tasted a cocktail or flew in a plane, who spoke only forty-four words on the radio and never used the telephone.[18] Only twice did she show signs of emotion in public. One occasion was at the coronation of King George VI; the other was at the solemn ceremony to the Unknown Warrior buried in Westminster Abbey. In true royal tradition she never spared herself: that was her conception of being a Queen.

BIBLIOGRAPHY

Aga Khan, *Memoirs* (1954).

Airlie, Mabell, Countess of, *Thatched with Gold* (1962).

Albert Victor, Prince, and George, Prince, of Wales, *The Cruise of HMS Bacchante, 1879–1882* (1886).

Alice, HRH Princess, of Athlone, *For My Grandchildren* (1966).

Alice, HRH Duchess of Gloucester, Princess, *Memoirs* (1983).

Alice, Grand Duchess of Hesse, *Letters to HM the Queen* (1885).

Anon, *The Vanished Pomps of Yesterday* (1919).

Anon, *Uncensored Recollections* (1924).

Antrim, Louisa, Countess of, *Recollections* (1937).

Aronson, Theo, *Royal Family* (1983).

Arthur, Sir George, *King George V* (1929).

Ashton, Rev. Patrick, *Sandringham Church*

Asquith, Lady Cynthia, *The Married Life of the Duchess of York* (1933).

—— *Queen Elizabeth* (1937).

Ayling, Stanley, *George the Third* (1972).

Battenberg, Prince Louis of, *Recollections 1854–1884* (Unpublished).

Battenberg, Princess Marie of, *Reminiscences* (1925).

Battersea, Lady Constance, *Reminiscences* (1922).

Battiscombe, Georgina, *Queen Alexandra* (1969).

Beaton, Cecil, *The Candid Eye of Cecil Beaton* (1961).

Benson, A. C. (Ed.), *Letters of Queen Victoria 1837–1901 (1st series)*.

Benson, E. F., *Daughters of Queen Victoria* (1939).

—— *King Edward VII* (1933).

—— *Queen Victoria* (1935).

Bloomfield, Lady, *Reminiscences of Court and Diplomatic Life* (1883).

Bolitho, Hector (Ed.), *Further Letters of Queen Victoria* (1938).

—— *The Reign of Queen Victoria* (1949).

Brett, M. V. (Ed.), *Journals and Letters of Reginald Viscount Esher* (1934).

Broad, Lewis, *The Abdication* (1961).

Brook-Shepherd, Gordon, *Uncle of Europe* (1975).

Brooke, John, *King George III* (1972).

Bryan, J., and Murphy, C. J. V., *The Windsor Story* (1979).
Bryant, Arthur, *George V* (1936).
Buchanan, Meriel, *Queen Victoria's Relations* (1954).
────── *Victorian Gallery* (1956).
Buckle, G. E. (Ed.), *Letters of Queen Victoria 1837–1901* (2nd and 3rd series).
Burghclere, Lady (Ed.), *A Great Lady's Friendships* (1933).
Buxton, Aubrey, *The King in His Country* (1955).

Carey, M. C., *Princess Mary* (1922).
Channon, Sir Henry, *Chips: The Diaries of Sir Henry Channon* (1967).
Chatwyn, Alys, *The Duchess of York* (1927).
Christopher, Prince of Greece, *Memoirs* (1938).
Collier, E. C. F., *A Victorian Diarist* (1946).
Colville, Lady Cynthia, *Crowded Life* (1963).
Connell, Brian, *Manifest Destiny* (1953).
Cookridge, E. H., *From Battenberg to Mountbatten* (1966).
Corti, Egon Caesar Conté, *The English Empress* (1957).
Crawford, Marion, *The Queen Mother* (1951).
Cresswell, Mrs G., *Eighteen Years on Sandringham Estate* (1887).
Creston, Dormer, *The Youthful Queen Victoria* (1952).
Curzon, Marchioness of Kedleston, *Reminiscences* (1955).

Dangerfield, George, *Victoria's Heir* (1941).
Darbyshire, Taylor, *King George VI* (1937).
Dennis, Geoffrey, *Coronation Commentary* (1937).
Dent, H. C., *Milestones to the Silver Jubilee* (1935).
Domville-Fife, Charles W., *King George VI and His Empire* (1937).
Donaldson, Frances, *Edward VIII* (1974).
Duff, David, *Alexandra: Princess and Queen* (1980).
────── *Elizabeth of Glamis* (1973).
────── *George and Elizabeth* (1983).
────── *Hessian Tapestry* (1967).
────── *The Shy Princess* (1958).
────── *Victoria Travels* (1970.

Eckardstein, Baron von, *Ten Years at the Court of St James* (1921).
Ellis, Jennifer, *The Royal Mother* (1954).
Elsberry, Terrence, *Marie of Romania* (1973).
Emden, Paul H., *Behind the Throne* (1934).

Felberman, Louis, *The House of Teck* (1911).

BIBLIOGRAPHY

Fischer, Henry W., *The Private Lives of William II and His Consort* (1904).

Fisher, Lord, Admiral of the Fleet, *Memories* (1919).

FitzGerald, Percy, *The Royal Dukes and Princesses of the Family of George III* (1882).

Frankland, Noble, *Prince Henry, Duke of Gloucester* (1980).

Fulford, Roger, *Darling Child* (1976).

——— *Dearest Child* (1964).

——— *Dearest Mama* (1968).

——— *Your Dear Letter* (1971).

Gernsheim, Alison, *Edward VII and Queen Alexandra* (1962).

Goldsmith, Barbara, *Little Gloria . . . Happy at Last* (1980).

Gore, John, *King George V* (1941).

Gorman, Major J. T., *George VI: King and Emperor* (1937).

Gould Lee, A., *The Royal House of Greece* (1948).

Gould Lee, A. (Ed.), *The Empress Frederick Writes to Sophie* (1955).

Hamilton, Lord Frederick, *The Days before Yesterday* (1920).

Harrison, Michael, *Clarence* (1972).

Hartnell, Norman, *Silver and Gold* (1955).

Hatch, Alden, *The Mountbattens* (1965).

Hibbert, Christopher, *Edward VII: A Portrait* (1976).

——— *The Court at Windsor* (1964).

Hohenlohe, Prince, *Memoirs* (1906).

Holmes, Sir Richard, *Edward VII* (1911).

Hough, Richard, *Louis and Victoria* (1974).

Huntly, Marquis of, *'Auld Acquaintance'* (Undated).

Jonas, Klaus, *The Life of Crown Prince William* (1961).

Jagow, Dr. (Ed.), *Letters of the Prince Consort 1831–1861* (1938).

'J.P.J.', *Reminiscences* (1929).

Judd, Denis, *George VI* (1982).

Kennedy, A. L., *'My Dear Duchess'* (1956).

Kinloch Cooke, Sir Clement, *HRH Princess Mary Adelaide, Duchess of Teck* (1900).

——— *Life of HM Queen Mary* (1911).

Knutsford, Viscount, *In Black and White* (1926).

Lacey, Robert, *Majesty* (1977).

Laird, Dorothy, *Queen Elizabeth the Queen Mother* (1966).

Lang, Theo, *The Darling Daisy Affair* (1966).

Lee, Sir Sidney, *King Edward VII* (1925).

—— *Queen Victoria* (1902).
Longford, Elizabeth, *Victoria RI* (1964).

Madol, Hans Roger, *The Private Life of Queen Alexandra* (1940).
Magnus, Philip, *King Edward the Seventh* (1964).
Makin, W. J., *The Life of King George the Fifth* (1936).
Mallet, Victor (Ed.), *Life with Queen Victoria* (1968).
Marie Louise, Princess, *My Memories of Six Reigns* (1956).
Massey, Gertrude, *Kings, Commoners and Me* (1934).
Massie, Robert K., *Nicholas and Alexandra* (1968).
Maurois, André, *King Edward and His Times* (1933).
Meynell, Lady Mary, *Sunshine and Shadows* (1933).
Middlemas, Keith, *The Life and Times of Edward VII* (1972).

Nicholas, Prince of Greece, *My Fifty Years* (1926).
Nicolson, Harold, *Diaries and Letters 1930–9* (1966).
—— *Diaries and Letters 1939–45* (1967).
—— *King George the Fifth* (1952).
Norwich, Viscount, *Old Men Forget* (1953).

Oman, Sir Charles, *Things I have Seen* (1933).
Ormathwaite, Lord, *When I was at Court* (1937).

Paoli, Xavier, *My Royal Clients* (Undated).
Petrie, Sir Charles, *Monarchy in the Twentieth Century* (1952).
Pless, Daisy, Princess of, *From My Private Diary* (1931).
Ponsonby, Arthur, *Henry Ponsonby: His Life from His Letters* (1942).
Ponsonby, Sir Frederick (Ed.), *Letters of the Empress Frederick* (1928).
—— *Recollections of Three Reigns* (1951).
Pope-Hennessy, James, *Queen Mary* (1959).
Pound, Reginald, *The Englishman* (1962).

Radnor, Helen, Dowager-Duchess of, *From a Great-Grandmother's Chair* (Undated).
Radziwill, Princess Catherine, *The Royal Marriage Mart of Europe* (1915).
Redesdale, Lord, *Memories* (1915).
Rendel, Lord, *The Personal Papers of* (1931).
Rose, Kenneth, *King George V* (1983).
Russell, G. W. E., *Collections and Recollections* (1903).

St. Aubyn, Giles, *Edward VII, Prince and King* (1979).

────── *The Royal George* (1963).
St. Helier, Lady, *Memories of Fifty Years* (1909).
Salusbury, F. G. H., *King Emperor's Jubilee* (1935).
Sanderson, Edgar, *King Edward VII* (1910).
Sheppard, Edgar (Ed.), *George, Duke of Cambridge* (1907).
Stuart, James (Viscount Stuart of Findhorn), *Within the Fringe* (1967).
Stuart, Dorothy Margaret, *King George the Sixth* (1937).
Sykes, Christopher, *Four Studies in Loyalty* (1946).

Taylor, Alistair and Henrietta, *The Book of the Duffs* (1914).
Thorndike, Russell, *Children of the Garter* (1937).
Topham, Anne, *Memories of the Kaiser's Court* (1914).
Trowbridge, W. R. H., *Queen Alexandra* (1921).
Tschumi, Gabriel, *Royal Chef* (1954).

Verney, Major F. F., *HRH* (1926).
Victoria, Queen, *More Leaves from the Journal of a Life in the Highlands* (1885).
Viktoria Luise, Princess of Prussia, *The Kaiser's Daughter* (1977).
Villiers, George, *A Vanished Victorian* (1938).

Wakeford, Geoffrey, *Thirty Years a Queen* (1968).
Watson, Francis, *Dawson of Penn* (1951).
Watson, Vera, *A Queen at Home* (1952).
Wheeler-Bennett, John W., *King George VI* (1958).
Williamson, David, *Before I Forget* (Undated).
Windsor, Duchess of, *The Heart has its Reasons* (1956).
Windsor, HRH Duke of, *A King's Story* (1951).
Woodward, Kathleen, *Queen Mary* (Undated).
Wortham, H. E., *The Delightful Profession* (1931).

Young, Gordon, *Voyage of State* (1939).

Zeigler, Philip, *Diana Cooper* (1981).

SOURCES

CHAPTER I

1 Ayling, p. 448 Brooke, p. 384.
2 Fitzgerald, Vol. II, p. 18.
3 Creevey, *Edward of Kent*, p. 243.
4 Creston, p. 429.
5 Ibid., p. 430.
6 Richardson: *My Dearest Uncle*, p. 155.
7 Kennedy, p. 210.
8 Pope-Hennessy, p. 35.
9 Eckhardstein, p. 73.
10 Madol: *The Private Life of Queen Alexandra*, p. 46.
11 Kennedy, p. 64.
12 Corti, pp. 225–7.
13 R.A. 12 April 1866, (Royal archives).
14 Sheppard, p. 267.

CHAPTER II

1 *Queen Victoria's Letters* (2nd series vol I)
2 Kennedy, p. 200.
3 Duff, *Hessian Tapestry*, p. 101.
4 Pope-Hennessy, p. 116.
5 Eckhardstein, p. 72.
6 Pope-Hennessy, p. 114.
7 St. Aubyn, *The Royal George*, p. 234.
8 Longford, p. 322.
9 Lee, *Queen Victoria*, p. 416.
10 Pope-Hennessy, p. 61.
11 Huntly, p. 47.
12 Woodward, p. 53.
13 Ibid.
14 Sykes, p. 59.
15 Woodward, p. 52.
16 Battenberg, Marie, p. 181.
17 Kinloch Cooke, Vol. II, p. 125.

CHAPTER III

1 *Diary*, 22 October 1883.
2 Ibid., 25 October 1883.
3 Ibid., 30 October 1883.
4 Pope-Hennessy, p. 123.
5 Sheppard, p. 127.
6 Pope-Hennessy, p. 129.
7 *Diary*, 7 July 1884.
8 Pope-Hennessy, p. 149.
9 Kinloch Cooke, p. 165.

CHAPTER IV

1 *Queen Victoria's Letters*, 18 March 1887.
2 Ibid., 3 December 1889.
3 Pope-Hennessy, p. 162.
4 Ibid., p. 165.
5 Kinloch Cooke, p. 170.
6 Pope-Hennessy, p. 179.
7 Woodward, p. 95.
8 Ibid., p. 54.
9 Ibid., p. 83.
10 Ibid., p. 85.
11 Holden: *Royal Quiz*.
12 Woodward, p. 103.
13 Sheppard, p. 200.
14 Nicolson, *King George V*, p. 14.
15 Magnus, p. 225.
16 *Punch*, 24 November 1883.
17 *Truth*, 25 December 1890.
18 Elsberry, p. 62.
19 Alexander: *Princess and Queen*, p. 182.

CHAPTER V

1 *Queen Victoria's Letters*, 5 December 1891.
2 Ibid., 7 December 1891.
3 Ibid., 8 December 1891.

4 Pope-Hennessy, p. 217.
5 Ibid., p. 222.
6 *Queen Victoria's Letters*, 13 January 1892.
7 Ponsonby, Arthur, p. 358.
8 Ibid.
9 Pope-Hennessy, p. 242.
10 Ibid., p. 155.
11 Ibid., p. 259.
12 *Queen Victoria's Letters*, 5 July 1893.
13 *Black and White*, (*magazines*) 10 July 1893.
14 *Queen Victoria's Letters*, 6 July 1893.

CHAPTER VI

1 Frankland, p. 4.
2 Duff, *Alexandra: Princess and Queen*, p. 194.
3 *Queen Victoria's Letters*, 26 June 1894.
4 Pope-Hennessy, p. 302.
5 Magnus, p. 309.
6 Frankland, p. 28.
7 *Queen Victoria's Letters*, 22 June 1897.
8 Pope-Hennessy, p. 335.
9 Kinloch Cooke, p. 313.

CHAPTER VII

1 Pope-Hennessy, p. 345.
2 *Queen Victoria's Letters*, 30 September 1897.
3 Ibid., 31 March 1900.
4 Duff, *George and Elizabeth*, p. 27.
5 Frankland, p. 7.
6 Gore, p. 128.
7 Rose, p. 34.
8 Mallet, p. 151.
9 Duff, Felberman, p. 27.
10 *Victoria Travels*, p. 264.
11 Benson, *Queen Victoria*, p. 382.
12 Collier, p. 68.
13 Pope-Hennessy, p. 353.
14 Longford, p. 563.
15 Duke of Argyll. Quoted in *Victoria Rex Imperatrix*, p. 396

CHAPTER VIII

1 Pope-Hennessy, p. 354.
2 Airlie, p. 107.
3 Duff, *George and Elizabeth*, p. 32.
4 Pope-Hennessy, p. 367.
5 Gore, p. 158.
6 Ibid., p. 159.
7 Pope-Hennessy, p. 372.
8 Princess Alice, *For My Grandchildren*, p. 115.
9 Duff, *The Shy Princess*, p. 218.
10 Gore, p. 212.
11 Pope-Hennessy, p. 405.
12 Information from the Marquess of Carisbrooke.

CHAPTER IX

1 Airlie, p. 112.
2 Aronson, p. 55.
3 Rose, p. 60.
4 Windsor, p. 24.
5 Rose, p. 72.
6 Pope-Hennessy, p. 392.
7 Battiscombe, p. 231.
8 Duff, *Alexandra: Princess and Queen*, p. 241.
9 Gore, p. 235.
10 Pope-Hennessy, p. 47.
11 Gore, p. 237.

CHAPTER X

1 Pope-Hennessy, p. 423.
2 Ibid.
3 Ponsonby, Frederick, *Recollections of Three Reigns*, p. 79.
4 Pope-Hennessy, p. 426.
5 Rose, p. 87.
6 Private information.
7 pp. 246–7.
8 Rose, p. 96.
9 Pope-Hennessy, p. 430.
10 Rose, p. 103.
11 Jonas, p. 67.
12 Ibid.
13 Duff, *Alexandra: Princess and Queen*, p. 254.

CHAPTER XI

1 Windsor, p. 102.
2 Ibid., p. 79.
3 Pope-Hennessy, p. 445.
4 Ibid., p. 456.
5 Gore, p. 264.
6 Ibid., pp. 264–5.
7 Pope-Hennessy, p. 469.
8 *The Diary of Arthur C. Benson*, p. 312.
9 Pope-Hennessy, p. 472.
10 Ibid., p. 467.
11 Ponsonby, Frederick, *Recollections of Three Reigns*, p. 293.
12 Ibid., p. 296.
13 Duff, *Alexandra: Princess and Queen*, p. 262.
14 Ponsonby, Frederick, *Recollections of Three Reigns*, p. 301.
15 Ibid.

CHAPTER XII

1 Windsor, p. 107.
2 Ibid., p. 108.
3 Woodward, p. 177.
4 Ibid., p. 190.
5 Ibid., p. 196.
6 Ibid., p. 186.
7 Ibid., p. 199.
8 Kinloch Cooke, *Queen Mary*, p. 245–6.
9 Elsberry, p. 158.
10 Woodward, p. 10.
11 Private information.
12 Ponsonby, Frederick, *Recollections of Three Reigns*, p. 329.
13 Woodward, p. 176.
14 Pope-Hennessy, p. 501.
15 Ibid., p. 505.
16 *The Times*, 21 April 1917.
17 Buchanan, *Victorian Gallery*, p. 183.
18 Pope-Hennessy, p. 509.

CHAPTER XIII

1 Pope-Hennessy, p. 511.
2 Aronson, p. 96.
3 Pope-Hennessy, p. 520.
4 Ibid., p. 522.
5 Rose, p. 292.
6 Ibid., p. 288.
7 Ibid.
8 Woodward, pp. 156–7.
9 Elsberry, p. 185.
10 Rose, p. 295.
11 Airlie, p. 166.
12 Ibid.
13 Princess Marie Louise, p. 163.
14 Duff, *Elizabeth of Glamis*, p. 58.

CHAPTER XIV

1 Rose, p. 294.
2 Ibid.
3 Pope-Hennessy, p. 528.
4 Princess Marie Louise, p. 281.
5 Pope-Hennessy, pp. 532–3.
6 Rose, p. 359.
7 Pope-Hennessy, p. 517.
8 Duff, *Alexandra: Princess and Queen*, p. 293.
9 Duff, *Elizabeth of Glamis*, p. 98.
10 Ibid.
11 Pope-Hennessy, p. 543.
12 Rose, p. 357.
13 Pope-Hennessy, p. 545.
14 Ibid., p. 546.

CHAPTER XV

1 Rose, p. 387.
2 Hibbert, *The Court at Windsor*, p. 264.
3 Airlie, p. 102.
4 Pope-Hennessy, p. 550.
5 Hibbert, *The Court at Windsor*, p. 264.
6 Ibid., p. 266.
7 Rose, p. 392.
8 Ibid.
9 Hatch, p. 124.
10 Rose, p. 292.
11 Ziegler, *Diana Cooper*.
12 Prince Nicholas of Greece, p. 164.

13 Duff, *Elizabeth of Glamis*,
   p. 94.
14 Bryan and Murphy, p. 103.
15 Rose, p. 302.
16 Bryan and Murphy, pp. 110–
   11.
17 Pope-Hennessy, p. 555.
18 Gore, p. 431.
19 Pope-Hennessy, p. 556.
20 Gore, p. 433.
21 Duff, *Elizabeth of Glamis*,
   p. 160.

CHAPTER XVI

 1 Pope-Hennessy, p. 560.
 2 Ibid., p. 567.
 3 Duff, *Elizabeth of Glamis*,
   p. 169.
 4 Windsor, p. 311.
 5 Ibid., p. 313.
 6 Wheeler-Bennett, p. 276.
 7 Pope-Hennessy, p. 574.
 8 Wheeler-Bennett, p. 277.
 9 Bryan and Murphy, p. 220.
10 Duff, *Elizabeth of Glamis*,
   p. 173.
11 Airlie, p. 198.
12 Pope-Hennessy, p. 576.
13 Donaldson, pp. 249–50.
14 Duff, *George and Elizabeth*,
   p. 115.
15 Pope-Hennessy, p. 578.
16 Windsor, p. 365.
17 Ibid., p. 404.
18 Lacey, p. 75.
19 Wheeler-Bennett, p. 286.
20 Duff, *Elizabeth of Glamis*,
   p. 176.
21 Crawford, p. 39.
22 *Daily Telegraph*, 21 April 1984.
23 Pope-Hennessy, p. 580.
24 Duff, *George and Elizabeth*,
   p. 124.

CHAPTER XVII

 1 Wheeler-Bennett, p. 294.
 2 Airlie, p. 226.

 3 *The Royal Family* (No. 19)
   (*Orbis* 1984).
 4 Airlie, p. 225.
 5 Cookridge, p. 267.
 6 Crawford, p. 20.
 7 Wheeler-Bennett, p. 296.
 8 Woodward, *The Lady of
   Marlborough House*, p. 185.
 9 Pope-Hennessy, p. 585.
10 Crawford, p. 99.
11 Pound, *The Englishman*,
   pp. 137–9.
12 Crawford, pp. 50–1.
13 Duff, *George and Elizabeth*,
   p. 163.
14 Duff, *Elizabeth of Glamis*,
   p. 196.
15 Wheeler-Bennett, p. 591.
16 Ibid., p. 592.
17 Ibid., p. 376.
18 Pope-Hennessy, p. 594.
19 Wheeler-Bennett, p. 378.
20 *Daily Sketch*, 25 March 1953.
21 Ibid.

CHAPTER XVIII

 1 Crawford, p. 110.
 2 Pope-Hennessy, p. 601.
 3 Wulf: *Her Majesty Queen
   Mary* (quoted in Crawford,
   The Queen Mother, p. 111).
 4 *Daily Telegraph*, 7 February
   1984.
 5 Pope-Hennessy, p. 609.
 6 Ibid., p. 614.
 7 Airlie, p. 224.
 8 Ibid., p. 227.
 9 Pope-Hennessy, p. 616.
10 *Daily Sketch*, 25 March 1953.
11 Tschumi, p. 205.
12 Pope-Hennessy, p. 617.
13 Ibid., p. 619.
14 Airlie, p. 235.
15 Pope-Hennessy, p. 620.
16 Airlie, p. 237.
17 *Daily Sketch*, 25 March 1953.
18 *Evening Standard*, 25 March
   1953.

INDEX